Regulating
Understanding the Issues

Introduced and edited by
Professor M. E. Beesley

Professor Martin Cave • Jon Stern
Professor Mark Armstrong • Professor George Yarrow
Professor Geoffrey Whittington
Professor David Newbery • Professor John Vickers
Dr Martin Howe • John Welsby

Comments by:
Sir Bryan Carsberg • Professor Michael Beesley
Dr Eileen Marshall • Ian Byatt
Professor Stephen Littlechild • Geoffrey Horton
John Bridgeman • Professor Colin Robinson
Chris Bolt

Published by The Institute of Economic Affairs in
association with the London Business School
1998

First published in September 1998 by
The Institute of Economic Affairs
2 Lord North Street
Westminster
London SW1P 3LB

in association with
The London Business School

IEA Readings 48
All rights reserved
ISSN 0305-814X
ISBN 0-255 36418-0

Printed in Great Britain by
Hartington Fine Arts Limited, Lancing, West Sussex
Set in Times Roman 11 on 12 point

Contents

iii

INTRODUCTION

M. E. Beesley
London Business School

AS RECORDED IN LAST YEAR'S REGULATION SERIES VI, UK-style regulation has entered a phase in which the debate no longer concerns whether it is to be preferred to rival systems, but rather how, in natural monopoly areas, to shape and monitor the 'regulatory contract', and, in potentially competitive areas, to ensure the emergence or continuance of rivals to incumbents. The current agenda concerns altering the regulatory structure, to support the 'contract', and how to enlist new competition law in the task of removing the remaining impediments to rivalry in newly opened markets. At the time of writing, the final outcome of the two principal developments – the Regulatory review and the Competition Bill, now passing through Parliament – have yet to appear. As the reader will see, however, these developments were well in the minds of our lecturers in the 1997 series. It is safe to predict that what does or does not emerge from them will be given close scrutiny in the current year's series.

The first lecture in the 1997 series, by **Professor Martin Cave**, was a timely reminder of the benefits which the UK legal framework confers on the UK's regulatory system. Developing countries rarely display the conditions we take for granted, and still less a full set of them. Martin explores the implications, and is left with the paradox of considerable foreign direct investment in utilities on what, in principle, is a highly dubious prospect in regulatory terms. The key, he thinks, is the exceptional growth prospects, and governments' care to avoid discouraging further investors. **Sir Bryan Carsberg,** from the chair, is struck by the similarities between UK and developing countries in the realities of privatisation and setting regulatory terms. He remains an advocate of competition even in circumstances, as in developing countries, where the temptation is to reduce particular investment risks by granting monopoly rights.

Many regulatory debates have centred around the means to

mitigate a very strong incumbent position on privatisation, as well as setting the balance between profit inducements and competitive structure. **Professor Mark Armstrong** takes up the case of the earliest, and unitary, utility privatisation, telecoms. The lack of local competition, he argues, still poses important questions for policy. While seeing many drawbacks when approached from the viewpoint of welfare economics, he has hopes that the effect of the UK's established policy, which has been to encourage the emergence of more local networks, even though likely to remain a far from complete challenge to incumbents, will ultimately reduce its market power. A close oligopolistic structure may, in this case, be quite competitive. He sees progress in requiring access to be given by all local operators, not only the incumbent, while warning against pressures towards reintegration. He explores several ways to eliminate the drawbacks of the inevitable 'rebalancing' which will occur. From the chair, I urge more attention to the particular business realities in telecoms involved in mounting challenges to the incumbents. In particular the issue of the current source of local network-based market power, strongly asymmetrical as between pick up and delivery, needs clearer confrontation and, possibly, a solution involving the threat of divestment.

Professor George Yarrow argues that the recent history of gas in particular demonstrates how far network industries are developing, and could further develop, new forms of contracting which will modify incumbent power. In gas, the work of ensuring access is nearly complete. The key point for the regulators now is that competition essentially means rivalry of all kinds. Behaviour will depend on the competitive rules, and in gas this includes the Network Code. The ways of making the rules in UK regulation, he argues, must be improved. **Dr Eileen Marshall** thinks that structural separation in gas was far more important than George allows, pointing to the unexpected speed of opening up the domestic gas markets. But she agrees on the significance now of removing the remaining obstacles to freer contracting. There remain difficulties, connected with the defensive use of rules by incumbents, including those on safety, and entrant shippers' wish to consolidate their market position.

Over the years, the lecture series has responded to the topics its largely professional regulatory audience wishes to discuss. Some of these topics have been hardy perennials. **Professor Geoffrey**

Whittington takes up two in his lecture on regulatory asset values (or regulatory asset base) and the cost of capital. He sees these as essential parts of the whole necessary set of regulators' information. The central issue is the time period over which the regulator seeks to drive out excess rates of return, which are partly due to the regulated firms' own efforts to improve efficiency. Cash flow forecasting provides a very important cross-check to accounting-based methods. As the regulator gets more expert in forecasting, emphasis on the regulatory asset base should lessen. But the recent emphasis on clarification of the 'regulatory contract' may be undesirable, as tending to a too legalistic, static position. **Mr Ian Byatt** greatly welcomes Geoffrey's general approach, which leads to proper articulation of financial accounting and essentially forward-looking information. Problems remain with evidence and theory about required rates of return, and the 'glide path' necessary to pass efficiency gains on to consumers through time. The underlying issue is the credibility of the regulatory régime as a whole, and in the regulator's clear exposition of his thinking.

A major issue in 1998 will be reform of the UK Electricity Pool: how far should this emphasise reform within the present structure or replacement by alternative trading arrangements? **Professor David Newbery** gives a comprehensive critique of the outcomes to date of the present Pool and trading arrangements. He sees judging the nature of competition as central. While entry will be the leading element in competition in generation, and ensuring future rivalry will eliminate the manifestations in Pool outcome of market power in that sector, entry will not remedy shortcomings in transmission. Mechanisms to allow substantial price adjustments in transmission are required. The locational signals thrown up by NGC should revisit the allocation of charges between generators and the customer, now arbitrary. Reforms in pool governance are a necessary condition to realise these improvements. The new powers in the Competition Bill should also assist the regulators to encourage market testing. **Professor Stephen Littlechild** welcomes David's reference to the need for changes in transmission prices, but thinks that his emphasis on the process of calculating prices is in general overdone. Real decentralised competitive markets do not work through calculating millions of prices; decisions are made on whatever is relevant to them, in which only a small number of prices may be central. The reason for differences in prices at peaks and other times would stem from firms discovering what is needed to survive. The paper underplays the possibility of more radical solutions, including trading outside the pool. Market alternatives, and not only reforms within the pool like demand-side bidding, must be explored.

As UK regulation assumes further responsibilities for the development of competition in their sectors, as envisaged in the Competition Bill, the need for clarity in basic notions about what constitutes the exercise of market power grows. **Professor John Vickers** takes the time-honoured question of when discrimination is 'undue' (the phrase universally used in licence conditions). He subjects it to a rigorous examination, proceeding from the neo-classical standpoint of divergences expected from perfect competition. Should a monopolist be allowed to engage in price discrimination, and how should 'fixed' costs be recovered? He shows how the possible answers have multiplied as research into the questions has been stimulated, largely in response to regulatory concerns; but some broad hints on preferred policy emerge. He finds that when actual regulatory policy is considered, as in domestic gas supply, the regulator has proceeded appropriately. An emphasis on assessing the effects of firms' pricing policy on future competition, rather than its particular forms, should be a constant regulatory theme. **John Bridgeman** agrees that the essence is to distinguish between anti- and pro-competitive behaviour. This is the approach taken in the Competition Bill; there is no presumption for or against particular instances of discrimination. He much welcomes the Bill also because of its provisions for better powers of investigation, interim powers to stop suspect behaviour, and better sanctions. In carrying out the new provisions, formulating guidelines will be important and in these, European Union jurisprudence will be absorbed, but interpretation of behaviour must be particular to the case at hand.

RPI-x, UK-style, depends to an important degree on the rights of appeal against the regulator's decision on prices to the MMC. **Dr Martin Howe** reviews the MMC's record in dealing with the six relevant utility cases so far; and considers the function of MMC inherent in airport regulation, used on five occasions. He finds MMC to be consistent in its support of RPI-x, as opposed to alternatives such as rate-of-return or profit-sharing schemes. The airport references to MMC, while not following the appeal model, have significantly helped the definition of how RPI-x should be applied. The Competition Bill presents new problems in preserving the MMC's current role in regulatory references. At the time this is written the question of whether, and how far, a regulator should be bound by MMC's conclusions in an appeal, or should retain discretion to modify them, is an issue before the High Court. Martin leans towards discretion but this should be tempered by the regulators not seeking to reopen decisions on issues of substance. **Professor Colin Robinson** considers that the seemingly inconsistent roles played by MMC in utility affairs may have some underlying logic. As Martin points out, there are in effect three models of MMC's role, depending on whether references to MMC are mandatory, and, where they are not, on the question of whether MMC findings are bound to be followed by the regulator (as in the exceptional case of water). These may reflect various responses to the regulators' own monopolistic positions. On the question of the impact of the Competition Bill, Colin welcomes the belated move to the originally intended 'regulation with a lighter touch' but, like Martin, sees in the Bill a potentially troublesome position on the appeal roles of the Competition Commission, which will inherit both regulatory price appeals and appeals on abuse of a competitive position.

Rail regulation is a subject on which the Lecture Series has provided one of the earlier forums for discussion. Rail is arguably technically the most interesting of all privatisations, and certainly among the most complex. Among the chief regulatory issues are resetting the Railtrack's price control and the approach to renewing rail passenger franchises. **John Welsby**, speaking as a principal protagonist in the process as well as an analyst, sees the root of the problem as a dilemma which has always confronted railway policy – on the one hand, controlling public subsidy and, on the other, sustaining a wide railway network, whose increases in output at any point in time are usually seen as socially desirable. He thinks the key to resolving the dilemma is the systematic application of value for money, in which social purposes are weighted appropriately. He sees the prediction of subsidy as a fit role for the proposed Strategic Authority for Railways. The resolution of the dilemma should recognise that putting the railways into the private sector was correct, whatever the difficulties from the form adopted. **Chris Bolt** thinks privatisation did succeed in separating government policy and railway operation more clearly. The old asymmetry in information in the structure control, weighted so heavily in favour of the Railways Board, is being corrected. The weakness in assessing costs of access is being dealt with. But John's vision of a division of functions between strategic determination of subsidy and private sector operation is problematic. The Regulator's assessment of future network needs, and OPRAF's new obligation to provide input to this, will be helpful. He hopes that there will be no need in the future to stick to the rigidities of specifying all terms of franchises.

The Series's tradition of promoting a timely discussion of regulatory affairs between active contributors to regulatory practice, and with the regulators responding from the chair, will be continued later this year, beginning on Tuesday 6 October 1998; as is customary, the papers and responses will then be published together. We believe this process is a useful stimulus to discussion, as I hope the reader will see in what follows.

London Business School   **M.E.B.**
July 1998

THE AUTHORS

Mark Armstrong is Official Fellow in Economics at Nuffield College, Oxford. He was educated at the Universities of Oxford and Cambridge, and until 1997 was Professor of Economic Policy at Southampton University. Much of his research concerns the theory of optimal pricing and tariffing decisions by firms with market power, including various forms of price discrimination, quantity discounts and auction schemes. The remaining research interests are to do with regulatory and competition policy, with a special focus on telecommunications and broadcasting; this includes, with Simon Cowan and John Vickers, *Regulatory Reform: Economic Analysis and British Experience* (1994). He is on the editorial boards of several leading academic journals, and has acted as an economic adviser to Oftel and to the Monopolies and Mergers Commission.

Michael Beesley is a founding Professor of Economics, now Emeritus, at the London Business School. Lecturer in Commerce at the University of Birmingham, then Reader in Economics at the LSE, he became the Department of Transport's Chief Economist for a spell in the 1960s. His recent work has centred on the issues of deregulation and privatisation in telecoms, transport, water and electricity, and he is currently Economic Adviser to Ofgas and Offer. Much of his work to 1996 in this area was summed up in *Privatisation, Regulation and Deregulation* (Routledge with the IEA, second edition, 1997).

His independent economic study of *Liberalisation of the Use of British Telecommunications' Network* was published in April 1981 by HMSO and he has since been active as an adviser to the Government in telecoms, the deregulation of buses and the privatisation of the water industry. For the IEA, of which he is a Managing Trustee, he wrote (with Bruce Laidlaw) *The Future of Telecommunications* (Research Monograph 42, 1989) and (with S.C. Littlechild) 'The Regulation of Privatised Monopolies in the United Kingdom', in *Regulators and the Market* (IEA Readings No.35, 1991). He contributed to and edited the IEA's *Markets and the Media* (IEA Readings No. 43, 1996), and he has edited all five of the previous volumes in this lecture series.

He was appointed CBE in the Birthday Honours List, 1985; from 1988 to 1994 he was a member of the Monopolies and Mergers Commission.

Chris Bolt is Director of the Economic Regulation Group at the Office of the Rail Regulator (ORR) which he joined in 1994. Having read economics at the University of Cambridge, he joined the Civil Service in 1975. He is responsible for policy on mergers and competition issues in the railway industry; policy on access charges for track, stations and depots; economic regulation of Railtrack (including preparing for the periodic review of Railtrack access charges); and advice to the Regulator on developments in regulatory policy generally. Before joining ORR, he was Head of Economic Regulation at Ofwat, the economic regulator for the water industry, and was responsible for developing the financial and economic aspects of the Periodic Review of price limits which took place in 1994. He has also worked in the Home Office, HM Treasury and the Department of the Environment.

John Bridgeman is the UK's Director General of Fair Trading. Prior to becoming Director General in 1995, he was managing director of British Alcan Aluminium plc. He joined Alcan Industries as a graduate trainee in 1966 and worked in Canada and Australia before becoming divisional managing director of Alcan Aluminium in 1981. From 1992 until 1993 he was director of corporate planning and development for Alcan Aluminium plc in Montreal, and in September 1993 was appointed Managing Director of British Alcan Aluminium plc.

Mr Bridgeman graduated from University College, Swansea, with an honours degree in chemistry. He undertook postgraduate training in economics and management studies at Oxford and Montreal and in 1992 became visiting professor of management at Keele University.

Commissioned into the Territorial Army in 1978, Mr Bridgeman is Honorary Colonel of the Queen's Own Oxfordshire Hussars. From 1991 until 1994 he served on the Defence Science Advisory Council as business director on the board of the Military Survey Defence Support Agency. He was appointed to the National

Employer Liaison Committee for Reserve Forces in 1992, and appointed Chairman in 1997. He was awarded the Territorial Decoration in 1995.

He has served as a member of the Monopolies and Mergers Commission and is currently vice-president of the UK-Canada Chamber of Commerce, a member of London's Canada Club and a Council Member of the Canada UK Colloquia.

He was appointed a Deputy Lieutenant of Oxfordshire in 1989 and was High Sheriff of Oxfordshire for 1995/96. Mr Bridgeman is married and has three daughters.

Ian Byatt was appointed as the first Director General of Water Services on 1 August 1989. He is an economist and an expert on the regulation of public utilities. His previous post was as Deputy Chief Economic Adviser to the Treasury (1978-89). He was born in 1932 and educated at Kirkham Grammar School and at St Edmund Hall and Nuffield College, Oxford. He also studied at Harvard University as a Commonwealth Fund Fellow. He has lectured in economics at both Durham University (1958-62) and the London School of Economics (1964-67).

He joined the Civil Service in 1967 as Senior Economic Adviser to the Department of Education and Science. His career in the Civil Service also included spells at the Ministry of Housing and Local Government and the Department of Environment, before joining the Treasury in 1972. In 1986 he chaired the Advisory Committee on Accounting for Economic Costs and Changing Prices. He is an Honorary Fellow of the Chartered Institution of Water and Environmental Management. In 1994 he was awarded an Honorary Doctorate by Brunel University.

He is a member of the Council of Management, National Institute of Economic and Social Research, Governor of Birkbeck College and President of The Economics and Business Education Association.

His publications include *The British Electrical Industry 1875-1914* (1979). For the IEA, he contributed a chapter, 'Ofwat: Regulation of Water and Sewage', to *Regulators and the Market* (IEA Readings No. 35, 1991), and another, 'Water: The Periodic Review Process', to *Utility Regulation: Challenge and Response* (IEA Readings No. 42, 1995), and a Comment to *Regulating Utilities: Broadening the Debate* (IEA Readings No. 46, 1997).

Sir Bryan Carsberg took up his post as Secretary-General of the International Accounting Standards Committee in May 1995. He held public office over the previous 11 years, as the first Director General of Telecommunications from 1984 and more recently as Director General of Fair Trading.

Sir Bryan became a member of the Institute of Chartered Accountants in England and Wales in 1960. He gained an MSc (Econ.) with distinction through part-time study at the London School of Economics in 1967. Between 1969 and 1981 Sir Bryan was Professor in the Department of Accounting and Business Finance at the University of Manchester. He was the Dean of its Faculty of Economics and Social Studies, 1977-78; and he was the Arthur Andersen Professor of Accounting at the London School of Economics, 1981-84. In 1974 he was a visiting Professor at the University of California (Berkeley). From 1978 to 1981 he was Assistant Director of the US Financial Accounting Standards Board. Sir Bryan was a member of the UK Accounting Standards Board, 1990-94, and was its deputy chairman between 1990 and 1992. He joined the Board of Cable and Wireless Communications plc in 1997. He was knighted in January 1989.

Sir Bryan is the author and co-author of 11 publications on accounting, economics and finance. For the IEA, he has contributed to five IEA Readings: No. 35, *Regulators and the Market* (1991); No. 40, *Major Issues in Regulation* (1993); No. 42, *Utility Regulation: Challenge and Response* (1995); No. 44, *Regulating Utilities: A Time For Change?* (1996); and to No. 46, *Regulating Utilities: Broadening the Debate* (1997). Sir Bryan also delivered the 1995 Wincott Memorial Lecture, *Competition Regulation the British Way: Jaguar or Dinosaur?* (IEA Occasional Paper No. 97, February 1996).

Martin Cave is Professor of Economics at Brunel University. He was educated at the University of Oxford and worked as a Research Fellow in the Centre for Russian and East European Studies at Birmingham, before going to Brunel. He has been a Visiting Professor at the University of Virginia and a Visiting Fellow at the Australian National University and La Trobe University.

Recently he has worked primarily on issues of regulation, especially of telecommunications and broadcasting, and the measurement of public sector performance. He has acted as a consultant to various government departments and regulatory bodies including Ofgas, Oftel and the Office of Fair Trading, and to a number of telecommunications firms. He is the author, with Robert Baldwin, of *Understanding Regulation* (Oxford University Press, 1999). Since 1996 he has been a member of the UK Monopolies and Mergers Commission.

Martin Howe is a graduate of the University of Leeds and obtained his PhD from the University of Sheffield in 1961. He was Director of the Competition Policy Division of the Office of Fair Trading from 1984 until his retirement at the end of 1996. For the final four months of his civil service career he was also Deputy Director General of the Office. Previous posts, after leaving academic life in 1972, included Senior Economic Adviser first at the Monopolies and Mergers Commission and then at the OFT, and, in the early 1980s, Assistant Secretary in the General Policy Division of the Department of Trade and Industry.

During his extensive career in UK competition policy, Martin Howe advised on countless cases, served on several official reviews of the law and policy and represented the UK on various international bodies. He was Vice–Chairman of the Competition Law and Policy Committee of the OECD from 1985 until 1996.

Martin Howe has been a Special Professor at the University of Nottingham since 1994 and a member of the Advisory Body on Fair Trading in Telecommunications since 1996. In early 1998 he was a visiting Adviser at the Australian Competition and Consumer Commission. He is currently a consultant with Europe Economics.

He is the author of many articles, mainly on competition policy topics, and, with A.J. Merrett and G.D. Newbold, of *New Issues and the London Capital Market* (1996).

Stephen Littlechild was appointed the first Director General of Electricity Supply on 1 September 1989. He has extensive experience of regulation both in the UK and abroad. He advised on the regulatory régime for British Telecom and the water industry. He was a member of the Monopolies and Mergers Commission for six years. Reports in which he participated included North and South of Scotland Electricity Boards, Manchester Airport and British Gas.

He has been Professor of Commerce, University of Birmingham, since 1975. He was formerly Professor of Applied Economics, University of Aston, 1973-75, and sometime Consultant to the Ministry of Transport, the Treasury, World Bank, Electricity Council, American Telephone & Telegraph Co., and Department of Energy. Professor Littlechild holds a BCom from the University of Birmingham and a PhD from the University of Texas.

He is author or co-author of *Operational Research for Managers* (1977), *Elements of Telecommunication Economics* (1979), and *Energy Strategies for the UK* (1982). For the IEA he wrote *The Fallacy of the Mixed Economy* (Hobart Paper 80, 1978, Second Edn. 1986), and contributed to *The Taming of Government* (IEA Readings 21, 1979) and *Agenda for Social Democracy* (Hobart Paperback 15, 1983). More recently, he contributed a chapter, 'Competition in Electricity: Retrospect and Prospect', to *Utility Regulation: Challenge and Response* (IEA Readings No. 42, 1995), and he also contributed to *Regulating Utilities: A Time For Change?* (IEA Readings No. 44, 1996), and to *Regulating Utilities: Broadening the Debate* (IEA Readings No. 46, 1997).

Eileen Marshall worked as a stockbroker in the City of London before becoming a lecturer at the University of Surrey, then Senior Lecturer in Industrial Economics at the University of Birmingham. Her research specialism was in Energy Economics, and she has acted as a consultant to many companies and bodies.

Dr Marshall took up the position of Director of Regulation and Business Affairs with the Office of Electricity Regulation (Offer) in October 1989. In April 1994 she was appointed as Chief Economic Adviser and Director of Regulation and Business Affairs at the Office of Gas Supply (Ofgas). Her responsibilities cover the full range of Ofgas policy issues, including the setting of price controls and the introduction of domestic competition. In January 1997, Dr Marshall became a part-time economic adviser to Offer, whilst retaining her responsiblities at Ofgas. She is presently leading the Offer/DTI Review of Electricity Trading Arrangements.

David Newbery PhD, FBA, has been Director of the Department of Applied Economics and Professor of Applied Economics at the University of Cambridge since 1988. He was educated at Trinity College, Cambridge, from 1961-65 and graduated with a degree in

Mathematics and also Economics. After a year working in the Treasury in Tanzania he returned to a Teaching Fellowship at Churchill College and an Assistant Lectureship in the Faculty of Economics and Politics at Cambridge in 1966. He spent two years as Division Chief, Public Economics, World Bank (1981-83), and has been a visiting Professor at Berkeley, Princeton, Stanford and Yale. He is a Fellow of the Centre for Economic Policy Research, a Fellow of the Econometric Society and of the British Academy. He was President of the European Economic Association in 1996. He was awarded the Frisch Medal of the Econometric Society in 1990 and the Harry Johnson Prize of the Canadian Economic Association in 1993. He has advised Offer on use-of-system pricing and earlier reforms of the Pool, and is currently an economic adviser to Ofgas and the Office of Rail Regulation. He is also a member of the Monopolies and Mergers Commission and on the academic panel of the Department of Transport and the Environment. He has managed a series of research projects on electricity and telecoms privatisation and regulation funded mostly by the UK Research Councils since 1988. His books include *The Theory of Commodity Price Stabilization: A Study in the Economics of Risk*, with J. Stiglitz (OUP, 1981), *The Theory of Taxation for Developing Countries*, edited with N. Stern (OUP, 1987), *Hungary; An Economy in Transition,* edited with I. Székely (CUP, 1993), and *Tax and Benefit Reform in Central and Eastern Europe*, ed. (CEPR, 1995), and his recent journal publications on electricity include 'Competition in the British Electricity Spot Market' (with R. Green), *JPE*, 1992, 'Restructuring and Privatising Electric Utilities in Eastern Europe', *Economics of Transition*, 1994, 'Power Markets and Market Power', *Energy Journal*, 1995, 'The Restructuring and Privatisation of the CEGB – Was it worth it?', with M. Pollitt, *JIE*, 1997, and 'Competition, Contracts and Entry in the Electricity Spot Market', *RAND Journal*, 1998.

Colin Robinson was educated at the University of Manchester, and then worked for 11 years as a business economist before being appointed to the Chair of Economics at the University of Surrey in 1968. He has been a member of the Electricity Supply Research Council, the Advisory Council for Research and Development in Fuel and Power (ACORD), and the electricity panel of the Monopolies and Mergers Commission. He has written widely on energy and regulation. His most recent IEA Papers are *Energy*

Policy: Errors, Illusions and Market Realities (IEA Occasional Paper No. 90, October 1993); 'Gas: What to Do After the MMC Verdict', in *Regulating Utilities: The Way Forward* (IEA Readings No. 41, 1994); 'Profit, Discovery and the Role of Entry: The Case of Electricity', in *Regulating Utilities: A Time For Change?* (IEA Readings No. 44, 1996), and 'Introducing Competition into Water', in *Regulating Utilities: Broadening the Debate* (IEA Readings No. 46, 1997).

Professor Robinson became a member of the IEA's Advisory Council in 1982 and was appointed its Editorial Director in 1992. He was appointed a Trustee of the Wincott Foundation in 1993. He received the British Institute of Energy Economists' award as 'Economist of the Year 1992'.

Jon Stern is a NERA Senior Adviser and an Affiliated Professor at the London Business School. He received his first degree in economics from the University of Cambridge and took an MSc from the University of Bristol.

Before joining NERA in 1989, he worked for a number of years as an economist in the Civil Service, with spells at the Treasury, the Department of Health and Social Security, and the Department of Employment where he was a Senior Economic Adviser and Director of the Employment Market Research Unit. His work was mainly concerned with policy appraisal and evaluation, particularly in the area of labour markets. He published a number of articles on unemployment and special employment measures, and was one of the joint authors of *The Nature of Unemployment in Britain: Studies of the DHSS Cohort* (1988).

Since joining NERA, he has worked on a variety of policy appraisal and evaluation projects both in the UK and Europe. In particular, he has played a leading role in building up NERA's practice in Central and Eastern Europe, including acting as a consultant to the World Bank. He has worked extensively both on regulatory governance issues and on utility and energy sector reform in Central and Eastern Europe. Recently, he has become increasingly involved with utility reform issues in Asian and other reforming economies. Recent publications include articles and contributions to published reports on electricity reform in Central and Eastern Europe, on East-West trade, on the Slovak economy, on regulatory governance in the UK and regulatory governance of infrastructure industries in developing Asian economies.

John Vickers is Chief Economist and Executive Director at the Bank of England (since April 1998). He is on leave from the Drummond Professorship of Political Economy at the University of Oxford, where he is a Fellow of All Souls College. After studying PPE at Oxford (BA, 1979), he worked for a while in the oil industry before returning to Oxford to pursue graduate economics (DPhil., 1985). From 1984 to 1990 he was Roy Harrod Fellow in the Economics of Business and Public Policy at Nuffield College, where he was also investment bursar for two years. He has held visiting positions at Harvard, Princeton and the London Business School. He has published numerous journal articles on industrial organisation, privatisation, regulation and competition. His books include (with George Yarrow) *Privatisation: An Economic Analysis* (1998) and (with Mark Armstrong and Simon Cowan) *Regulatory Reform* (1994).

John Welsby is the part-time Chairman of the British Railways Board, re-appointed in May 1998 following a three-year appointment as full-time Chairman and Chief Executive, Railways.

After studying at Exeter and London, he joined the Electricity Council as an Economist, and then moved to the then Ministry of Transport as an Economic Adviser in 1966. From 1969 to 1971 he was Assistant Professor at the Business School of the University of Columbia, Canada, and returned to the Department of Transport as a Senior Economic Adviser.

He was seconded from the Department of Transport to BR, joining in 1979 as Director, Strategic Studies, before becoming Development Officer (Business Policy). When the sector organisation was set up in 1982 he was appointed Director, Provincial. Early in 1984 he became Director, Manufacturing and Maintenance Policy, and the following year moved to the new post of Managing Director, Procurement and Special Projects.

As a member of the Board he was responsible for private sector initiatives and the Channel Tunnel project up to 1 January 1990, when he took over the day-to-day management of the BR system as Chief Executive, Railways. He was awarded the CBE in the Queen's Birthday Honours List, 1990, is a Fellow of the Chartered

Institute of Transport and Chairman elect of the Chartered Institute of Transport in the United Kingdom. He is also a Fellow of the Royal Society of Arts and a companion of the Institute of Management.

Geoffrey Whittington is the Price Waterhouse Professor of Financial Accounting at the University of Cambridge, a Fellow of Fitzwilliam College, and a Professorial Research Fellow of the Institute of Chartered Accountants of Scotland. He is currently a member of the Accounting Standards Board. He is a Chartered Accountant and also holds a doctorate in Economics.

He was a member of the Monopolies and Mergers Commission from 1987 to 1996. He has also served as a member of the Technical and Research Committees of the Institute of Chartered Accountants in England and Wales, as a part-time economic adviser to the Office of Fair Trading (in connection with the 'Big Bang' stock exchange case) and as a member of the Oftel Advisory Body on Competition in Telecommunications.

George Yarrow is Director of the Regulatory Policy Institute; Visiting Professor at Queen Mary College, London, and at Newcastle University; and Senior Research Fellow at Hertford College, Oxford. He is also an economic adviser to the Director General of Gas Supply.

After studying economics at St. John's College, Cambridge, he held appointments at Warwick and Newcastle Universities before becoming a Fellow in Economics at Hertford College, Oxford, in 1978. He has also held visiting positions at Harvard University and the University of California at San Diego.

His early research was centred mainly on the economics of the firm, with secondary interests in monetary economics, including theories of hyperinflation, and environmental policy. During the 1980s and 1990s he published extensively on issues concerning privatisation, regulation, and competition, including (with John Vickers) *Privatisation: An Economic Analysis* (1988) and (with Piotr Jasinski) the four-volume anthology *Privatization* (1996). Most recently he has extended these interests to analysis of problems surrounding the reform of the welfare state, most notably in the monographs *Welfare, Mutuality and Self-Help* (1996) and *On Welfare Reform* (1997).

1

REGULATORY INSTITUTIONS AND REGULATORY POLICY FOR ECONOMIES IN TRANSITION[1]

Martin Cave

Brunel University

and

Jon Stern

NERA and London Business School

ENERGY, TELECOMMUNICATIONS, TRANSPORT AND WATER are crucial to economic progress in all economies. It is therefore vital to devise institutions and policies for these sectors which promote efficiency. This paper is concerned with the problems which arise in the utilities sector in economies in transition, where the peculiar history of economic structure and institutional forms creates special challenges for regulatory reform.

Section 1 of the paper discusses the problem of regulatory design in general terms, but with a special focus on economies in transition. Section 2 reviews problems of adjustment related to the telecommunications industry, and the regulatory framework in which they are being addressed. Section 3 covers the same ground with respect to the electricity industry, and Section 4 contains conclusions.

1. Designing Regulatory Institutions

The Problem
Mass-market network industries (which we shall refer to as utilities) share three critical technical and economic characteristics which

---

[1] This paper was presented by Martin Cave.

make their regulation a matter of some difficulty (see Levy and Spiller, 1994):

- Utilities are capital intensive and the assets which they require are both durable and – in many cases – sunk, not in the sense of lying underground, although this is true of many of them, but in the sense of not being capable of sale and redeployment. As a result, such assets are something of a hostage to fortune made by the providers of investment capital.

- Many, if not all, network utilities are characterised by economies of scale, which place a limit on the number of firms which can provide service to any particular area. These economies of scale typically apply primarily (but not invariably) to distribution networks, rather than to activities such as extraction of energy and generation of electricity (at one end of the supply chain) and to retailing and 'supply' (at the other). In between, however, there is likely to be scope for only one, or a limited number of networks. As a consequence, governments cannot rely upon the operation of the competitive process to police incumbents. In addition, some network industries are characterised by economies of scope, which add further to the concentration of market power in the hands of the incumbent.

- The services provided by network utilities, especially transport, water and energy, but to an increasing extent telecommunications too, are consumed by and necessary to the welfare of a large proportion of the population and, at any approximately cost-based prices can represent a significant proportion of household budgets, especially in the case of poorer households. Utility pricing thus has a major impact on real incomes and price changes have major redistributive effects. Utility services are also of fundamental importance as an intermediate input into almost all other sectors of the economy. Their prices and the financial policies used to support them thus have a major impact on, for example, international competitiveness.

These three characteristics have had a major influence upon the organisation of the sector. Over the last century, an 'American' model was developed of investor-owned monopoly utilities, whose activities – especially pricing – were regulated through politically accountable regulatory authorities which were, however, often captured by the regulatee. The traditional 'Western European' model is of a state-owned monopoly utility, acting either as a government department or as a public enterprise subject to controls imposed by government on its pricing and investment policy. Each of these models has changed radically in the past 20 years with privatisation, the introduction of competition and new forms of incentive regulation, and it is to this new variant that many economies in transition now aspire. However, their starting point has been an even more centrally controlled and heavily distorted variant of the Western European model.

Utilities under Central Planning

In most East European countries, national networks were created from regional utility companies in the later 1940s and early 1950s (see Cave and Valentiny, 1994). Because of their size and importance, public utilities became departments of ministries or even constituted a whole ministry. The ruling ideology required that their services should be cheap and available to all. However, only the first part of this injunction was fulfilled. Tariff structures typically favoured households, so that residential consumption was constantly under-priced compared to industrial use, and cross-subsidisation of consumers became a permanent feature of the tariff structure. Moreover, tariffs in general failed to cover economic costs. This was sustainable due to the lack of a feedback mechanism between prices and investment. As occurred generally in these economies, investments were covered by the central budget through taxation without any reference to revenues raised by the utilities; the Planning Office's choices among new projects were not based on rate-of-return analysis but on administratively set output targets.

Prevailing economic doctrine and the needs of industrialisation resulted in separation of 'productive' and 'non-productive' activities within the economy. The former were assumed to create wealth, while the latter were assumed to consume it. Giving preference to 'material' production or 'material' services was a pervasive feature of economic policy under central planning. Although most public utilities fell into the category of 'productive' activities, some of them were considered less productive than others.

Energy industries (gas and electric utilities) were in a more

3

advantageous position as they provided an input central to material production. In the early stages of industrialisation, energy shortages created bottlenecks and 'black-outs' in periods of rapid growth. Subsequently, the problem became one of extravagance in energy use. The transport and particularly the telecommunications industries suffered more from the rules of central allocation of investments, as planners first satisfied the requirements of 'material production', while services only received residual financial resources.

An equivalent hierarchy of customers can also be detected within each sector. While network expansion in electricity or gas supply already showed some sign of preferential treatment of industrial or bulk consumers, the development of transport and telecommunication services made the distinction between industrial and residential consumers more directly.

As a result, public utilities, with the exception of energy, were relatively weak sectors in the centrally planned economies. Because of their low prestige, which was reflected in the investment allocation system, they were provided with fewer and fewer resources. Their performance lagged behind that of utilities in market economies. In many areas their relative backwardness became a major factor contributing to the inefficient use of resources. At the same time, inflexible and relatively low tariffs led to excess demand, and the levels of service utilisation were much higher in Eastern Europe than in Western economies.

In telecommunications particularly, Eastern Europe was at the bottom of the European league, in terms of lines per 100 population. The networks also suffered from technological backwardness due to autarchic development. The lack of technology transfer eliminated competitive pressure, often raised costs and cut Eastern public utilities off from the rapid changes in technology in the West. The annual loss of GDP in Hungary due to the low level of telecommunications was estimated as 4 to 5 per cent of GDP at the end of the socialist régime (Major, 1992, p. 78).

In summary, severe shortages, poor quality of service and lack of investment characterised the public utilities as they entered the era of transition to a market economy. The bureaucratic style of government of the previous system had affected utilities in fundamental ways. This raised the isssue of the problems which are likely to arise in moving from this traditional arrangement of the utility sector in a centrally planned economy towards the dominant régime emerging in the rest of the world, which, as noted above, is characterised by privatisation, the development of competition and the introduction of a more economically efficient pricing policy.

As far as pricing and the development of competition are concerned, we discuss in more detail in Sections 2 and 3 below the policies adopted by economies in transition in relation to the telecommunications and electricity sectors. Such separate treatment is necessitated by major differences in the characteristics of the industry. However, all utilities sectors share in common the first of the characteristics noted at the start of this section – the necessity for substantial levels of investment in assets which are non-salvageable, or sunk, and which therefore make the investor vulnerable to some form of expropriation. This could simply be achieved, for example, by tightening price controls so that the investor in the utility receives just sufficient revenue to cover its operating costs, but neither earns a rate of return on its investments, nor has the value of them returned to it through the incorporation in prices of depreciation charges. That this is more than a theoretical possibility is shown by the experience of certain countries, noted below.

Enforcing the Regulatory Contract

A frequently proposed solution to this familiar problem is by means of the so-called regulatory contract. This is an informal agreement between, on the one hand, government and regulators acting as agents for their principals, customers and citizens and, on the other hand, the management of the regulated firm acting as agents for their principals, the stockholders. Under the contract, the regulatory body commits to providing an adequate rate of return on investments, if those investments are efficiently chosen and managed; at the same time, to protect consumers from exploitation, it further commits itself to some form of control over prices and related areas such as quality of service, although the details of the arrangements, notably the power of the incentive mechanisms built into them, may involve significant departures from simple remuneration of cost.

The necessity for some quasi-contractual relationship of this kind seems obvious. If it is absent, firms will either refuse to invest or require a return on their investment so high as to make it unlikely

5

that the regulator will accede to it by authorising the corresponding prices. A major crux of the problem of regulatory design therefore becomes how best to structure arrangements for the specification and – even more importantly – the enforcement of the regulatory contract.

The major contribution of Levy and Spiller and their associates to this debate has been their attempt systematically to identify alternative methods for implementing the regulatory contract, characterised by different ways of providing the crucial enforcement mechanism in particular (Levy and Spiller, 1996). We first review this work in general terms, before applying to the circumstances of economies in transition.

To be provided with comfort that their assets will not be expropriated, private investors require the existence of regulatory arrangements which impose some restraint on the regulators' discretion in operating a given system, restraints on changing the system, and institutions to enforce those restraints. Satisfying these requirements involves imposing demands upon three types of agents:

- the parliament, which enacts primary legislation governing the allocation of regulatory functions and the duties and powers of the various regulators;

- the administration, including officials in government departments or appointees to more or less independent regulatory bodies, who implement the legislative arrangements;

- the courts, to whom aggrieved parties can appeal in the event they believe that the administration is not acting in accordance with the legislation.

Designing an efficient regulatory mechanism involves allocating functions among the three sets of agents in order to provide the necessary comfort to investors, while at the same time discouraging regulatory capture.

As far as the *Parliamentary system* is concerned, two key distinctions are whether the system of government is unified or has a federal structure in which power is distributed, and whether the voting system leads to radical alternations of government, rather than more minor adjustments of coalitions. Thus federal systems such as the United States, Australia and the European Union generate frameworks in which regulated industries are controlled by legislation originating from a number of sources. This makes sudden and radical change less likely. Equally, voting systems such as first-past-the-post accentuate changes in popular preference and are likely to lead to radical changes in government, as compared with proportional representation, which tends to generate coalition governments.

As far as the *administrative system* is concerned, countries differ considerably in the capacity, tenure and degree of independence of their public servants. Thus in some countries, a change of government will lead to a major change in administrative personnel, including those involved in quasi-judicial functions, as well as ministers' policy advisers. In other countries, the core personnel in the bureaucracy do not change as governments change, and key regulatory appointees may have been placed by statute in positions of independence. Thus Directors General of UK regulatory agencies are appointed by the Secretary of State, generally for a five-year period, and may not be dismissed except in the case of incapacity or malfeasance. As a result, the recent change of government in the UK did not lead to any immediate change in the identity of the regulators. If, on the other hand, regulatory functions are discharged by departmental officials subject to rotation at will, this safeguard does not exist. This important distinction is quite separate from one based upon the level of competence of the officials involved, which places a limitation upon the degree of complexity of the regulatory issues which can be made subject to their discretion.

As far as the *legal system* is concerned, a country's regulatory endowment can differ in a number of important ways. The key element is, of course, the independence or lack of independence of the judiciary. In the absence of judicial independence, a legal safeguard is of little value. Other important distinctions concern the development of administrative and contract law. A highly developed system of administrative law will diminish the risk of abuse of the administrative process. Equally, the availability of contracts between the government and the regulator, enforced by the courts, is an alternative route to providing security for investors.

For illustrative purposes, we now describe some of the permutations of the Parliamentary, administrative and legal

7

institutions which can be found in three countries outside Eastern Europe, as a prelude to discussing the problems which exist in relation to economies in transition.

The United Kingdom exhibits a highly centralised system of government, although increasingly subject to restraints imposed by its membership of the European Union. It is subject to radical alternations in the governing party. This is compensated to some extent by assigning substantial independence through existing legislation to independent regulatory agencies. But the independent regulators (single individuals) thus appointed have considerable discretionary power. They do not have to follow precedent, nor are they tied to any particular 'rate base' in setting prices. Although the system of administrative law is relatively undeveloped, there is little doubt about the independence of the judiciary. The contractual option described below has not been implemented. The overall framework is thus vulnerable to Parliamentary changes, but protected to some degree by the non-partisan nature of the public service.

Jamaica, on the other hand, is also subject to swings in government composition, but lacks a tradition of independent regulation, although an Office of Utility Regulation has recently been established, with limited powers. The most dramatic events in Jamaica have concerned telecommunications regulation, where private investors in the 1970s were subject to what Spiller and Sampson (1996) refer to as quasi-expropriation. Following the withdrawal of the private operator, a new company, Tele-communications of Jamaica, was created, subject to licences which formalise a system of rate-of-return regulation subject to arbitration in the event of disagreement. In other words, the system relies primarily upon operating licences with an automatic arbitration procedure, supervised by an independent judiciary with a history of protection of property rights to give investors comfort. In some other countries, this arbitration procedure may be extra-territorial.

In the United States, as a first approximation, the system of sharing of powers between Congress and the Executive, and between Federal and State levels of government generates a degree of stability and inertia not found in either the United Kingdom or Jamaica. At the same time, the courts play a fundamental role in regulatory processes – not only policing procedural issues as in the UK, but also enforcing property rights and ensuring an adequate return on capital, and in many cases taking over the substance of regulatory decision-making. (An example is Judge Greene's taking over of the break-up of the Bell system.) At the state level the independent regulatory agencies themselves are in some cases directly politically accountable, leading to a situation in which short-run political considerations may lead to breaches of the regulatory contract.

Regulatory Design for Economies in Transition

What lessons does this analysis have for economies in transition? Clearly, as well as suffering from the weak infrastructure illustrated above, such economies also have to develop institutional arrangements against a background of lack of trust and the absence of a properly developed 'civil society'. In terms of the characteristics of the three types of agent identified above, economies in transition typically have centralised states inherited from their previous existence, and electoral systems which, when combined with a relatively volatile electorate, produce transfers of power between rival parties or coalitions. In some states, notably Russia, this instability is blunted by a separation of powers between president and Parliament. Transfers of power do not necessarily mean a radical overhaul of policy towards utilities, nor lead to expropriation of private investors. Militating against such conduct is a common desire among governments of all kinds to secure significant revenues, including foreign direct investment, from their highly valuable utility assets.

As far as the judiciary is concerned, economies in transition naturally vary in the degree of independence enjoyed by the judges and in the stability and level of development of their legal codes. As a generalisation, however, it is unlikely that much reliance can be placed upon the judiciary to uphold property rights, especially in circumstances where commercial and property law are in a relatively early stage of development, and the judiciary lacks knowledge and experience of handling economic issues.

These two characteristics impose a heavy burden on the administrative system in generating favourable expectations on the part of investors concerning the security of their assets. Much of the discussion on this issue has revolved around the desirability of establishing independent regulatory agencies, which are capable of implementing necessarily somewhat vague legislative principles in

9

a manner consistent with the implicit regulatory contract. This is contrasted with the alternative of regulation undertaken directly by government departments, whose decisions are inseparable from those of the governing party.

Experience teaches, however, that there may be no real difference between these alternatives, unless the 'independent regulator' really enjoys security of tenure and an assured level of funding. Although evidence on this point from independent utility regulators is limited, there is a longer and more systematic history of independent competition offices in economies in transition. A study by Fingleton *et al.* (1996) of competition legislation in four countries (the Czech Republic, Hungary, Poland and Slovakia) showed a broadly similar system of law in all four cases, heavily influenced by Articles 85 and 86 of the Treaty of Rome, and broadly identical institutional arrangements, in the shape of a nominally independent Anti-Monopoly Office. However, the outcomes were quite different. In the first three countries, the President of the Office enjoyed comparatively long tenure and came to exercise a degree of authority in the field of economic policy-making. In Slovakia, by contrast, there was a quick turnover of personnel, with four holders of the post of President in a four-year period. In effect, the Anti-Monopoly Office, although independent, found itself quite incapable of resisting government policy when that policy conflicted with the Office's interpretation of its legislative mandate. The ability of the government summarily to fire the President made any apparent independence ineffective.

However, the fact that independence can in some circumstances be subverted does not automatically undermine all arguments in its favour (Stern, 1997). In particular, independent regulators have more opportunities than government officials to gain legitimacy and power by seeking an independent political constituency for themselves, by developing mechanisms for accountability to bodies other than the government departments with which they are associated, and by seeking to protect their independence through the development of transparent procedures. The first task would naturally be achieved by appealing to the constituency of consumers (as regulators in Western countries have done), although the task is made more difficult for regulators in economies in transition by the pricing policies likely to be required of them. (This is discussed in the following sections.) Whether alternative routes of accountability can be found will depend upon the details of the legislation, but an independent regulator has an opportunity to develop a direct link with Parliament, which is absent when regulation is administered within a government department. Thirdly, an independent regulator often has the capacity to develop its own procedures, which ideally will involve such familiar methods for publicising decisions as a consultation process, open hearings, and the giving of reasons for decisions. Such procedures can make it more difficult for governments or regulated firms to suborn the regulatory process for their own ends.

The analysis in this section has underlined the fragility of regulatory processes throughout the world. Because of uncertainties about the future, all long-term contracts tend to be incomplete. Where they involve relations between investors in sunk assets and a second contracting party which is in some degree politically accountable, the uncertainties multiply.

But even against this general background of difficulty, the situation in economies in transition is particularly fraught. Their Parliamentary and legal systems are often embryonic, and their administrative capacities limited. The risk of loss of credibility is always present. Moreover, the decisions to be taken in relation to utilities are often hard and unpopular. We now illustrate these problems further with respect to the telecommunications and energy sectors.

2. Policy and Regulation Towards Telecommunications

Policy Options

The telecommunications sector of economies in transition in Central and Eastern Europe and the former Soviet Union exhibited a discouraging picture in the early 1990s, with penetration rates of less than one-third the average of the OECD countries, and payphone access also extremely poor. Waiting lists for lines were considerable, and in many countries average waiting times were between five and 15 years. Even those who had lines enjoyed very patchy service, with high levels of fault incidence and of call blocking, linked to the outdated equipment to be found in the region, itself a consequence of Western technology embargoes.

Tariffs were also low and unbalanced, although comparisons of level are bedevilled by problems in obtaining meaningful exchange

11

rates. At nominal exchange rates revenue per line in the former Soviet Union was only $15 per year in 1992. As in most European countries, but to an even greater degree, tariffs were unbalanced, with residential line rentals typically less than $40 per year and long-distance and international call rates exceptionally high.

According to estimates made at the time, the attainment of government objectives by the year 2000 would require an annual rate of line growth of 11 per cent and investment of over $100 billion over the 1993–2000 period. This would raise penetration to roughly one-half the OECD average. It was clear that the internal resources of the region were quite inadequate to achieve these objectives. The shortfall not only covered finance but also technology and management skills. In the circumstances, designing a regulatory framework capable of encouraging the necessary investment became a key priority.

The strain placed upon the regulatory system would, however, depend upon the nature of the strategy employed. Given that the *status quo* was unacceptable, governments in economies in transition were faced by two main options – a radical strategy of immediately liberalising markets or a more conventional strategy of allocating a temporary monopoly to the incumbent, accompanied by privatisation through a trade sale to a consortium of overseas operators. Both of these would involve use of radio-based technologies (fixed or mobile), which speed up the provision of service, diminish up-front investment, generate significant revenue given the high willingness to pay when waiting lists for fixed line service are high, and generate revenue for the government through the sale of franchises for mobile services.

A study undertaken for the European Bank for Reconstruction and Development (EBRD) has evaluated these two alternatives, the characteristics of which are shown in Table 1 (Davies *et al.*, 1996). The study concluded that the desirability in terms of standard welfare analysis of the two alternatives depended significantly on the extent of network externality. The fast-track privatisation option gives the government an opportunity to require high levels of network build in the early stages which confer major benefits if there are network externalities. Clearly, however, any such comparisons depend critically upon the detailed assumptions made in the analysis.

A review of policies adopted by economies in transition shows a preference for the fast-track privatisation option. Many have adopted, and others intend to adopt, a policy of privatisation involving a strategic partner.

In terms of the stresses placed upon the regulatory régime, fast-track privatisation requires the conclusion of a contract between the strategic investor and the regulatory body, the main elements of which cover pricing, the timing of the introduction of competition, and the speed of network build-out. This contract can clearly go wrong in a number of ways. First, the network operator may exercise excessive influence over the regulator, leading the latter to set insufficiently demanding targets, to fail to enforce the agreement reached or to defer unnecessarily the introduction of competition. Alternatively, the government or regulator may practise an opportunistic policy of enforcing high network build targets, during which the operator incurs losses, then reneging on agreements to defer competition, especially in profitable long-distance and international calls.

The Regulatory Framework

The development of regulatory régimes to deal with these issues is still at an early stage. As Table 2 indicates, of the countries under consideration for membership of the EU, all have retained the sector-specific regulatory function within the relevant government department, although some propose to allocate it in the near future to an agency enjoying a degree of independence but largely confined to an advisory capacity. It is too early to say how these arrangements will work out. At present, and for the foreseeable future, governments in the regions are unlikely to cede ultimate power to control prices to a genuinely independent regulator.

Slovakia represents a particularly interesting example (see Jurzyca, 1997). In many ways it is characteristic of the region, with low penetration rates, a significant waiting time for lines and relatively low productivity. Like other economies in transition, the country has an ambitious plan, approved in 1995, to develop the sector by 2000. This would increase penetration to 2.5 times the 1991 level and produce a largely digital network. Waiting times would be eliminated.

However, this ambitious plan necessitates considerable investment and, in effect, the involvement of a strategic partner. The

TABLE 1:
The Two Principal Options

1. Competition
<ul><li>Immediate liberalisation of all telecoms markets, including local and long-distance telephony: mobile telephone, cable TV service providers, utility companies and others permitted to supply fixed telephony services.</li><li>One-off increase in average price levels at the time of liberalisation.</li><li>Telecommunications Operator (TO) prices remain subject to regulation until active competition erodes its market power.</li><li>Rapid rebalancing of TO prices towards cost.</li></ul>

2. Fast-track Privatisation
<ul><li>Fast-track privatisation of TO.</li><li>Sale of controlling interest in TO to a consortium including a Western telecoms operator.</li><li>Rights and obligations of privatised operator specified in licence or concession.</li><li>TO retains a monopoly over telephony for 5–10 years; all other telecom markets opened up to competition.</li><li>TO commits to ambitious targets for network expansion and service quality improvement.</li><li>One-off increase in average price levels prior to privatisation.</li><li>TO subject to price cap regulation.</li><li>Gradual rebalancing of prices towards costs.</li></ul>

Source: Adapted from Davies *et al.* (1996).

14

TABLE 2:

Country	State Owner-ship %	Independent Regulator	Regulatory Institution	Stage of Regulatory Development in Price Setting[†]
Czech Republic	51	No	Czech Telecommunications Bureau, Ministry of Transport and Communications	2
Hungary	33	No	Ministry of Transport and Communications	3
Poland	100	No*	Ministry of Telcoms	2
Slovak Republic	100	No*	Ministry of Transport, Post and Telecoms	2
Estonia	51	No	Ministry of Transport and Communications	2
Latvia	51	No	Ministry of Post and Telecommunications	2
Lithuania	100	No	Ministry of Communications and Informatics	2
Bulgaria	100	No	Committee of Post and Telecoms	2
Romania	100	No*	Ministry of Communications	2
Slovenia	100	No*	Ministry of Transport and Communications	1

*Indications of an independent regulator by end 1998.

† Key: 1: Ministry sets Tariffs
2: Ministry approves Tariffs set by firm.
3: Tariffs set according to price cap formula.

Source: Analysys (1997); *Public Network Europe, 1998 Yearbook.*

situation is complicated by a decision taken by the government in 1996 not to privatise a number of key state enterprises, including the telecommunications operator. This decision will have to be changed or circumvented.

Inevitably, any strategic investor will be concerned with regulatory arrangements. To date, these are uncertain. There is a plan to create an independent regulatory body, but it has not yet been put forward. Even if it is, it is doubtful whether it will be credible. When the European Commission evaluated the degree of readiness for accession to the EU of a number of economies in transition, it delivered a broadly favourable judgement on Slovakia's economic situation, but found its political institutions wanting and noted the need for fuller independence of the judicial system (Transition, 1997). The experience noted above of the Slovak Anti-Monopoly Office is a case in point. Despite this, a number of Western European operators, including France Telecom, have expressed considerable interest in taking a major stake in Slovak telecommunications.

In some countries the anti-monopoly authority has been more influential in the regulation of the sector than any sector-specific regulator. For example, in Poland, the Anti-Monopoly Office has made a number of interventions in telecommunications markets. These include action requiring the dominant operator to provide access to underground telephone lines (Fingleton *et al.*, 1996, p. 120).

In summary, the design of a regulatory framework for telecommunications in economies in transition presents considerable challenges. Massive levels of investment are required, as well as a significant increase in the level and a change in the structure of tariffs. Rather than using competition as an enforcer of immediate rebalancing, governments have generally preferred the more gradual approach which relies upon an arrangement with a strategic partner, which makes a commitment to invest in return for a temporary monopoly. Because of the potentially high profits available from the industry, there has been no shortage of strategic partners, and heavy competition among them for the franchise. This suggests that, so far, lack of certainty about the regulatory arrangements in Slovakia has not discouraged investment, although it may of course have increased the cost of capital. This is despite the fact that the degree of protection provided to investors through the Parliamentary process, the administrative system and the courts is not particularly high. In countries with more 'reliable' institutions, the competition among strategic partners to invest will be even more intense.

3. Policy and Regulation Towards Electricity

Regulatory Developments

The context in which energy and electricity regulation is developing in economies in transition clearly has many similarities with that for telecommunications, but also some significant differences. The most obvious similarity is the need for significant increases in the level and changes in the structure of tariffs. The development of effective economic regulation will, in the short to medium term, bring two- or three-fold increases in tariffs to household consumers rather than reductions. The most obvious difference with telecommunications is the high levels of spare capacity – at least in Central Europe. Hence, in practice, there is much less current need for large-scale investment in electricity to meet demand, although such a need will re-emerge over the next 5-10 years.

Stern (1994) presents a survey of the development of formal and independent economic regulation in Central and Eastern European (CEE) economies – or, to be more precise, a survey and exploration of the very limited progress that had been made in its development. At that time, Hungary was the only country that had passed laws that provided for economic regulation. The Czech Republic was debating it, as were Slovakia, Latvia, Bulgaria and some other CEE economies.

The picture is little different three years later (see Table 3 for a summary). In Hungary, there is a relatively independent electricity and gas regulator, the Hungarian Energy Office (HEO), whose powers and duties are established by parliamentary statute. In Latvia, there is also an energy sector regulatory agency which has been developed out of the Anti-Monopoly Committee, and Lithuania has set up an Energy Pricing Council. Neither of them is set up by parliamentary statute. The Czech Republic passed an Electricity Law in 1994, but this law left issues of economic regulation to the Ministry of Finance to cover under the generic Prices Law. Recent years have seen renewed and, to date, inconclusive debate about amending the Czech Electricity and Gas Laws to include economic regulation.

17

There is no sign, or any early expectation, of laws to provide for economic regulation of the energy sector in the Slovak Republic or Bulgaria, where price regulation remains under the control of the Ministries of Finance. However, the major new development since 1994 is that, early in 1997, Poland passed a new Energy Law which set up the Energy Regulatory Authority (ERA) from the beginning of 1998.

What is even clearer now than in 1994 is that the regulatory authorities that have been set up are all *advisory*, particularly on regulation of prices, which is the core regulatory issue in CEE economies. Thus, in Hungary, the HEO advises the Ministry of Industry on price rises. The Electricity Law requires that regulated electricity companies are allowed an 8 per cent rate of return on capital. It does not, though, specify or define the base to which the 8 per cent should be applied. In 1996, the HEO carried out a tariff review under which it recommended price increases that would have significantly raised prices in real terms. The Ministry sent this for review. The review reduced the costs in the rate base sufficiently for the 8 per cent rate of return not to give a real-terms price increase to final consumers.

In Latvia and Lithuania, the regulatory bodies are advisory. They are meant to be strongly advisory – that is, the intention is that their recommendations will be accepted unless there are good reasons not to do so. Nevertheless, the lack of any formal legal powers or financial independence plus the high political profile of energy prices, particularly to households, means that they do not have any effective independence. In Poland, ERA advises the Ministry of Finance on energy price changes for the first two years, before becoming the regulatory decision-maker in 2000.

Dependence for funding on Ministries and/or the imposition of civil service pay scales for regulatory staff is another way in which governments limit the effective autonomy of regulatory agencies. In Hungary, the HEO is significantly limited in this way and these issues were one of the major battlegrounds in the Polish Energy Law, but one on which the Polish proponents of independent regulatory bodies were more successful.

Other areas where regulatory practice is little developed in CEE economies are:

* **Appeals**. There are typically no formal legal appeal rights against regulatory decisions by Ministries. Appeals against regu-

TABLE 3:
Regulation of Electricity in Ten Economies in Transition

Country	Independent Economic Regulation	Regulatory Institution	Stage of Regulatory Development	Powers of Independent Regulator Concerning Prices
Czech Republic	No	MIT; MoF	*	N/A
Hungary	Yes	MIT, Hungarian Energy Office (HEO)	†	Advisory
Poland	Yes, 1998	Office for Competition and Consumer Protection, MoF, MoE, Regulatory Agency (ERA after 1998)	†	Advisory for 2 years
Slovak Republic	No	MoF, MoE, Energy Inspection Office	*	N/A
Estonia	No	Energy Market Inspectorate; MoE	‡	N/A
Latvia	Developing	Energy Council; Anti–Monopoly Committee	†	Advisory
Lithuania	Embryonic	Energy Agency and Energy Pricing Council	‡	Advisory
Bulgaria	No	MoF	*	N/A
Romania	No	MoF, MoE	*	N/A
Slovenia	No		*	N/A

* The regulatory function is integrated with the ownership function.
† Regulatory system for private utilities is in operation.
‡ Regulatory system is being established in connection with increased private participation, privatisation or liberalisation.

Sources: Various.

latory decisions by regulatory bodies (on price or non-price issues) tend to go initially to the Ministry of Industry or equivalent and not to the courts. In Hungary, Poland and elsewhere there are, though, the conventional administrative law appeal rights under Continental Law;

- **Obligations to Publish and Justify.** For Ministerial regulators, there are understandably no obligations to publish, explain or give reasons for their decisions. Unfortunately, the same is true for the advisory regulatory agencies. HEO in Hungary has developed into a more open institution, but, in general, regulatory procedures are, as yet, under-developed relative to the UK.

In the former Soviet Union, there are some embryonic electricity regulatory institutions in Russia, Ukraine and Kazakhstan (for example, the Federal Energy Commission in Russia and the National Energy Regulatory Commission in the Ukraine). However, none of them seems yet to have achieved any real degree of autonomy *de facto* and none is as yet assigned powers and duties by parliamentary statute. Political influences appear still to be dominant as evidenced by the 1997 price and trading structure interventions in Russia by Deputy Prime Minister Nemstov.

Regulation of Electricity Prices

The criteria by which electricity and other energy sector prices are to be regulated are probably the single most difficult issue for price regulation. The Hungarian Law uses the term 'justified costs'. Other countries refer to 'objectively determined' or to 'rationalised' costs. These are nowhere defined in primary legislation and the new regulatory agencies have not been given the authority to define them. In Poland, the first major task for price regulation will be to conclude the secondary legislation on prices and, in particular, to define the basis of and criteria for price regulation. ERA can expect to be involved in this process – possibly intensively. Nevertheless, the legal responsibility for formulating and enacting this secondary legislation has been given to the Ministry of Finance and the Ministry of Economy.

Thus far, no government has been prepared to accept the replacement cost of assets as the basis for 'justified' or 'objectively determined' capital costs. No regulatory agency has yet achieved the legal powers or general influence to do so, whether the regulatory agencies discussed above or the Ministerial regulators in the other economies. Stern (1994) argued that the development of effective economic regulation in energy would need to await the emergence of the need for large-scale investment.

One of the main features of economic regulation as practised in the UK and elsewhere is that price regulation is combined with some regulatory oversight of costs. In the US, there has been explicit prior approval of investments, in the UK the regulatory offices evaluate the business plans of regulated businesses. Indeed, the bringing together of regulatory oversight on investment and pricing is seen as being at the heart of economic regulation.

In electricity regulation, the responsibilities for price regulation and investment approval/regulation are typically separate. Thus, in the Czech and Slovak Republics, the Ministry of Finance is responsible for price regulation and the Ministry of Industry and Trade (the Ministry of Economy in the Slovak Republic) is responsible for all electricity investment issues. Indeed, the latter are responsible for licensing and all issues of technical regulation. The same is true in Romania and elsewhere.

In Hungary, the HEO has to consider investment programmes when carrying out its duties on price regulation and it has to prepare system-wide development plans. It is, though, the Ministry of Industry and Trade that is responsible for investment approvals; the HEO has no formal legal role and, particularly where foreign investment proposals are concerned, appears to play little part. In Poland, ERA is to be given the duty to regulate development plans of regulated companies. However, the content and form of this regulation is yet to be determined in secondary legislation to be prepared by the Ministry of Economy.

Competition and Structure

Within many CEE countries, the notion is regularly put forward that regulation is merely a temporary phenomenon until competition has been established, for example by former Prime Minister Klaus in the Czech Republic. However, regulatory practice has shown that competition and general competition law cannot replace regulation until: (i) there are enough competitors and potential new entrants to the competitive parts of the industry (generation and supply for electricity) to ensure that there is no serious risk of abuse of market power; and (ii) it is possible to duplicate networks.

While competition depends on access to monopoly network facilities, economic regulation is required to ensure that network access and pricing support competition. This can clearly be very difficult where transmission and generation are combined, but remains a significant issue even when they are separate – and similarly for distribution and supply. Indeed, the need for and difficulty of regulation can increase as competition over networks is increased. The nature of regulation changes considerably but the need for it does not.

For electricity, there is no sign as yet of competing high-voltage transmission or low-voltage transmission networks. This is in contrast to telecommunications, where radio telephony and internet telephony offer competition and it can be economic to build competing fixed link networks. Even in gas, given sufficient demand growth, it can be economic to build competing high-pressure pipeline networks. That is not the case in electricity.

Access issues, access pricing and competition issues have become important in Hungary and a concern to the Hungarian Energy Office. The main problem is that the Hungarian electricity law does not impose any obligations on the transmission company (MVM) to supply access. In Poland, the energy law requires third-party access – at least for Polish companies.

In other countries, the issue has not yet been properly addressed, not least because neither competition in generation nor the construction of new independently owned plants has yet become a serious concern. In general, these competition and access issues tend to be confounded with (unresolved) debates over the structure of the industry, as in the Czech Republic. It is likely that the regulatory dimensions will only be tackled seriously when debates on the industry and trading structure have been concluded.

Economic regulation is by no means yet a settled part of the institutional arrangements in the energy sector. It not only remains difficult and controversial, but the long-term, probably permanent, need for regulation of network access and pricing is far from accepted.

4. Conclusions and Prospects

We began this paper by using the helpful framework developed by Spiller and his associates to identify the potential strength of institutional arrangements to sustain the regulatory contract in industries characterised by durable sunk investments. The requirements for this problem to be solved satisfactorily seem fairly stringent: the contract has to be enforceable, must be invulnerable to post-contractual opportunism by one of the parties, and, for this reason, must be relatively explicit. Strict satisfaction of all these conditions is likely to be unattainable, not least because in the limit a government with control over Parliament can enact legislation which overturns any contractual underpinnings to a regulatory contract. Moreover, where enforcement is through administrative procedures rather than through a legal contract, a government may be able in practice to subvert the administrative process by personnel changes. By this standard, the development of satisfactory regulatory arrangements seems highly problematic even in countries like the United Kingdom or the USA which are often regarded as exhibiting relatively stable regulatory contracts which provide a reasonable amount of security to investors.

When the analysis is applied to economies in transition, the difficulties multiply. They are exacerbated by two forms of inheritance from the previous régime. One concerns weaknesses of the infrastructure built under socialism, which is inadequate in some sectors and poorly designed and operated in others. On top of these technical difficulties are inherited prices which are not only below cost but are also unbalanced, both with respect to groups of customers and with respect to the services provided.

The second damaging inheritance takes the forms of new and untried Parliamentary procedures, administrative personnel untested in the operation of market systems and a system of law which has to establish its independence as well as develop a legal framework appropriate to a market economy. By any count, the task of developing regulatory institutions in such economies seems unusually difficult.

Yet, despite these difficulties, economies in transition have so far encountered relatively few problems in attracting foreign direct investment. This applies both to the telecommunications sector and the energy sector, the experiences of which have been briefly summarised above. One would expect the return required from such investments to be higher than would apply in traditional market economies. But that still leaves open the question of why investors have been willing to invest at all, given the apparent risks of gradual expropriation which they face.

A number of possible explanations can be found for this puzzle:

- In the case of the electricity sector, over-capacity and waste of energy under the old régime have limited the need for further investment. As a result, Western investors have been able to limit their risks. This does not apply, however, to telecommunications where massive additional investments are required. But international experience shows that telecommunications is potentially a highly profitable industry. Investors must therefore balance the downside risk of expropriation against considerable upside opportunities.

- Many economies in transition are so large and have such potential for growth that companies are willing to take risks even against a background of regulatory uncertainty. A massive investment made by George Soros and his associates in the Russian long-distance operator Svyazinvest falls into this category. It is also noticeable that Western firms are eager to invest in China, despite continuing uncertainties concerning the country's commitment to privatisation of the infrastructure and a regulatory régime which is extremely opaque.

- All countries and governments will also be aware of reputational effects. A single blatant breach of the regulatory contract involving expropriation of foreign investors' sunk assets may jeopardise future prospects of foreign investment in all sectors subject to similar risk or even more broadly. So far, governments in economies in transition have apparently been prepared to preserve their countries' financial reputations, even in the case of short-term temptations in particular industries. Some firms may also be able to take retaliatory measures in the event of expropriation, in the limit by withdrawal of necessary technical inputs or by making it difficult for the networks concerned to get access to spare parts or upgrades.

As with many other aspects of economic reform in economies in transition the optimist can point to evidence that the glass is at least half-full whereas the sceptic can cite evidence that it is at least half-empty. Clearly, major progress has been made in devising regulatory arrangements to support foreign and domestic non-governmental investment into network industries in the Central European countries (particularly in Hungary and Poland) and in the Baltic states. But, the structures are fragile and much remains to be done. The Slovak Republic is an obvious example of a Central European country which has made relatively little progress.

Looking eastwards from Central Europe, the Balkan countries have not yet established any effective regulatory arrangements and network industry investment levels remain low, although the position in Romania must now be much more hopeful. Russia and other countries of the former Soviet Union lag further and there appears to be some evidence of regulatory capture of the embryonic institutions by the powerful utilities. When these countries will make the necessary reforms to utility regulation (as to other areas of economic policy) is an open question.

We should, however, remember that the development of effective regulatory institutions is the response to a demand for them to support investment in the industries. The optimist will expect a response to this demand when the need for large-scale private investment in network industries becomes sufficiently strong.

Events in Asia in the second half of 1997 show the risks of eschewing formal regulatory arrangements in favour of relying on a reputation for sustained growth. Where stock exchanges operate in economies in transition, utility stocks are very important, and the backlash from events in Asia has introduced considerable volatility into returns to those stocks. A more reliable regulatory framework to protect investors should reduce the likelihood of shocks to the availability and cost of private investment funds.

References

Analysys (1997): *Network Operators in Central and Eastern Europe,* Analysys Publications, Cambridge.

Cave, M. and Valentiny, P. (1994): 'Privatisation and Regulation of Utilities in Economies in Transition', in S. Estrin (ed.), *Privatisation in Central and Eastern Europe,* Longmans.

Davies, G., *et al.* (1996): 'Technology and Policy Options for the Telecommunications Sector. The Situation in Central and Eastern Europe and the Former Soviet Union', *Telecommunications Policy,* Vol. 20, No.2, pp. 101-24.

Fingleton, J. *et al.* (1996): *Competition Policy and the Transformation of Eastern Europe,* CEPR.

Jurzyca, E. (1997): *Prospects for Privatisation of Slovak Telecommunications,* Mimeo, CFD, Bratislava.

Levy, B. and Spiller, P. (eds.) (1996): *Regulations, Institutions and Commitment,* Cambridge University Press.

Major, I. (1992): 'Private and Public Infrastructure in Eastern Europe', *Oxford Review of Economic Policy,* Vol. 7, No. 4, pp. 76-92.

Spiller, P. and Sampson, C. (1996): 'Telecommunications Regulations in Jamaica': pp. 36-78 of Levy, B. and Spiller, P. (eds.), *Regulations, Institutions and Commitment.*

Stern, Jon (1994): 'Economic Regulation in Central and Eastern Europe?', *Economics of Transition,* Vol. 2, pp. 391-97.

Stern, Jon (1997): 'What Makes an Independent Regulator Independent', *Business Strategy Review,* Vol. 8, No. 2, pp. 67-74.

Transition (1997): 'The Commission's Report Card', *Transition,* August, pp. 5-8.

CHAIRMAN'S COMMENTS

Sir Bryan Carsberg

I FOUND MARTIN'S PAPER EXTRAORDINARILY INTERESTING. Had he begun by saying, 'I am going to talk tonight about a situation in which we start with prices very much out of balance; where regulators are going to have to make some tough decisions that will put up the bills for consumers; and people are worried about whether businesses will invest because there is a danger that arrangements may change politically and they are not sure about getting their money back in five years or whatever', it would *not* have been clear that he was not talking about the UK. What he has described is a situation that differs only in degree from the one we know in the West. Most of these problems have been present in one form or another in most countries and the division between countries in transition for developing countries and others is itself not clear.

Will a particular set of arrangements that seems to work in one country work in another? When I was at OFTEL, for example, I was invited to visit India, a country which showed many of the same problems and many of the same issues as I confronted in the UK. The international telephone company which invited me to lecture in India was very frustrated by the domestic telephone operators' inability to give a good performance. I asked whether a country in the position of India should promote competition. Are the arguments for doing that the same as they are in the UK? Should one look for the same kind of incentive regulation? Should privatisation be part of the solution?. As I went through the analysis it seemed to me that a lot of the time we were saying that the solutions *should* be the same.

The special problem of such countries is the extraordinarily low penetration rate and low levels of wealth. But judged on the numbers Martin gave, the situation is rather that not everybody who can afford a telephone can get one, a strange paradox. On competition, you indicated that the actual development had not been to promote competition, although you did not actually say that competition would not have been a good idea. It seems to me that a government wishing to promote consumer welfare would very much want competition. Whether or not you could persuade the companies to go along with it is another question. Competitors will vie with each other to get a network rolled out quickly so that they can get the customers signed up, hoping that once they have got the customers there will be some customer loyalty, from which they will reap the benefits later. An entrant from abroad, if it had the choice, would probably prefer to have a monopoly, and indeed might insist on it. But that may be a mistaken policy on its part. Anyone who observed, as I did, the initial stages of the mobile telephone business in the UK cannot avoid the impression that not only did competition mean that the network was rolled out, and customers signed up faster than would otherwise have been the case, but possibly both participants in the first round of competition came out better than they would have done as a monopolist, because of the market excitement that was developed by the competitive activity, as well as the stimulation of fighting for market share.

Thinking about the mobile system leads me on to say that one is not necessarily looking just for head-to-head competition, but also for competition among technologies. In telecoms, as opposed to other utilities, there seem to be particularly great gains from this aspect of competition. I understand such competition is taking place in these countries. Mobile systems are developing, effectively competing with the fixed systems. The mobile systems provide a particular opportunity for getting service out quickly and at relatively low investment compared to what would be needed with the fixed systems. This seems a very good strategy for these countries. At OFTEL we sometimes thought that mobile systems would compete with the fixed systems head on effectively before long, and might actually be the mode for all telecoms services for some people. If so, mobile systems have a very important role in countries in transition, because they can avoid the false trail of developing fixed-link systems.

As far as incentive regulation is concerned, the second leg of the three-legged policy stool, again, if one has a monopoly situation the same strong argument for having it in countries in transition seems to apply. Surely it is always better to have incentive regulation than the sort of regulation that does not provide incentives? The third leg – privatisation – is presumably needed in much the same way, to make incentive regulation competition work, and particularly perhaps, to draw in the capital that is needed for the investment that will not be available on state budgets.

If the same three solutions *are* applied, you run into some particularly interesting issues concerning the difficulty of instability in the political situation, as it bears on having an adequate regulatory contract. It is interesting to speculate about what kind of defensive reactions by companies you would expect to find in that kind of situation, to compare with what you actually observed. It is surprising that it has not been more difficult for these countries to get a willing participant in the operating systems. As Martin has said, it is impossible to get an absolutely firm assurance about these matters, anywhere. But checks and balances are some assurance. I suppose the UK situation does this, with independent regulation and certain limited appeal mechanisms. Under its present structure, things have to go wrong under two or three different heads before you are in really deep trouble. But as Martin said, Parliament cannot be stopped from passing laws. The whole situation could be changed if people wanted it to be so. I was interested particularly by the characterisation of the political situation in the UK as 'volatile' and the comparison with the United States, where there is a balance of powers which gives rather stronger protection.

By way of protection, one move for companies investing in these transitional economies would be to form largish consortia, so that they could spread the risk, with no one company investing too much in any one country. If I understand it correctly, that has not happened a great deal. A number of companies have had rather large individual investments; the risk has not been spread in that way. If that is the case, perhaps it is because the companies think that the diversification takes place at the level of their investors. But one would expect in that situation that management would want to diversify. Certainly, one supposes that the companies investing in economies in transition expect to get a higher than normal rate of return. I suppose time will prove whether or not their expectations have been realistic.

The idea of the regulatory contract that was made explicit in Jamaica's case was also very interesting – one would expect companies to try to secure such a contract, and to try to write into the contractual terms some form of guaranteed compensation if there is a fundamental change in the situation. As we both have recognised, none of those things gives absolutely firm protection because the government can always pass new laws overriding existing contracts; and a revolutionary situation is possible. But I guess a contract at least strengthens the companies' moral position.

When one looks at it through the analytical vehicle Martin has given, I am a bit surprised that so much has happened so promisingly in these countries in transition and that the operators have not been more reluctant to invest. They seem to me to be putting a very high reliance on the future potential. This presumably does promise a very high upside to set against the downside. But I might have been a bit more cautious than some of them appear to have been!

2

LOCAL COMPETITION IN UK TELECOMMUNICATIONS[1]

Mark Armstrong

Nuffield College, Oxford

1. Introduction

THIS PAPER WILL DISCUSS SOME ASPECTS OF RECENT POLICY TOWARDS THE TELECOMMUNICATIONS INDUSTRY in the UK. Specifically, I will largely be concerned with policy towards the basic voice telephony service over fixed networks and how the introduction of local network competition, and the manner of its introduction, affects this policy.[2] Local competition is now a fact in the UK and a few other countries, and many subscribers in Britain currently have a choice between BT, the cable companies, Mercury (or Cable and Wireless Communications as it now is), Ionica and others to provide their connection to the public network. (In addition, they may connect via a mobile network, but this lies outside the scope of the paper.) Questions discussed in the paper include:

- What are the benefits of local competition? In particular, to what extent can the successful introduction of such competition remove the need for retail price regulation and the control of interconnection pricing?

- What are the costs of local competition? In particular, what are the physical costs involved in the duplication of local networks?

---

[1] I am grateful for information and discussion to David Lewin, Geoffrey Myers, Michael Ryan and John Vickers. However, all views and any errors are my own.

[2] For recent discussions of the important developments in the USA, see Crandall and Waverman (1995, Chapter 7) and Vogelsang and Mitchell (1997).

- What effect does BT's current structure of tariffs have on the pattern of entry (and vice versa)?

- Should policy be designed to 'assist' entry into local telecommunications, and what are the costs associated with entry assistance?

These three questions are addressed in sections 4, 5 and 6 respectively. In section 2 I summarise the current state of the UK market, and in section 3 some aspects of costs and technology involved in local network construction are briefly discussed. Finally, section 7 offers some thoughts on future policy towards local competition. Although for simplicity most of the discussion is in terms of basic voice telephony, many of the arguments can easily be extended to include other enhanced services (of which TV services are an important example).

2. The State of the Local Market in the UK

Policy towards competition in the UK market falls into two distinct periods: from 1984 until 1991 (the 'duopoly policy' era) Mercury, or MCL, was BT's only nationwide competitor (and the only other operator permitted to offer international services), whereas from 1991 onwards entry was permitted into virtually all sectors of the industry.[3] During the duopoly policy era, Mercury's entry was largely in the long-distance and international sectors, at least for residential subscribers, and there was very little local network competition. Some summary statistics for the year 1992/3 (just after the ending of the duopoly policy) are given in Table 1. Thus, at the end of the duopoly policy era, BT had the overwhelming majority of direct connections to subscribers, and a slightly more moderate market share for long-distance and international calls.

The reason for these differences in Mercury's market shares, of course, is that it was possible to use Mercury's network without being directly connected to it: if a person so desired she could use Mercury's network by keeping her BT line (on which she continued

---

[3] See Armstrong, Cowan and Vickers (1994, Chapter 7) and Armstrong (1997a) for more detail on the UK industry since BT's privatisation in 1984. In fact, the international sector remained a duopoly until 1996 when many firms were granted licences to provide such services.

TABLE 1: Market Shares of BT and Mercury in 1992/3 (Business and Residential) (per cent)

	BT	*Mercury*
(directly connected) Subscribers:	98.7	0.5
Local call minutes:	95.6	3.0
National call minutes:	89.2	10.5
International call minutes:	77.4	21.9

Source: Oftel, 1997b, Tables 2 and 4.

to pay the standard rate for quarterly line rental and local calls) and access Mercury's network by dialling a rather lengthy access code for each long-distance call.[4] Therefore, although there was a degree of competition in the long-distance market, it is fair to say that because of the asymmetric nature of the two trunk operators – to make a call on Mercury's network required substantial extra dialling – the market was, at least in this respect, heavily tilted in BT's favour.[5] This asymmetry comes not just from the extra dialling required, but also from the fact that the 'default' option was to use BT's network so that if a subscriber did nothing, she was directed to BT's trunk network. In sum, to use the industry jargon, there did not exist 'equal access' to Mercury's network. Thus, the industry structure was roughly as depicted in Figure 1A below. (In Figures 1A and 1B a *solid* line indicates that a subscriber on the local network can easily use the associated trunk network, and a *dotted* line signifies that a subscriber on BT's local network can use the rival trunk network(s), but only by incurring significantly greater inconvenience.)

---

[4] Alternatively, she could purchase a special 'blue button' telephone that dialled the access code automatically.

[5] Mercury also had advantages in its battle against BT: BT's retail tariff in the early post-privatisation era was relatively unbalanced and it used revenues from trunk services to cross-subsidise local services. In section 5 below I argue that unbalanced tariffs also aid the entry of local networks.

Figure 1A
The Market Pre-1991

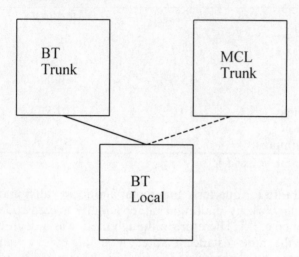

Figure 1B
The Market Post-1991

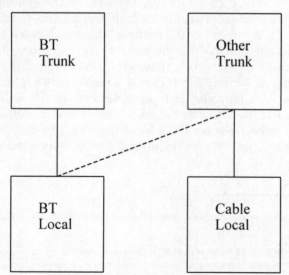

With the ending of the duopoly policy, however, many more firms entered the industry, both in the long-distance and local markets. In the latter case, the most significant entrants so far have been the cable TV companies. Prior to 1991, cable TV was introduced to many regions of the country in competition with terrestrial broadcast and satellite TV, and a single cable company was licensed to operate in each of the franchise areas. Because of the duopoly policy that then existed, however, these firms were not permitted to offer telephony services over their networks, something that was possible at little extra cost. In 1991, however, cable telephony was permitted, and since that time the companies have managed to achieve a substantial market share in local telephony. BT is not itself permitted to provide TV services over its telephony network (although it is permitted to own cable companies), a feature which is discussed further in section 6 below.

Since the cable companies are only local companies, the vast bulk of long-distance traffic originating on cable networks must be carried by other companies such as Mercury.[6] However, this is organised at the wholesale level by the cable networks themselves, and their subscribers typically do not have a choice of long-distance network.[7] Thus, for instance a cable company may arrange that Mercury's long-distance network is used wherever possible and will negotiate terms of carriage with Mercury to this end. Its subscribers, though, only deal with the cable company. In particular, a cable subscriber cannot use BT's long-distance network by, for instance, dialling some access code. In sum, the current state of the market is schematically shown in Figure 1B above, and a BT subscriber can use other long-distance carriers by dialling an access code (as in Figure 1A), but a cable subscriber has no such choice.

As well as the liberalisation of the market, another important policy development since 1991 has been to make it much easier to access rival trunk networks from BT's local network. Thus, instead

---

[6]   In fact, in April 1997 Mercury merged with three of the largest cable companies (Bell Cablemedia, Nynex CableComms and Videotron) to form Cable and Wireless Communications. Thus there is now a major vertically integrated competitor to BT in the residential sector.

[7]   An exception to this is that cable subscribers can access the independent international companies, but they typically have to do so using a very lengthy dialling sequence (e.g. a 10-digit freephone number, followed by a 12- digit customer identification number, followed by the desired international number itself).

of dialling a lengthy access code, a BT subscriber typically needs only to dial '133' to gain access to Mercury's network (once contact has been made with Mercury). Oftel uses the term 'easy access' for this procedure. This still, however, falls some way short of any form of fully 'equal access' since, for instance, the default option is still for a BT subscriber to use BT's long-distance network.[8]

Tables 2 and 3 describe the recent state of the market, as a whole and just for residential subscribers, following these policy developments. When interpreting these tables, note that the market share for calls for cable companies measures the share of calls *billed* to cable subscribers, and many of the long-distance and international calls made by cable subscribers will in fact be physically carried on Mercury's trunk network. Thus, the main differences with the duopoly era market are the arrival of the cable companies together with a very significant increase in competition in international telephony from independent operators (which has had the effect of reducing the market share of both BT and Mercury since 1992/3).

TABLE 2

Market Shares in December 1996 (Business and Residential)

(per cent)

	BT	*Mercury*	*Cable*	*Others*
Subscribers:	90.6	1.0	7.5	0.9
Local call minutes:	86.1	2.4	9.8	1.7
National call minutes:	79.1	10.7	5.1	5.1
International call minutes:	57.9	15.6	5.1	21.4

Source: Oftel, 1997a, Tables 5 and 7.

---

[8] In addition, the cost to the user of dialling just a few extra digits may still be significant: Oftel (1996c, p. 21) reports evidence that users believe that the cost of dialling an extra four digits is equivalent to a price disadvantage of about 4 per cent. In addition, if a user is not paying the telephone bill herself (say, when she uses the phone at work), then she has little incentive to incur even a small inconvenience.

TABLE 3:
Market Shares in December 1996 (residential subscribers only)

	BT	Mercury	Cable	Others
Subscribers:	90.4	0.0	9.0	0.6
Local call minutes:	88.3	0.1	11.5	0.1
National call minutes:	88.3	5.0	6.4	0.3
International call minutes:	77.0	8.1	8.0	6.9

Source: Oftel, 1997a, Tables 8 and 10.

Table 3 shows that cable subscribers tend to have slightly different calling patterns from the average residential subscriber, and make more local calls (perhaps because the broadband cable networks are well-suited for using the internet, and also because many cable companies offer free local calls to other subscribers on the same network) and fewer longer distance calls. When interpreting the market share of the cable companies, it should be remembered that cable is only licensed in a limited number of geographic areas, although new franchises are being granted from time to time. In July 1997 around 17 million homes lay within cable franchise areas, or about 75 per cent of all homes in the UK. Of these 17 million, about 9.5 million homes had actually been 'passed' by cable, that is, were able to subscribe to TV and/or telephone services from the local cable company. In other words, only about 40 per cent of homes could subscribe to cable services in July 1997, and of those homes around 26 per cent actually subscribed to telephony services.[9] Thus, as the cable companies

---

[9] These data are taken from a News Release from the Independent Television Commission dated 4 September 1997. In MMC (1995, paragraph 4.11) it is stated that virtually all cable companies do offer telephony as well as TV services, or plan to do so. Of the two franchisees that do not, in the areas of Westminster, Aberdeen and Coventry, one is a subsidiary of BT and the other leases the cable network from BT.

TABLE 4
Net Residential Subscriber Growth, December 1995 to December 1996

	BT	*Cable*
Net number of new residential subscribers:	27,000	727,000
Residential subscriber growth rate (per cent):	0.1	55.5

Source: Oftel, 1997a, Table 12.

continue to build their networks their overall market share can be expected to rise considerably, as is illustrated in Table 4.

In addition to the cable companies, the main other source of local network competition in the near future is expected to come from the 'fixed wireless' entrants, such as Ionica, which use radio links to provide the final connection into homes and business. As discussed in the next section, this technology has several attractive features, but entrants using the technology are at a very early stage in their launch, and whether they will eventually be successful remains to be seen.

3. Local Network Technology

The transmission technologies used in (fixed) local networks fall into two categories: wire networks and wireless networks. The former may be based on the traditional copper technology, which has only moderate carrying capacity (although there have been marked improvements in recent years), on coaxial cable, which has much higher carrying capacity, and on fibre-optic cables. Wireless networks, on the other hand, use radio links to carry the signal into a person's home or business (but in contrast to mobile networks, fixed wireless networks do not allow subscribers to roam from their premises).

For the present analysis, the three most important aspects of technology in the local network are the sunk-cost nature of much of the required investment, the prevalence of economies of density in network construction, and the extent of economies of scope between TV and telephony provision on a single network. Wire-based networks of all types involve a very large degree of sunk costs. For instance, if a network operator has already laid a cable into a person's house which cost, say, £500 in 1990, and which had a useful life of 30 years, and a rival firm lays a new cable and signs up the subscriber, then the original cable no longer generates revenue for the original company. The fact that costs are sunk implies that, if free to do so, a network will only lay a new cable into a person's premises if it believes that future revenues generated by the connection will cover the initial cost.

The local telecommunications networks installed by the cable companies are not precisely *sunk* – for that to be true there would have to be no significant other use for the network – since the networks can also be used for television service provision. A very rough figure for the per-line cost of installing a cable network is obtained by dividing the cable companies' reported annual investment – which was approximately £2.2 billion in the year 1996 – by the increase in the number of homes passed by the networks, which was about 2.3 million in 1996. Thus the approximate incremental cost of laying a (broadband) cable network is £950 per line.[10]

Alternatively, an approximate measure of the cost of BT's local network can be computed: according to BT (1997, p. 10) the 'mean capital employed' in BT's 'access' network (which is defined to be the business associated with providing connections, take-over and maintenance of exchange lines) was £9.3 billion in the year 1995/6 as measured in current cost terms, and in that period it had about 27 million exchange lines. Therefore, the capital employed per line in this year, as measured in current cost terms, was about £345. The large difference between these two numbers is due to a number of factors, including (i) the fact that the cable companies are still building their networks, and economies of density will probably cause their average cost to fall, (ii) the cable networks are technologically more advanced, broadband networks, whereas BT's

---

[10] See *The Financial Times*, 11 June 1997, and statistics provided on the web-site of the Cable Communications Association. The figure obtained represents an order-of-magnitude estimate, and in one sense will be an over-estimate of the cost of installing a new telecommunications local network (since the networks also provide TV services which require additional investment), and in another will be an under-estimate (since a modest further investment is required actually to connect a home which has been passed by the network).

access network still uses predominantly copper technology, and (iii) BT's network is of an older vintage. But however it is measured, it is clear that the average cost of constructing a wire-based local network is several hundred pounds per connection.

The costs associated with providing a wireless network, however, involve much lower sunk costs, since pavements do not have to be dug up, cables laid, and so on. Also, many of the connection costs, such as the receiving station in a premises, could be removed and used elsewhere if the subscriber chooses to disconnect. In sum, a basic difference between wire-based and wireless local networks is that former have significant subscriber-specific sunk costs which cannot be recovered in the event of the subscriber disconnecting, whereas the latter have no such significant costs. This may have important implications for tariff structures in a competitive marketplace, as discussed further in section 7 below.

The second important feature of local network technology is the presence of economies of density. Thus, especially for wire-based networks, the average cost of network construction decreases as the density of subscribers, that is, the number of subscribers per square mile, increases. This is because in a dense network many savings can be made, in terms of digging up pavements and so on, by concentrating several wires in a single cable/duct and using remote concentrators to split up wires close to a premises. This effect is much less pronounced for wireless networks, and the cost characteristics of the two technologies are schematically illustrated in Figure 2.

Thus, in many situations it is cheaper to build a wireless (rather than a wire-based) network when subscribers are sparsely situated. Bearing in mind that the relevant parameter is *subscriber* density (rather than total population density), even in urban areas it may well be cost-effective for a new entrant, which does not expect to achieve a large market share, to invest in a wireless network, especially given the small degree of sunk costs involved in such a strategy.

Finally, there is the question of the extent of economies of scope in providing cable TV services and telephony over the same broadband network. Little public information is available on this point, but there can be little doubt that the incremental cost of upgrading BT's largely copper-based local network to carry a full range of TV services, while substantial, is very much less than the

Figure 2: Economies of Density in Local Networks

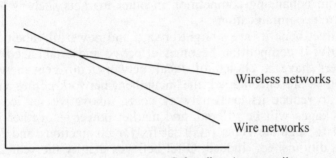

Cost per subscriber

Subscribers/square mile

stand-alone cost of constructing a cable network from scratch (which was estimated above to be roughly £950 per line), if for no other reason than that the necessary ducts and rights-of-way are already in place. Similarly, the incremental cost of converting a cable TV network to provide telephony is modest.[11]

Taking these three factors together, for the foreseeable future it is hard to imagine more than two significant wire-based local networks competing for residential subscribers in any given region, these being BT and the local cable operator. It is an open question whether any fixed wireless operator will be able to make a significant impact. Unlike other sectors in telecommunications, therefore, we must expect a significant degree of market concentration in the local market, even in the longer term.

---

[11] In DTI (1990, p. 31), the then Director General of Telecommunications reported that Oftel carried out a study into this question, and concluded that: 'If the cable operator's trench and duct costs were fully recovered from entertainment revenues, and taking into account the potential loss of economies of scale by the incumbent operator, the introduction of competition would result in only a small increase in the overall cost of providing telephony services.' However, it is important to note that the comparison was between the situations where (i) cable companies offered entertainment services and BT offered telephony, and (ii) where cable companies offered both entertainment services and telephony, and BT offered telephony, and the possibility of a single firm, BT, offering both entertainment and telephony, was not considered.

4. Benefits of Local Competition

There are two broad sources of benefits from local competition: the *direct* benefit from introducing choice in this hitherto monopolised sector of the industry, and the possible *indirect* benefit which may result from enhancing competition in other markets such as long-distance telecommunications.

The direct benefits are straightforward and powerful, albeit hard to quantify: if competition becomes effective and established then subscribers have a choice of local network, different network technologies are encouraged, the incumbent network comes under pressure to reduce its local network costs, innovative service and tariff packages will be offered, and market power – together with the need to regulate BT's retail tariffs for connections and local calls – is diminished. Indeed, Oftel believes that by the year 2001 competition will be so well established that no formal retail price controls for BT will be required.[12]

Another, somewhat controversial benefit – or cost depending on one's viewpoint – is that competition will bring pressure to make BT's retail tariffs more cost-reflective. (At present, for instance, BT is required to set geographically uniform tariffs despite the fact that its cost of serving subscribers differs widely.) We return to this point later.

A more subtle kind of benefit from local competition concerns its potentially desirable effect on other markets such as long-distance telecommunications. Behind this possibility is the basic idea that whichever firm controls the point of access of a subscriber to the network also to a large extent controls other services consumed by that subscriber. This may be the case for at least two reasons: (i) subscribers may place a large premium on receiving all services from, and paying a bill to, a single supplier, that is, they like using a 'one-stop shop' which might naturally be considered to be the chosen local network, and (ii) regulation, no matter how benevolent, may be unable to prevent completely a vertically integrated operator from distorting competition in potentially competitive markets in its favour. (The second reason was the main motive for the dramatic break-up of AT&T in 1984.) The theoretical literature on this latter point, both in regulated and unregulated settings, is extensive, and

---

12 See Oftel (1996a, p. 1).

this is not the place to discuss it in depth.[13] However, Oftel's view on the matter is illustrated in the following (Oftel, 1996b, p. 11):

'Oftel considers that greater competition in the international and national markets will have little impact for most residential customers, since they generally take all their calls as a combined package of local/national/international calls from their local access provider . . . Residential customers will, therefore, in most cases only be able to take advantage of the greater competition in national and international calls when they have effective competition amongst alternative local access providers.'[14]

It is worth investigating the above argument in more detail. The costs and benefits of using Mercury's long-distance network while remaining connected to BT's network are summarised in Table 5. Thus the costs comprise (i) the cost of making contact with Mercury, (ii) the per-call cost of extra dialling (which is needed if 'equal access' is not introduced), and (iii) the increased transactions cost of dealing with two operators. Of course, it is important to remember that costs (ii) and (iii) are *endogenous* and can be affected by policy (for example, 'equal access' could be introduced together with all billing functions being performed by the local operator). On the other hand, if a subscriber switches from BT to a combined cable/long-distance operator, the costs and benefits are set out in Table 6.

Thus some of the costs and benefits are the same in the two cases. What is different is that (i) there is now no cost associated with dealing with two operators, and (ii) there is a new cost associated with having to change telephone number (if 'number portability' has not been introduced). The above quote from Oftel suggests that not many subscribers believe the benefits outweigh the costs in Table 5 whereas more subscribers believe there is a net benefit in Table 6.

---

[13] See Armstrong, Cowan and Vickers (1994, Chapter 4) for an overview of this topic.

[14] In fact, Oftel's position on the benefits of indirect access seems ambiguous: later in the same document (p. 61) it states that it 'remains of the view that indirect access will make a significant contribution to a competitive market for a substantial number of residential and small business customers.'

TABLE 5
Costs and Benefits of Using Mercury's Long-Distance Network While Remaining a BT Subscriber

Benefits	*Costs*
Lower call charges	Cost of arranging contractual relationship with new operator
Possibly superior quality	Possible per-call cost of extra dialling
	Possible cost of paying bills to two networks rather than one

TABLE 6
Costs and Benefits of Switching to Cable/Trunk Operator from BT

Benefits	*Costs*
Lower call charges	Cost of arranging contractual relationship with new operator
Possibly superior quality/ enhanced range of services	Possible cost of having to change telephone number

This is especially likely to be true if (a) 'equal access' is not introduced for indirect access to trunk networks, and (b) 'number portability' is introduced. If these twin conditions are satisfied, as is the case currently, then it is indeed likely that the introduction of local competition will increase competition in the long-distance market.

Of course, it is arguable that a more *direct* method of enhancing competition in trunk services would be to undertake a policy such as 'equal access' – see Oftel (1996c) for an economic analysis of the desirability of such a policy. In fact, in Department of Trade and Industry (1991, para. 7.12) the then Director General of

Telecommunications concluded that 'equal access should be introduced as soon as possible'. One illustration of the effectiveness of equal access comes from the city of Hull, which for historical reasons has its own local telecommunications operator (Kingston Communications). There, a subscriber can use Mercury's long-distance network on a call-by-call basis by dialling a two-digit access code, and if no code is dialled BT carries the call by default. (Thus, even here there is not full equal access.) The local carrier does all the billing, and so subscribers do not receive a separate bill from Mercury. Thus there is no significant cost of arranging a contractual relationship with Mercury. According to Oftel (1996c, p. 24), in Hull Mercury receives over *half* of outgoing long-distance calls, which compares with about 10 per cent across the country as a whole (see Table 2 above).

However, the analysis commissioned by Oftel concluded (in Oftel, 1996c, p. 74) that 'there is *no conclusive evidence* that, in the UK at this present time, equal access ... has benefits that exceed its costs' (emphasis in original). Of course, the predicted benefits of equal access depend crucially on its predicted effect on long-distance market shares. The central assumption in Oftel (1996c) was that the introduction of equal access would cause the number of BT exchange lines using indirect services from other long-distance operators to increase only by about 1 million from 1.5 million to 2.5 million, that is, the vast majority of BT subscribers would continue to use BT's long-distance services. It is possible that this assumption was unduly conservative, especially given the experience in Hull. In any event, as a result of its study Oftel has no plans to introduce equal access in the foreseeable future.[15] (Another possible motive for its reluctance to introduce equal access, namely

---

[15] This policy of Oftel's may well run into conflict with European Union policy towards the industry. For instance, a recent Green Paper (CEC, 1996) proposes that 'carrier pre-selection', which is a form of equal access, should be mandatory in all EU member states from the year 2000. In addition, CEC (1996, section IV.1) estimates that the benefits of equal access outweigh the costs by a factor of 10 to 1, in stark contrast with the economic analysis in Oftel (1996c). However, no details of these estimates are available. It is likely, though, that many of the benefits are assumed to arise from a dramatic rebalancing of long-distance call charges in continental Europe, something that has already occurred to a large extent in the UK. Moreover, the UK already has in place 'easy access' which goes some way towards realising the benefits of equal access.

the damage it may do to the profitability of local network entrants, is discussed in section 6 below.)

Finally, although well understood by Oftel and others but nevertheless worth emphasising, competition in local networks, even if highly vigorous, does not necessarily do away with the need to regulate *some* aspects of pricing. Even if a local network has a small number of subscribers, it still holds a monopoly on delivering calls from other networks to those subscribers. Since its own subscribers do not pay for the cost of delivering their calls (at least with current arrangements), they do not care especially about what it costs callers to make calls to them. There will, therefore, be a strong incentive for *any* local operator to set an excessive price for delivering calls, and this will require control. (However, one highly speculative method of overcoming this ultimate bottleneck problem is discussed in the concluding section.)

5. Drawbacks of Local Competition

The main potential disadvantages of local competition are to do with the duplication of sunk-cost infrastructure and the losses of economies of density and scope, as discussed in section 3 above. These two effects are logically quite distinct. The first is essentially a *dynamic* issue: given that BT has already ducts and wires in place for the majority of households and businesses, and this investment has no other useful purpose, it is wasteful for a second operator to build another network and lay a second cable duct into homes and businesses. (We have already seen that the cost of local network construction is of the order of several hundred pounds per connection.) BT's local infrastructure for those subscribers it loses to rivals is then worthless. The second effect – the losses of economies of density and scope – is essentially *static* and would be an issue regardless of whether infrastructure investment was sunk: all else equal it is cheaper to build (i) a single local telephony network in a given region than for two networks to split the market, and (ii) a single network providing both TV and telephony services than to have two networks specialising in the two services.

There are two methods which might be considered to ameliorate these drawbacks: rivals could have access to BT's ducts when laying their own cables, and rivals could buy or rent BT's local connection into a home or business. Oftel (1996d) discusses the pros and cons of duct and pole sharing, a practice that is quite common in North America. BT is unwilling to share its ducts on public land, claiming that allowing such access could damage network security, and also that it has a very uneven pattern of spare duct capacity. In any event, there are clearly substantial practical problems with mandating duct sharing, albeit problems which seem to have been overcome in other countries, and Oftel has not yet come to any firm conclusion about its policy in this area.

An alternative, which is currently being considered in the United States and elsewhere, is to allow local operators to buy or rent BT's local connection to a subscriber (at some regulated price) should a subscriber decide to switch operator from BT. In practical terms what would happen is that the rival would take over the local connection up to roughly the point where it meets BT's local exchange, and then divert the signal to its own (nearby) local exchange, thus saving the substantial cost of installing its own local connection. (Oftel uses the term 'direct connection to the access network' for this practice, though the term 'line-side interconnection' is also used within the industry.) On the surface, this seems a desirable policy since much sunk investment continues to be utilised. However, Oftel's policy on this question is clear (Oftel, 1996e, pp. 8-9):

> 'Although Oftel recognises that direct connection to the Access Network is feasible, it would run counter to the UK policy of encouraging alternative infrastructure ... It would undermine the value of the investment other operators, particularly cable companies, have made in building their own infrastructure... Any move to allow operators to take over BT exchange lines would undermine past investments and jeopardise future plans.'

Thus the issue is again one of sunk costs, this time concerning the *cable* networks: the fact that cable companies have already invested substantially in their networks, including the provision of their own local connections, makes Oftel unwilling to devalue this investment by making it easier for *future* entrants to construct their own networks. Moreover, it is unlikely that the cable companies (or the wireless entrants) would make substantial use of the ability to take over BT's copper connections, since these wires are not easily capable of carrying TV signals. Therefore, a policy of allowing local operators to take over BT's local connections would have little benefit for the cable companies and some possible drawbacks. As a result, Oftel has no plans to allow direct connection to the access network for the foreseeable future.

Another cost of local competition is the probable need to introduce number portability when there are multiple local operators, so that a subscriber can keep her old telephone number if she changes to a rival network (and remains at the same address).[16] If this policy is not implemented then many residential and business subscribers will be reluctant to switch operator even if they prefer the price/service package on offer from the rival. For instance, MMC (1995, Table 7.4) reports evidence that a residential subscriber would typically require an additional price discount of 10 per cent from a rival network to consider seriously changing if she could not keep her number, compared to the case where she could keep the number. However, introducing number portability incurs costs, not just due to increased regulatory activity, but also physical costs of more complicated call routing and software requirements.

Another cost of *laissez-faire* local competition arises if the current structure of BT's retail tariffs – in particular, the requirement that BT sets geographically uniform tariffs – is maintained, which is the danger of 'cream-skimming' entry. To illustrate this, suppose there are two types of subscribers, 'rural' and 'urban', who are identical in every way except for the cost of supplying services to them. Suppose that BT receives the same revenue R from each type of subscriber (because of geographical uniformity of its tariff), and that it incurs the total cost C_H when supplying a rural subscriber and cost $C_L < C_H$ when supplying an urban subscriber. It is natural to assume that $C_L < R < C_H$ so that it is profitable for BT to serve urban but not rural subscribers at its mandated tariff. Suppose an entrant provides an identical set of services to BT, and that there is no subscriber inertia (for example, because there is number portability). Therefore, the entrant can obtain (almost) the same revenue R from a subscriber by slightly undercutting BT's tariff and causing the subscriber to switch operator. Then the entrant will find it profitable to supply an urban subscriber if its own cost of supplying services, denoted c_L, satisfies $c_L < R$ whereas productive efficiency requires that it should supply the subscriber only if $c_L < C_L$. Thus if

---

[16] More generally, the complexity of numbering administration arrangements, at least for geographic numbers, is much increased by local competition.

$C_L < c_L < R$ the entrant finds it profitable to serve urban subscribers even though it is *less* efficient than BT. Similarly, if $R < c_H < C_H$ then the entrant will not find it profitable to serve a rural subscriber even though it is *more* efficient than BT.

As well as the danger of inefficient entry (and inefficient lack of entry) when BT's tariff is not cost-reflective, there is also the danger that with significant entry BT will lose much of its profitable urban market and be unable to finance its loss-making rural subscribers. These twin dangers combine to make a significant drawback for *laissez-faire* local competition in the longer term. There are two natural remedies for this: (i) allow BT to charge different tariffs (for instance, different connection and line rental charges) for high-cost and low-cost subscribers, or (ii) require entrants to face the same implicit tax/subsidy scheme as that imposed on BT. The former response may be 'politically unacceptable', at least in the medium term, and is discussed a little more in section 7 below. The second would, for instance, impose a tax on urban entry of $T = R - C_L$ per subscriber, which implies that an entrant with costs c_L would serve an urban subscriber if

$$0 < R - c_L - T$$
$$= C_L - c_L$$

that is, if and only if the entrant is more efficient. As well as ensuring productive efficiency, this tax would ensure that BT remains able to finance its loss-making obligations. However, this scheme would be complex and controversial to operate, and a long way from Oftel's plan to withdraw from detailed regulation.[17]

A response which does *not* by itself solve both these problems, however, is to maintain the present geographically uniform structure of BT's tariff and to establish a 'universal service fund' which compensates the providers of loss-making services (in practice, BT), which is financed by all firms in the industry. Such a system would

---

[17].This tax is an instance of what is known as the 'efficient component pricing rule'– see for instance Armstrong, Doyle and Vickers (1996) for a detailed discussion of this rule. Oftel's earlier régime of 'access deficit contributions', which bore many similarities with the efficient component pricing rule, has recently been abandoned – see Armstrong, Cowan and Vickers (1994, section 7.5.6) for a discussion of controversies surrounding the levying of these charges.

solve the financing issue but would still give entrants the wrong price signals, and the danger of inefficient entry into the profitable markets would remain.[18]

6. Entry Assistance in Local Telecoms

Oftel, together with the previous Conservative Government, has clearly been pursuing a policy of actively assisting entry into local telecommunications, with the aim of ensuring that the new entrants eventually reach a strength that they can compete effectively, and presumably without assistance, against BT. Oftel's vision of the future state of local competition is clear (Oftel, 1996e, p. 8):

'The UK's aim is that all consumers should have the choice of at least three operators. These might comprise BT, a cable operator, a radio access operator and/or an indirect access operator.'

The main strands of this assistance policy have been:

- A prohibition on BT and Mercury providing TV services over their telecommunications networks, while allowing the cable companies to provide both TV and telephony since 1991. (This ban was provisionally until the year 2001, but the new Labour Government has indicated that it may abandon the policy.) This has the effect of assisting entry into telephony since it (greatly) increases the profitability of the supply of TV services by cable companies – their only rivals in the pay TV market are from satellite provision – which can then be extended at little incremental cost to provide telephony as well.[19] Of course, such

---

[18] The introduction of a universal service fund was considered in Oftel (1995). However, Oftel judged that at the present time BT did not incur a net cost in providing its social obligations – it received various intangible benefits such as ubiquity and brandname recognition which compensated for its costs – and in Oftel (1997e) it decided against the use of such a fund for the time being.

[19] In 1996, BT tried indirectly to compete in the market for joint supply of TV and telephony by announcing a promotion whereby any subscriber who also subscribed to the satellite provider BSkyB would obtain a total discount of £99 on what she would normally pay for telephony and TV separately. (Such an offer would clearly be tempting to a subscriber considering whether to switch to a cable company.) However, Oftel determined that such a promotion was 'unduly preferential in that it targeted, and offered continuing benefits to, only those who became and remained customers both of BT and of BSkyB. ... the arrangements could have

a policy incurs significant efficiency costs – which may or may not be recouped by the future benefits of a more competitive industry – since it prevents BT from jointly supplying TV and telephony services even though it may be more efficient than the cable companies in doing so.

• A prohibition on BT and Mercury using fixed wireless technology in their networks (other than in sparsely populated rural areas where competition is unlikely to materialise in any event). This clearly encourages entry from rival fixed wireless networks such as Ionica.

• An unwillingness to require BT to offer equal access to rivals in the long-distance and international markets, at least for the time being. The reason that this benefits local entrants (both cable and wireless operators) is that many subscribers will switch to, say, a cable operator in large part because of the cheaper long-distance and international calls on offer, services which are then *not* conveniently available from BT's network.[20]

• Finally, the current requirement that BT sets geographically uniform tariffs encourages entry in those regions (for example, urban regions) where local network costs tend to be low (see previous section). While the maintenance of uniform tariffs may be politically desirable for quite independent 'equity' reasons,[21] it certainly also has the effect of imposing high profit

---

had the effect of unfairly distorting or reducing competition in the supply of telephone services', and BT was ordered to cease the promotion – see Oftel (1997c, pp. 11-12).

[20] For a clear statement that one factor in Oftel's decision not to pursue equal access was the adverse effect on local competition, Oftel (1996e, p. 5) states: 'Oftel is concerned that its [that is, equal access] introduction could discourage operators from developing alternative access networks if they risked the benefits of their investments to competing operators.' This statement contrasts with earlier statements in DTI (1991, paragraphs 7.1 to 7.12), in particular paragraph 7.6 states that 'The [then] Director General believes that the doubts expressed about the potential adverse effect on local competition of the introduction of equal access are over-stated.'

[21] For instance, in DTI (1990, p. 69) it states: 'Neither the Government nor the Director General [of Telecommunications] would find [geographical deaveraging] acceptable.' It is interesting to note that Oftel (1997d, paragraph 61) recognises that geographical averaging of tariffs is a form of price discrimination.

margins in, say, urban markets which will attract more entry than would more cost-reflective pricing. Although uniform pricing has the superficially desirable property that it 'brings the benefits of competition to those subscribers who do not directly have a choice of operator', this seems a very blunt and inefficient instrument for encouraging entry.

Naturally, each of these four policies has the effect of sacrificing short-run efficiency in one form or another in return for hoped-for increased benefits from more vigorous competition at some point in the future. It is probably true that a degree of entry assistance is required if there is to be effective local competition. Local entry requires very substantial sunk-cost investments, not just in network infrastructure but also in advertising and so on, and this investment is vulnerable to future changes in regulatory and licensing policy. Therefore, some up-front inducements are needed to counteract the riskiness of the investments. In addition, there are substantial positive *externalities* from competition, such as the reduced need for costly regulation, which can justify 'tilting the playing field' in favour of entrants.[22] However, whether the scale of the assistance was warranted is debatable, and it is an open question whether competition fostered in the current 'hothouse' environment will be able to withstand *laissez-faire* competition in the future.

7. Questions for Future Policy

Many of the main policy decisions concerning local competition have, in the UK at least, already been taken. This concluding

---

[22] See Armstrong, Cowan and Vickers (1994, section 4.2) for a more detailed overview of the issues of barriers to entry and the possible need for entry assistance. In the duopoly period before 1991, Oftel and the Government also had a policy of encouraging infrastructure investment, this time on the part of Mercury: although BT was required to provide access to its local network to Mercury, it had no such obligation to provide Mercury with long-distance links on request. The effect was to encourage Mercury to provide a competing trunk infrastructure to BT's. However, when the duopoly was reviewed, the Government abandoned this policy (DTI, 1991, paragraph 9.3): 'The purpose of the ... restriction was to ensure that competing operators developed competing facilities. The Government and the Director General continue to favour such facilities-based competition. Experience has shown, however, that the rigid application of such regulatory constraints may impede otherwise efficient and beneficial arrangements.' (I am grateful to Michael Ryan for pointing out this previous policy.) The same point might apply equally to the present regulatory constraints aimed at encouraging entry.

section addresses some important further questions for future policy. Turning first to the question of equal access, there is a basic question of what form of industry 'architecture' is desirable for the industry in the long run. Two possibilities are illustrated in Figures 3A and 3B.

As before, a line from a trunk operator to a local operator implies that a subscriber on the local network can easily access the trunk network if desired. In Figure 3A, a subscriber on a given local network has no choice over the trunk network used (for example, because the trunk and local networks are vertically integrated or have exclusive dealing arrangements), whereas in Figure 3B, the choice of local network does not determine the choice of trunk network. Thus in this latter situation, which one might term 'unbundled' competition, a subscriber has six options, corresponding to which combination of local/trunk network is made, whereas in Figure 3A, which one might term 'vertically integrated' competition, a subscriber has just two options.

Given the technological features of local networks at present, it seems unlikely that local competition will involve more than just two or three firms in the residential sector, whereas the long-distance and international markets have the potential to be more competitive. While oligopolies with two or three firms *might* be quite competitive, this is by no means guaranteed, and semi-collusive outcomes are also possible (especially given the nature of telecommunications where networks must interact in various ways to agree details of network interconnection, network interfaces, numbering databases, and so on). The disadvantage of vertical integration (Figure 3A) is that competition in the trunk sector is limited by that in the local sector, with the result that subscribers are denied choice and the benefits of vigorous price (and non-price) competition for trunk calls. Therefore, one policy that seems attractive in the near future is to require equal (or near equal) access from *all* local operators.[23] Of the two broad options, unbundled network competition seems to fulfil better Oftel's principal duty (under the 1984 Telecommunications Act) to 'promote the interests

---

[23] There has been some theoretical work done on the closely related issue of whether vertically integrated firms should, or will, make components of their products compatible with either others' products (for example, cameras, lenses and film, or computers and software). For instance, see Matutes and Regibeau (1988).

Figure 3A: Vertically-integrated Competition

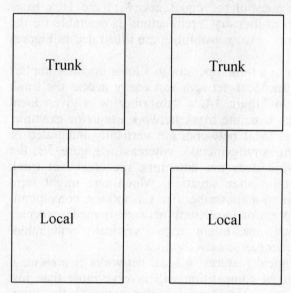

Figure 3B: Unbundled Competition

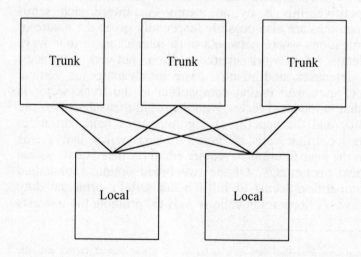

of consumers ... in respect of the prices charged for, and the quality and variety of, telecommunications services provided'. There is the danger, however, that current policies, if pursued for much longer, will lead the industry towards vertical integration (and the recent merger between Mercury and three cable companies is a major step in this direction).

Other questions involve the future structure of retail tariffs, especially those of BT. For instance, one issue that may arise is whether BT (and other operators) should be permitted to make its call charges depend on whether a subscriber's call is made to another BT subscriber or to a subscriber on a rival network (say, a cable network).[24] Of course, BT is already allowed to charge more for calls to mobile networks, but this is mainly justified by the high call termination charges currently paid by BT to mobile networks. The cable companies currently do price discriminate in this way, since they often offer free calls to other subscribers on their local networks (but not for local calls to BT subscribers). But because of its very large share of subscribers it would be highly controversial if BT were to do the same. Consider, for instance, the outcome of BT increasing its charge to its subscribers for calling cable customers and decreasing its charge for calling other BT subscribers. There would then be at least two effects (assuming cable tariffs remain as now): (i) becoming a cable customer would become more attractive since the cost of calling other cable customers is then lower, and (ii) becoming a cable customer would become less attractive since the cost of calling BT subscribers is relatively higher on a cable network. Given that BT has the majority of customers, it seems likely that the latter effect would dominate for many subscribers and this kind of price discrimination would be anti-competitive.[25]

The next question is how long other features of BT's retail tariff can be maintained. This has two aspects: the extent of geographical

---

[24] In a general sense, the issue is again one of 'equal access', this time one of equal access to subscribers on all (fixed) networks. This kind of price discrimination does not appear to be explicitly prohibited under BT's Licence, although it could well be interpreted as falling foul of the prohibition on undue preference and undue discrimination. One way in which BT could easily implement such a discriminatory strategy would be to allow its 'Friends and Family' discount scheme to apply only for calls to its own subscribers.

[25] See Laffont, Rey and Tirole (1996) for a theoretical analysis of this form of price discrimination.

uniformity, and the balance between connection charges and other (rental, call) charges. The first of these has already been discussed in sections 5 and 6 above, and there it was argued that placing restrictions on the incumbent firm such as geographical uniformity while leaving entrants free to pick and choose their subscribers is undesirable in the long run, partly because of the danger of inefficient entry in profitable markets and partly because the incumbent may have difficulty in funding its loss-making obligations.

While a 'universal service fund' might solve the latter problem, it does nothing for the former and is not an ideal solution. One alternative is a complex tax/subsidy scheme on entrants, but this will be contentious and goes against the present de-regulatory philosophy in the UK and elsewhere. Another option might be to impose the same constraints on entrants as well, so that cable companies, say, are eventually required to supply services to *everyone* who wants supply in their franchise areas on the same terms. However, this ignores the fact that cable will cover only about 75 per cent of the population (and the most profitable 75 per cent at that), and also that cable franchise areas are quite small and cost conditions will vary widely from one area to another. Perhaps the only remaining long-run solution, then, is to permit the incumbent to make its tariff somewhat more cost-reflective, so that many subscribers in sparsely populated rural areas end up paying more and others paying less.

Orthodox economic theory suggests that the benefit to those who gain will outweigh the losses of those who lose, but there is obvious unpopularity in moving away from the *status quo* as far as the losers are concerned. In addition, there are good arguments for subsidising network access for those in sparsely populated areas – such as promoting 'national cohesiveness', maintaining access to emergency services, and so on. (However, such arguments do not imply that tariffs should be *uniform*, only that certain loss-making services be subsidised in some way.) Perhaps a suitable compromise might be to (i) require BT to offer some fairly minimal set of services across the country at some regulated tariff (maybe even geographically uniform), (ii) make all firms in the industry contribute to any losses incurred in providing these social obligations, and (iii) allow BT to make other tariffs it offers depend more directly on the costs of service. For this not to cause too much inefficiency in the long run, however, it seems necessary to make the set of social obligations not too broad, so that the majority of the population prefers other service packages on offer.[26]

The second kind of rebalancing is more specific to local competition with wire-based networks (rather than fixed wireless networks where subscriber-specific sunk costs are much less significant). If competition becomes vigorous and the rate of 'churn' – the fraction of subscribers who change local supplier in a year – becomes high, then it is unlikely that present charging arrangements, whereby a subscriber pays a modest connection fee and a significant quarterly fixed charge, can remain. If a network is considering whether to lay a cable into a new subscriber's house then because the cost is sunk it will wish as far as possible to guarantee that future revenues recover the cost of connection. The most obvious ways to do this are (a) to charge an up-front one-off connection fee which covers the sunk investment, or (b) to maintain the current quarterly charging arrangements but to impose a minimum contract period (say, one or two years). Although a move to either of these methods of cost recovery on the part of BT would probably be regarded as undesirable by Oftel at present (for instance, the latter method will act to 'lock in' subscribers to BT), the current system, where a subscriber does not pay up-front for connection but can stop service with only minimal notice, is simply not sustainable in a competitive environment.[27]

Finally, the fact that wire-based local networks are sunk investments raises an intriguing possibility. In the vast majority of cases where a subscriber switches from BT to a cable company for telephone service, that subscriber will continue to have BT's local line physically in place, a line which may continue to be of potential use for many further years. As was discussed in section 4 above,

---

[26] In essence, this is similar to the approach followed in Oftel (1997e). However, it is not yet clear whether only the basic services defined in the definition of 'universal services' are to be provided at geographically uniform rates, or whether *all* voice telephony services (such as optional discount schemes for big residential users) are also required to be offered at the same terms throughout the country.

[27] The mobile market in the UK, which is quite competitive, is instructive in this regard. A new subscriber either pays for her mobile handset up front, or is offered a handset at a greatly subsidised rate but signs a contract for one or two years. See Armstrong (1997b) for an analysis of the mobile market in the UK.

conventional wisdom has it that local networks hold a monopoly over call termination to their subscribers, and that this ultimate bottleneck will always require control of some form. But if a subscriber has two or more lines into her house, this is not necessarily so. For instance, it seems feasible for BT, say, to *continue* to deliver calls from its own network to a subscriber who has switched to cable, and thereby bypass the cable network (and remove the need to pay the cable company call termination payments). If this were possible, it would at least partially overcome a cable company's ability to set excessive charges for call termination.

Of course, BT would have to ensure that its ex-subscriber was willing to keep an active BT line into her house, but some small payment should suffice for this (which BT could afford to pay out of its savings on call termination charges). In addition, it would be undesirable for the ex-subscriber to need two telephone numbers – one for calls from cable customers and one for calls from BT customers – but the development of sophisticated numbering databases and 'intelligent networks' should overcome this need. Thus, it is possible that the UK's policy of strongly encouraging competing local infrastructure, while costly to implement in terms of duplicating sunk costs, once in place may ultimately serve to overcome even the most resilient of bottlenecks in the industry.

In conclusion, Britain has embarked on a distinctive policy of encouraging local competition, a policy that contrasts with many aspects of recent policy in the United States towards the industry. Other countries will watch with interest the outcome of this experiment in industrial policy.

References

(Note that most Oftel documents are available on the internet at www.oftel.gov.uk.)

Armstrong, M. (1997a): 'Competition in Telecommunications', *Oxford Review of Economic Policy* 13, pp. 64-82.

Armstrong, M. (1997b): 'Mobile Telephony in the UK', mimeo, Nuffield College, Oxford.

Armstrong, M., S. Cowan and J. Vickers (1994): *Regulatory Reform*, MIT Press.

Armstrong, M., C. Doyle and J. Vickers (1996): 'The Access Pricing Problem: A Synthesis', *Journal of Industrial Economics* 44, pp. 131-50.

BT (1997): *Current Cost Financial Statements for the Businesses 1996*, British Telecommunications plc.

Commission of the European Communities (1996): *Green Paper on a Numbering Policy for Telecommunications Services in Europe*, Brussels.

Crandall, R. and L. Waverman (1995): *Talk Is Cheap: The Promise of Regulatory Reform in North American Telecommunications*, Washington DC: The Brookings Institution.

Department of Trade and Industry (1990): *Competition and Choice: Telecommunications Policy for the 1990s: A Consultative Document*, London: HMSO.

Department of Trade and Industry (1991): *Competition and Choice: Telecommunications Policy for the 1990s*, London: HMSO.

Laffont, J.-J., P. Rey and J. Tirole (1996): 'Network Competition: II. Price Discrimination', *Rand Journal of Economics*.

Matutes, C. and P. Regibeau (1988): 'Mix and Match: Product Compatibility Without Network Externalities', *Rand Journal of Economics* 19, pp. 221-34.

MMC (1995): *Telephone Number Portability*, London: HMSO.

Oftel (1995): *Universal Telecommunications Services: A Consultative Document*.

Oftel (1996a): *Pricing of Telecommunications Services From 1997: A Statement.*

Oftel (1996b): *Pricing of Telecommunications Services From 1997: A Consultative Document.*

Oftel (1996c): *Cost-Benefit Analysis of Equal Access: A Study Prepared for Oftel by NERA.*

Oftel (1996d): *Duct and Pole Sharing: A Consultative Document.*

Oftel (1996e): *Oftel's Policy on Indirect Access, Equal Access and Direct Connection to the Access Network: A Statement.*

Oftel (1997a): *Market Information Update: July 1997.*

Oftel (1997b): *Market Information 1992/3 to 1995/6.*

Oftel (1997c): *Competition Bulletin, January 1997.*

Oftel (1997d): *Guidelines on the Operation of the Fair Trading Condition.*

Oftel (1997e): *Universal Telecommunications Services: A Statement.*

Vogelsang, I. and B. Mitchell (1997): *Telecommunications Competition: The Last Ten Miles*, MIT Press.

CHAIRMAN'S COMMENTS

Michael Beesley

IN A FASCINATING PAPER, Mark has covered so many of the current telecoms issues that it is difficult to know where to start. Let me concentrate first on the local loop, the lowest level in the network hierarchy. In the early days of telephone competition, the conventional wisdom was that all natural monopoly problems started with natural monopoly there. As Mark has said, much of policy was then geared to changing that. Yet we cannot now shift to the opposite assumption - of effective competition in it. There is all the more reason to be clear where the rivalry in supply now exists, and what the prospects are for its development. I have some questions bearing on these prospects.

As a background to understanding tariff structures in a competitive market place, Mark makes a good deal of the comparisons between, and contrasts of, 'sunk costs' of investment which may involve different technology, as between suppliers, and what then determines competition. I wonder whether a better place to start might be the question: Under what conditions will rival local networks appear at all? From the viewpoint of a potential entrant, the critical comparisons about *costs* concern the contrast between what outlays the entrant must now face in order to produce, against what the incumbent(s) must now outlay to continue producing. The prospective entrant has all costs to cover, and hopes also to make a profit, otherwise he will not enter. What proportion of these outlays will be 'sunk' cost in the event depends entirely on whether he succeeds or not. If he does, nothing will prove to be 'sunk' or 'lost' – he can always sell a successful business. He knows the incumbent has put down a lot of money in the past, but the significant point for him is – What must the incumbent now spend to keep in this market? That is, what are the incumbent's forward-looking, or in another word 'avoidable costs'? It will be a comfort to the potential entrant if the price he, the entrant, can charge is below the incumbent's avoidable costs. This is one part of the incentive bearing on whether the entrant decides to 'have a go'.

Though subject to uncertainty about each other's costs, the broad relation will be known to each side. But prospective costs are only part of the story, and of the incentive. Potential entrants normally innovate at the same time, providing quite a lot that is different from the incumbents, or believe that they can do so. My question is: To what extent are these business realities reflected in the current discussion on policy? So much of rationalisation to support policy seems to me to focus on the idea of outright substitution of incumbents' services. In the real world, differentiation and complementarity abound.

A number of further questions arise – about the realities of entry, for example. I am just as impressed by the 75 per cent of cabled houses which did *not* in 1995 take telephony services as the 25 per cent which did. Are there many subscribers who have actually given up a BT line when taking TV cable telephone offers? And what of mobile and so-called 'fixed wireless'? Where are the statistics of multiple-network households, rather like one-two etc. household car owners? What do we know about these manifestations of differentiated markets? In broader terms, do you feel that the demand side is understood well enough?

When it comes to the discussion on the 'drawbacks of local competition' it seems to me there is perhaps too much emphasis by economists on the 'drawbacks' supposed to attend entry by rival (of at least *new*) networks. This is often presented as, on the one side, the 'waste' if BT is not forced to price down to avoidable costs, and, on the other, some supposed sacrifice of economies of density and/ or scope if they do not and entrants arrive. A lot of this worry seems to arise from forgetting that 'static' propositions about the efficiency of alternative configurations of networks refer to a green-field comparison, when all outlays have yet to be made. Whomever this refers to, it is unlikely to be the incumbent for whom only future costs are relevant. Entry can only be understood in a dynamic context. Can economists really make convincing statements about what will and what will not be in the consumer interest without a huge investment in understanding real entry decisions?

That aside, the practical questions now seem to boil down to: How secure is BT's market power arising from ownership of the local loop, and how long will it last? I was especially intrigued by your last remarks on BT's local lines being still there after a switch to cable. Unless these can be bought or hired by rivals, this seems a potential reinforcement for the incumbent. Yet BT's market power nowadays essentially consists of the use of its local loops for delivery of calls as opposed to collection of calls. Universal delivery is a prerequisite for all serious players. Collection is in part rivalrous and getting more so. In conventional regulatory terms, this spells out a formidable problem of attribution of costs and relative mark-ups for services, looked at not as hypothetical green-field costs, but as truly avoidable outlays, because the plant and other inputs very largely serve both pick-up and delivery. It would be interesting to hear where the debate now stands on this.

More fundamentally, since many of the benefits of competition arise from the clash of ownership interests with different views on costs, demands, market potential and everything else relevant to making money out of telecoms, do we need to consider again the terms on which networks, or their subdivisions, can be owned, operated, and be made subject to market challenge for ownership? We are all invited to embrace the European approach to competition via Articles 85 and 86. But the admitted weakness of that approach is the lack of means to enlist divestment as at least a fall-back threat to monopoly power. Do you, or some of the audience, feel uneasy about this?

3

PROGRESS IN GAS COMPETITION

George Yarrow

Regulatory Policy Institute, Oxford

1. Introduction

THE PRIVATISATION OF BRITISH GAS (BG) was probably the most extensively criticised of the major divestitures of the UK privatisation programme, and the reasons for this are not hard to find. More than in any other case, the government was perceived to have turned a public monopoly into a private monopoly and to have neglected regulatory options, such as separate regulation of transportation and storage and trading/supply, that would have facilitated the introduction of greater competition into gas markets.

Looking at the position from, say, 1990, the outlook for competition would have appeared bleak. Whereas in the electricity industry, privatised four years later than gas, there had been unbundling of transmission and distribution from supply, and there was a plan to eliminate all monopoly supply franchises by 1998, in gas a fully integrated company was subject to challenge in only that part of the market comprising loads above 25,000 therms per annum, with no immediate plans to change that limit.

The obstacles to competition immediately after privatisation can be seen by looking at the problems facing any new entrant. First, the entrant would need to negotiate a supply contract from offshore producers in circumstances where (i) existing gas fields were already committed to British Gas under long-term contracts, (ii) new fields tended to be smaller, higher-cost sources of supply, and (iii) there was competition for new supplies from a dominant incumbent firm with a deep pocket.

Supposing supplies could be obtained, an entrant would also have to (i) first identify and then negotiate with potential customers and (ii) enter into access negotiations with BG for use of the latter's pipelines and storage facilities in supplying the targeted customers. Thus, information would be given to BG at an early stage concerning the entrant's intentions, yielding opportunities for British Gas to approach the targeted customers and offer discount prices.

Viewing matters from the perspective of October 1997, the situation looks radically different. The gas supply/trading business of British Gas has been divested, most industrial and commercial (including power generation) demand for gas is met by companies that have entered the market in the past few years, and, barring major mishaps, within nine months franchised monopoly will be a thing of the past in Britain.

The first part of what follows is a very brief history of the first stages of this remarkable transition. It is followed by an evaluation of the development of competition thus far in the industrial and commercial market, and by a discussion of the evidence on competition in the domestic/residential sector. The final sections set out some views on issues for the future.

2. Early Regulatory Developments

Not surprisingly given the way in which British Gas was privatised, competition did not spontaneously emerge in the UK gas market in the period immediately following divestiture. Yet the 'contract' market (for supplies in excess of 25,000 therms per annum) had been deregulated on the basis that it was not naturally monopolistic and hence price determination could safely be left to competitive forces.[1]

2.1 The First MMC Report

The problem – a *de facto* gas monopoly in an unregulated market – was, however, soon taken up by the competition policy authorities. A year after flotation, in late 1987, the Director General of Fair Trading referred British Gas's behaviour in the contract market to the Monopolies and Mergers Commission (MMC) for investigation and report. The initiative was made under general competition law,

---

[1] Some customers could switch easily between alternative fuels, so there was a degree of inter-fuel competition in the market-place. However, intra-fuel (or gas-on-gas) competition was absent, and the many gas consumers who were unable to switch easily to other fuels were left facing a monopolist.

since Ofgas had not been granted jurisdiction over pricing matters in the contract market.

The MMC reported in October 1988,[2] concluding that a number of British Gas's practices were anti-competitive, particularly price discrimination whereby BG charged higher prices to customers who had limited abilities to switch to a substitute fuel and lower prices to those for whom switching was a much lower-cost operation.

Among the regulatory measures implemented as a result of the MMC's recommendations were:

- limitations on British Gas's ability to contract for supplies from whole gas fields on the United Kingdom Continental Shelf, a measure directed at the problem of the availability of gas supplies to potential entrants. More specifically, British Gas was required not to contract for more than 90 per cent of the gas coming to market from 'new' UKCS fields (the so-called 90/10 rule);

- a requirement that British Gas offer supplies in the contract market on the basis of non-discriminatory, published price schedules;

- a requirement that British Gas publish more information about common carriage terms for use of its pipeline and storage facilities.

Each of these measures was targeted at one of three major barriers to entry:

- limited availability of gas supplies;

- targeted price discounting by the dominant, incumbent firm;

- BG's control of common-carriage terms.

The common-carriage requirements were, however, relatively weak: while publication of information about carriage terms may help in monitoring anti-competitive behaviour, it does nothing in itself to prevent anti-competitive behaviour.

---

2   Monopolies and Mergers Commission, *Gas*, Cm. 500, London: HMSO, 1988.

The publication of the MMC report roughly corresponded with the first signs of a substantial shift in BG's pricing behaviour. The principal target of the regulatory interventions was BG's conduct in the 'firm' contract market, comprising supplies to large customers who typically have significant inter-fuel switching costs. The chart shows estimates of British Gas's implicit charges (per cubic metre) for transport and supply of firm gas to industrial users, at 1992 prices (using the GDP deflator). These 'gross margin' figures are calculated by subtracting BG's average gas input costs – the price per cubic metre which it purchases from offshore producers, inclusive of taxation – from its final selling prices to the relevant industrial consumers.

As is illustrated in Figure 1, the privatisation of British Gas in late 1986 was not immediately accompanied by any major change in pricing behaviour. There was, however, a sharp fall in BG's gross margin in 1988, and the steep decline continued in subsequent years. By 1994 the real gross margin had fallen to around 40 per cent of its 1987 value.

2.2 The OFT Report

When the Monopolies and Mergers Commission makes recommendations that are subsequently implemented, the Office of Fair Trading (OFT) takes general responsibility for monitoring compliance with, and assessing the effectiveness of, the relevant measures. In the case of the 1988 MMC Report on Gas, the measures were reviewed by the OFT in 1991, and the results of the review were set out in a Report published in October of that year.[3]

Notwithstanding the shift in pricing policy in the firm contract market, the OFT reached the general conclusion that the measures were not working as intended. For example, the OFT argued that although British Gas was contracting for substantially less new gas than was allowed under the 90/10 rule, most of the independent purchases were for power generation purposes. Treating power generation as a separate market, the OFT argued that penetration of the firm and (short-term) interruptible markets by independent traders was relatively slight.

---

[3] Discussed in Monopolies and Mergers Commission, *Gas and British Gas plc*, Cm. 2314-2317 (three volumes), London: HMSO, August 1993, Vol. 2.

Figure 1: Real Gross Margin, Firm Industrial Market, 1985-94 (pence per cu. m.)

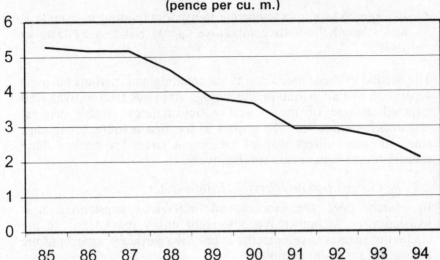

It is interesting to note the emphasis placed by the OFT on market shares as an indicator of competition, and the corresponding neglect of other indicators such as performance data (for example, the changes in firm contract prices described above). A similar concern over market shares had also characterised many of the pronouncements of the then Director General of Gas Supply (DGGS) on these matters, and prior to the OFT review the DGGS was on record as setting out the market shares that he hoped would be achieved by independent traders in the early 1990s.

Following its Report, the OFT entered into negotiations with British Gas in order to extract undertakings from the Company that would further erode its market power. Underlying these negotiations was the threat of a reference to the MMC, which could potentially open up issues concerning the post-privatisation structure of the Company. In the event, in early 1992, British Gas ended up agreeing to some quite significant regulatory measures. In particular:

- the emphasis on market shares led the Office of Fair Trading to set out a market share target for BG: BG was to aim to reduce its share of the contract market (excluding power generation) to 40 per cent by 1995 and was to release gas to competitors in order

69

to ensure that this target was achieved.

• BG agreed to set up a separate transportation unit, to operate at arm's length from its competitive supply business by October 1993.

The second of these measures, the accounting and (partial) business separation of transportation and storage from gas trading, was well targeted at one of the central policy failings of the original privatisation exercise. The impact of the first is more ambiguous, since the most direct way of meeting a target for market share reduction is to behave *less* competitively.

2.3 The Competition and Service (Utilities) Act

In March 1992 the Government introduced substantive new legislation to strengthen the powers of utility regulators. In the context of market developments in gas, two particular aspects of the legislation are worth noting:

• The Act gave powers to the Secretary of State for Industry to lower the threshold volume of supply that divides the franchised monopoly (tariff) market from the competitive contract market. This power was used more or less immediately in that the monopoly threshold was reduced from 25,000 therms per annum to 2,500 therms per annum in the Autumn of 1992, and the Government announced the general aim of reducing it further in future years. As a result of the initial step, approximately a quarter of a million more customers were allowed a choice of supplier.

• The Act contained provisions allowing the development of explicit, separate regulation of the transportation and storage and trading activities of British Gas.

The immediate consequence of the reduction in the threshold in 1992 was a rapid increase in the number of sites supplied by British Gas's rivals. That is, there was substantial, immediate entry into that section of the overall market that had just been opened up to competition. The (approximate) total number of sites supplied by new entrants increased as follows: October 1991, 1,000; September 1992, 6,000; March 1993, 34,000.

2.4 The 1992 MMC Reference

The trigger for the second MMC reference appears to have been the then Director General's dissatisfaction with the way in which the details of more sophisticated tariffs for use of British Gas's pipeline and storage system were being developed by BG. Whatever the cause, and despite previous statements that he did not favour breaking up the company, the Director General asked the MMC to address the question of whether British Gas should, in the public interest, be required to divest its pipeline and storage operations.

This issue of vertical separation was precisely the issue that British Gas had for so long been trying to avoid. Given that it was now unavoidable, British Gas sought to widen the MMC investigation so that it could also re-open earlier questions surrounding the price-cap formula, particularly the impact on its revenues of the OFT and DTI interventions. This it succeeded in doing by persuading the Secretary of State for Industry himself to make wide-ranging references to the MMC.

In the event, the MMC recommended that:

• British Gas be required to divest its trading business by 31 March 1997;

• the remaining tariff monopoly, for supplies below 2,500 therms per annum, be ended some time between the years 2000 and 2002.

That is, priority was given to vertical separation over early introduction of competition for small consumers.

The Secretary of State did not accept these priorities, preferring instead to require:

• only an internal separation of transportation and storage from supply;

• a more rapid introduction of competition to the market as a whole, on a phased basis, between 1996 and 1998.

The new DGGS also took a relatively relaxed view of the issue of ownership separation between transportation and storage and supply/trading, arguing that British Gas would eventually find it to be in its own best commercial interests to divest trading.

71

2.5 Comments

At the time, a number of commentators interpreted the Secretary of State's decisions as being a retreat from the more pro-competitive recommendations of the MMC. Here, as is so often the case in competition policy matters, it is crucial to distinguish intention from effect. Whatever the intentions, whether of the MMC panel or of the Secretary of State, the latter's decisions have, with a high degree of probability, led more quickly to a competitive outcome than would have been the case if the former's recommendations had been implemented. The trading business of British Gas has been divested according to the MMC schedule *and* the tariff monopoly is being ended several years ahead of the proposed schedule.

There is, I think, a major lesson to be learned from this experience, and one that is directly relevant to the draft competition bill now being finalised. Over recent years many economists have placed a great deal of emphasis on the importance of structural remedies in dealing with perceived failings of competition. In this context, 'structure' is generally taken to mean market characteristics such as the degree of concentration, the height of barriers to entry, and the degree of vertical integration in the relevant industry.

These elements of structure *are* important determinants of economic behaviour, but they are far from the only influences, and the relationships between some of these variables (for example, concentration, vertical integration) and economic behaviour are generally both weaker and more complex than popularised variants of 'structuralism' would have us believe.

Arguably the major lesson to be learned is that competition policy should focus more on the 'rules of the competitive game'. Among other things, these rules define the boundaries of acceptable conduct, and such defined boundaries are, in a very real sense, part of the structure of the market. Over time, the rules of the game also influence other aspects of the market structure, such as concentration and vertical arrangements. If, for example, a particular form of industrial organisation has a tendency to induce conduct that is in breach of the defined rules of the game, then provided only that public policy has the sanctions necessary to enforce the rules, self-interested companies will have incentives to change industrial organisation.[4] Moreover, the resulting structural change might be expected to occur more efficiently than when the details of change are imposed by outside agencies.

3. Competition in the Industrial and Commercial Market

As a consequence of the regulatory events described above, there has been a transformation in the nature of the market-place over the past few years. Whereas in the late 1980s, seven years after the first attempted liberalisation of the market (the Oil and Gas (Enterprise) Act), British Gas faced no rivals in the contract market, by early Spring 1993, 15 independent shippers (traders) were competing with British Gas and 47 transportation agreements were in place, of which 33 were concluded in early 1993. By the first quarter of 1993 these independent shippers were supplying over 50 per cent of the firm contract market.

By April 1995, BG's share of the large firm contract market had fallen to around 10 per cent, although it recovered to around 19 per cent in June 1996, in part influenced by the relaxation of constraints on price discrimination 'first imposed in response to the 1988 MMC Report' that had taken place in the previous two years.

Changes in market shares in other sections of the industrial and commercial market have also been quite dramatic, as Tables 1 and 3 show. The development of gas-on-gas competition in the interruptibles sector lagged that in the firm gas sector, but by 1996 BG's share had fallen to close to one-third. Table 3 indicates that, by the mid-1990s, substantial year-on-year changes in BG's sector shares were occurring in both directions.

As noted earlier, the decline in firm contract prices, measured relative to beach prices of gas, started much earlier than these changes in market share, but, whatever the precise mechanisms through which the competitive constraints have been transmitted, there is little doubt that the development of gas-on-gas competition has had powerful effects on pricing behaviour.

The pricing implications of the changes have been much less dramatic in the interruptible sector, for obvious reasons. Inter-fuel competition was much stronger at the outset, as is illustrated by the sharp fall in interruptible margins following the oil price collapse in

---

[4] In the case of gas, it is crucial for the argument here that Ofgas did have the means effectively to enforce the 'rules' of business separation.

the mid-1980s, well ahead of any of the possible effects of gas market liberalisation. The existence of gas-on-gas competition does, however, provide some protection for customers in the event that the developments of the mid-1980s are reversed and heavy fuel oil prices rise relative to beach prices of gas (that is, if the pressures of inter-fuel competition are relaxed for a period).

4. Competition in the Domestic/Residential Market

Once started, the transition to a fully liberalised gas market for all sizes of consumer proceeded at a remarkable pace. Whereas the 1993 Monopolies and Mergers Commission Report envisaged that the process would be completed between the years 2000 and 2002, in the event it is likely that it will be completed in 1998.

Domestic competition was introduced in the first pilot area, the South West of England, in April 1996. There were further significant extensions of the competitive market in February and March 1997, which saw both an enlargement of the area of competition in the South West and liberalisation in the South East. Scotland and the North East are scheduled to follow in late 1997, with a roll-out through the rest of the country during the first half of 1998, reaching the last of the areas, London, in June.

The introduction of domestic competition has necessarily been an experimental process, with learning on all sides as events have developed and with inevitable problems along the way. There have, for example, been complaints about marketing methods, of a type not dissimilar to the kinds of problem that are routinely dealt with by the Office of Fair Trading in other markets. Other issues that have arisen have concerned the initial dominance of BGT/Centrica and its possible effects on the development of competition, and problems surrounding the services provided by Transco to shippers.

5. Market Dominance and Prices

A pessimist looking forward to the first introduction of domestic competition might have analysed the prospects as follows.

British Gas Trading (BGT) starts from a position of market dominance. It has first-mover advantages in name/brand recognition, in established customer relationships, and in the systems required to serve large numbers of small accounts. As a result of some of these factors, switching costs will be significant in relation to the likely gains from switching (since the accounts are

TABLE 1
BG's Shares of Loads in Excess of 2,500 Therms Per Annum

Market sector (above 2,500 therms p.a.)	BG's share (June 1996)
Industrial and commercial	29%
Power generation	24%

TABLE 2
Shares in the Industrial and Commercial Sector

Industrial and commercial sub-sectors	BG's share (number of competitors)
Large firm (> 25,000 therms p.a.)	19% (>35)
Small firm (2,500 to 25,000 therms p.a.)	43% (> 40)
2,500 - 5,000	63%
5,000 - 10,000	37%
10,000 - 25,000	29%
Interruptible	34% (>25)

TABLE 3
Changes in Sector Shares

Market sector	Change in BG share (4/95 to 6/96)
Industrial and commercial	-6%
Large firm	+9%
Small firm	-2%
Interruptible	-23%
Power generation	-8%

small, a price advantage of, say, 5 per cent does not add up to an enormous amount in terms of pounds per annum). New competitors will, therefore, have to offer very substantial discounts to gain a significant foothold in the market, and BGT will be able to prevent this happening by ensuring that the price gap between its own offerings and those of its competitors remains small. In the worst-case scenario, *ex ante* anticipation of this post-entry outcome will deter entry, and the introduction of competition will have little effect on economic performance.

The early introduction of domestic competition in the South West means that we already have a substantial body of evidence to test out this kind of view of the world. On the basis of this evidence it is possible to recognise that the pessimistic view does contain elements of truth. Entrants *have* found it necessary to offer substantial discounts to gain significant market share; BGT *has* reacted to market developments by cutting its own prices (through the ValuePlus tariff); and the reaction *has* made life tougher for new entrants. Going further, it is more than likely that, over time, there will be exit of a significant number of suppliers from the market, and it is quite possible that the final equilibrium will see the bulk of the market being supplied by Centrica and only one, two or three major competitors.

From the public policy perspective, however, the crucial test of competition is not the number of major suppliers that can be sustained in the market, nor is it whether or not individual competitors get hurt in the process. The key questions concern consumer welfare. Does competition lead to lower prices and better quality of service?

On these crucial tests, the available evidence suggests a positive verdict on the experiment so far. New entry *has* taken place, with some companies showing themselves willing to make substantial financial commitments to establish their positions. By April 1997, it is estimated that new entrants had captured over 20 per cent of the market in the South West and over 11 per cent in the areas that had been opened to competition only in February and March of that year.

These numbers may not look very impressive when interpreted statically, as if looking at an equilibrium position: the pessimist can, for example, point to the fact that Centrica still supplied nearly 80 per cent of the South West market. But consider any manager who reports back to head office that his or her division has lost 20 per cent of its market in less than a year, or over 10 per cent of its market in a couple of months. That magnitude of effect can concentrate minds wonderfully; which is just a way of saying that competitive pressures are real.

A MORI survey (December 1996) undertaken for Ofgas indicates that, notwithstanding the existence of problems connected with marketing, meter reading, and the like, only 4 per cent of those who had switched suppliers were dissatisfied with the outcome. Around 79 per cent had found it easy to switch, and only around 12 per cent reported that it was not easy. The overwhelming reason for switching was lower prices (92 per cent), although 6 per cent gave poor service (from BG) as a reason.

Among those gas consumers who had not switched in the first few months of competition, a significant minority (27 per cent) indicated to MORI that they had considered switching. Some of these indicated that they were 'waiting to see' how things developed, while others said they were 'still deciding'. Around 15 per cent of non-switchers said they expected to change supplier over the next 12 months.

Turning to prices, it is clear that consumers have, in aggregate, benefited substantially from competition. The initial prices offered by entrants were of the order of 10 per cent to 20 per cent below BGT's standard tariff (see Table 4), and when BGT reacted by introducing the ValuePlus tariff, the benefits of lower prices were spread to a much larger fraction of consumers.

There have been complaints from the Gas Consumers Council and others that the benefits have not been evenly spread among different classes of customer, and that pre-payment customers in particular are not doing very well. That is certainly true, but the central issue here is cost-to-serve. From the perspective of economic efficiency at least, the rebalancing of tariff structures that is occurring as a result of competition is only problematic if it is leading to major distortions of price–cost relationships.

Economic efficiency is not the only concern of public policy, and many of the complaints about changes in tariff structures are to do with questions of distribution or equity. All that I will say on this is that I do not believe that industry specific regulatory agencies are the right bodies to deal with *major* questions of income distribution. I addressed this issue in detail two years ago in an IEA/LBS lecture on social obligations in telecoms,[5] and my views have not changed since then.

Distributional issues cannot be avoided entirely, however, and it should be noted that the DGGS anticipated a number of the rebalancing issues at the time of the last supply price review. Maintenance of price controls based upon an average or total revenue formula would, in the absence of further constraints, have allowed BGT to compensate for price cuts to one class of customer by increasing prices to other classes of customer. For example, reduced revenue yields from direct debit customers would have opened the way to price increases (relative to a pre-change benchmark) to pre-payment customers.

The introduction of individual price caps on the main tariffs, however, eliminated this option. Price cuts to direct debit customers do not adversely affect the position of pre-payment customers. The latter may not yet have gained a great deal from the introduction of competition, but the regulatory constraints have ensured that they have not suffered from it either. It is appropriate to acknowledge, therefore, that the Director General has taken active steps to protect the position of poorer customers, and the effects of that protection are no less real for being the result of technical decisions taken *ex ante* rather than the result of *ex post* interventions in media spotlights.

There remains the question of whether price competition in the domestic market will continue to be strong once the initial experimental stages are over. I think there are some reasons to be concerned about this, but, in my view, they are less to do with dominance of the market by Centrica and more to do with market conditions conducive to tacit co-ordination. I will return to this point below.

6. The Network Code and the Rules of Competition

The Transco Network Code is a legal document that forms the basis of the arrangements between the Public Gas Transporter (PGT) and shippers whose gas is transported. It is an important determinant of the 'rules' of competition in gas, and hence upon competitive

---

[5] George Yarrow, 'Dealing with Social Obligations in Telecoms', in M. E. Beesley (ed.), *Regulating Utilities: A Time for Change?*, IEA Readings 44, Institute of Economic Affairs, 1996.

TABLE 4
Competing Tariff Offers in the South West

Tariffs	Index, BGT DirectPay = 100	Index, BGT ValuePlus = 100
Amerada Hess – Band A	91.02	96.06
British Fuels Gas – DD	90.12	95.12
Eastern – Standard less 6%	80.51	84.97
Total – Monthly DD	85.85	90.61
Southern Electric – DD	86.43	91.22
SWEB – Blue Saver DD – Red Saver DD	85.34 83.93	90.07 88.58
Calortex – DD Saver Plus	86.04	90.81
Midlands – DD	84.03	88.68
Northern Electric – Energy Club DD	87.23	92.06
Beacon – DD	95.01	100.27
BGT – DirectPay BGT – ValuePlus	100.00 (£297.50) 94.75 (£281.88)	100.00

conduct and the economic performance to which that conduct leads. Different rules of competition can materially affect the nature of competition, and the Network Code is, or should be, a matter of great importance to policy-makers.

For the same reasons, the procedures by which the code is modified are also of considerable significance for competition: they too influence the rules of the game in operation at any one time. To illustrate, suppose the development of some innovative service was infeasible as a result of particular aspects of the Network Code. Innovation will depend upon modifications of the Code, and if this is difficult for some reason or another, or if there is unnecessary delay, the innovation may be blocked.

The current modification rules enable:

• shippers and the PGT to make proposals for change;

• shippers and other interested parties who are likely to be materially affected to make representations concerning proposed changes.

There is a Modification Panel with Transco and shipper membership, and non-voting representatives from Ofgas and delivery facility operators. The Panel determines procedural issues to do with how a proposed change should be dealt with under the rules. Transco convenes the Panel to consider modification proposals. In the end, however, it is Transco that is responsible for preparing modification reports, which recommend acceptance or rejection of a proposal, and for obtaining Ofgas consent to any changes.

If we stand back from the detail of these arrangements for the moment, it should be obvious that the Network Code is a rather special type of vertical supply arrangement between a monopoly supplier of services (Transco) and a *group* of buyers of those services. Now even those economists who are most relaxed about the likely economic implications of vertical agreements (for example, members of the Chicago school of economics) generally accept that there can be competitive failures when the vertical arrangements are, in effect, part of a buyers' 'cartel'. The idea is simply that, by signing up to the same terms and conditions, the downstream industry suppresses competition in the purchase of the input. And the more important the input is as a cost component for the downstream product, the greater the anti-competitive effect.

Let us take this one step further. There has been a line of argument that vertical separation is essential for the development of competition in the utility industries because, without it, the monopolistic network operator will have both the incentive and the capacity to distort downstream competition. In the course of the vertical reform of the electricity and gas industries, however, contractual arrangements have been developed that re-introduce the same problem. To the extent that downstream suppliers have influence over the operation of the networks, they can potentially use that influence to distort downstream competition to their advantage.

Consider, for example, a shipper that seeks to gain competitive advantage by means of its conduct in respect of the purchase and use of upstream services. In unregulated industries, the ways forward here are fairly clear. The downstream firm would open negotiations with suppliers to seek to obtain better prices than rivals, perhaps by offering the supplier something attractive in return (for example, a high volume of purchases, or a long-term contract, or support for a joint promotion), or, alternatively, by negotiating with the supplier for new products and services that the buyer, from experience of the retail market, has identified as potential winners.

Now consider a similar problem in the gas industry. Negotiating bespoke discounts would be difficult, not least because regulatory authorities tend to be worried about the implications of undue discrimination among customers or classes of customers. All buyers therefore face the same input prices, which eliminates one source of competition. In the alternative case, where the shipper seeks to encourage the PGT to develop new services, if the development of those new services requires modification of the network code, then the modification procedures may, as already noted, be such as to attenuate the returns from innovation. The shipper will not only have to persuade the PGT and Ofgas to implement the change but will also have to reveal its hand to competitors.

There are concerns, therefore, about the possible longer-term consequences of the Network Code. To put the case at its most extreme, the arrangements could be seen as conducive to the longer-term development of a 'club culture' among shippers, and between shippers and Transco, that had the effect of:

- raising entry barriers to newcomers;

- impeding individual, competitive actions that might threaten the 'orderly' marketing and supply of gas;

- impeding innovation.

7. Transco Incentives

These points lead naturally into the question of Transco incentives. We are all now familiar with the problems of regulating for quality of service to the final consumer, but, in relation to Transco and to suppliers of network services in other industries, the quality of the service provided has a very major impact on downstream competition.

Consider, for example, the question of the supply of information from Transco to shippers (meter reading being the most obvious example). The supply of abundant, correct and timely information has very major implications for what happens at the level of the final customer. If meter reads are inaccurate, shippers will potentially find themselves in all sorts of difficulties with their own customers; and in circumstances of transition to a competitive market, such difficulties may raise switching costs and serve as barriers to mobility and to entry.

There is no simple answer to the quality of service problem, and regulatory policy will need to continue to work away at providing better incentives for Transco. If innovations in the operation of the network have important and generally positive effects on competition in related markets, then the incentive structure should be such as to provide significant rewards for successful innovation. While price-cap regulation has been moderately effective in providing incentives for cost-reducing innovation, perhaps the greater challenge for the future is to establish appropriate rewards for innovative improvements in services.

Pressures on Transco to innovate will also increasingly emanate from both suppliers and customers in related markets (shippers, suppliers, end-users of gas), as these various companies seek competitive advantage in their own activities. The strength of such pressures can, however, be greatly affected by institutional structures, and here there are grounds for believing that current institutional arrangements are not entirely satisfactory. The Network Code club needs to be opened up. Greater participation of end-users is one option, but probably the most powerful instrument available is the exposure of the arrangements to the rigour of reformed competition law.

8. Regulation and Competition Policy

Industry-specific regulators are increasingly dealing with problems that have traditionally fallen to more general competition policy. The decision of the DGGS in relation to the acceptability of BG's new ValuePlus tariff is a good illustration of this, being based, as it was, on assessments of dominance, predation, and price discrimination.

As this shift in regulatory focus has proceeded, a whole new vocabulary has emerged. Particularly noticeable has been the proliferation of adjectival qualifications to the notion of competition. Workable competition and effective competition are old, if chameleon-like, friends, but nowadays there is choice from a wide array of alternatives: sustainable competition, self-sustaining competition, commercially sustainable competition; incipient competition; established competition; normal competition; full competition; and so on. Vanilla competition probably lurks in some document or other (if only in a PhD thesis), and maybe someone will offer chocolate and strawberry alternatives.

There is huge potential for nonsense in all of this, and considerable scope for inconsistency among the relevant authorities. The latter possibility has led, for example, to calls for the amalgamation of Ofgas and Offer. To my mind, however, the big questions to be confronted have less to do with the interactions between convergent gas and electricity industries, and rather more to do with the convergence of *issues* among *all* the network industries where competition has become or is becoming a major factor.

The key point is this. In gas, as in other industries, the behavioural effects of competition depend upon the rules of the game. The intuition here is basic. Competition simply means rivalry: the rewards of one player or set of players depend upon performance relative to another player or set of players. Conduct can be powerfully affected by rivalry, but how rivalry is channelled depends on the rules. Given competition, the rules themselves therefore have strong effects on conduct and performance. And nowhere is this effect more significant than in the network industries, where the rules tend to be complex in order to deal with the problems of co-ordination among complementary activities. The motto in respect of competition should be: forget the adjectives, do not try to engineer the outcomes, focus on the rules.

In gas, the Transco Network Code is an important element of the rules of the game. It should, therefore, be exposed to evaluation under general competition policy. In other sectors of the economy a group of companies would not normally be allowed to have such a major influence over the rules under which they compete.

The rules *are,* of course, scrutinised by Ofgas, but what I am suggesting is that the rule-making process leaves much to be desired. As in respect of other UK institutional arrangements in competition and regulatory policy, there is much to be done to improve access to, and consistency and due process in, the making of the rules of competition. And, given the increasing complexity of industrial organisation in the network industries as new possibilities are opened up by advancing technologies, much will depend upon the success of this venture.

9. In Conclusion

After a slow start, the post-privatisation history of the UK gas industry has been a history of very rapid change, and there is unlikely to be a slowing of the process in the near future. In many areas, public policy is struggling to keep up with the opportunities offered by new technological developments and, even in well-informed circles, I think there is not always a full appreciation of just how far the network industries have moved, and are moving, away from their traditional forms of industrial organisation.

To provide a rough guide, and at the risk of gross over-simplification, let me set out what might be called the 'main deregulatory sequence' through which we are moving. It goes as follows:

Traditional franchised monopoly, based upon supply by fully integrated companies protected from competition. Supply prices are regulated.

Franchised monopoly plus limited third party access: third parties are allowed access to 'the network' for the purposes of supplying larger consumers at deregulated prices. Supply prices to smaller customers remain regulated. Network charges are regulated.

Full, regulated access: third parties have access to 'the network' to supply *all* parts of the market. Supply prices are deregulated.

Network charges are regulated.

Network competition: competing, interconnecting networks offer consumers choices in some, but not necessarily all, network services. There is deregulation of the prices of some network services, but continuing price controls in other areas. There may be blurring of some boundaries between networks.

Network component (or facilities-based) competition: there is some degree of competition in the supply of all (unbundled) network components and comprehensive, or near comprehensive, deregulation of prices. Market governance is provided by general competition law (relating to agreements, dominance, essential facilities). There may be further integration among networks.

The Oil and Gas (Enterprise) Act marked a transition from stage one to stage two in this sequence. In the absence of an effective framework of regulation and competition policy, that transition had no effect on gas prices. When, starting in 1988, more activist policy measures to promote competition were implemented, there was a substantial improvement in BG's pricing performance in the firm contract market.

The introduction of domestic market competition can be viewed as the completion of the move from stage two to stage three of the sequence, although in some areas progress towards the later stages is already being made (for instance, the unbundling of storage). This phase of the transition is of particular significance in that, for network operators, it marks a shift from a situation in which utilities are responsible for supplying very large numbers of small customers to one in which they supply a relatively small number of large buyers. The implications of this transition to *oligopsony* on the demand side of regulated markets have yet to be fully worked through, and they will, government willing, present plenty of problems to challenge the DGGS for the foreseeable future.

The initial results from the liberalisation of domestic gas markets are, however, encouraging. Despite substantial technical problems, competition has been introduced, without major mishap, to millions of customers across the country, and they have benefited from the resulting price reductions. Lower beach-head prices are an important part of this story, but, as in earlier periods, competitive pressures on margins also appear to have been a significant, contributory factor.

Finally, as the sequence set out above indicates, there remain substantial further opportunities for increasing the role of competitive forces in the gas industry, and there are many who argue that the greatest benefits from the introduction of competition will lie in the transition to network-component or facilities-based competition. That is a topic for another day, however.

CHAIRMAN'S COMMENTS

Eileen Marshall

MY FIRST POINT IS ON THE QUESTION OF WHETHER VERTICAL SEPARATION WAS IMPORTANT OR NOT. I think it is true that, after the MMC report and the Secretary of State's decision, there was a slight change of emphasis away from a clean business separation and divestment of supplies and transportation. It remains a total mystery to me why the MMC recommended the separation of supply and not transportation. Nevertheless, the separation that we did put in place at that time was pretty stringent. It was as close to a separate subsidiary as you could possibly get, involving physical separation between supply and transportation, prevention of leaks of information and a compliance officer who did an exceptionally good job. I think that separation was more important than George allows. In particular, it gave competitors the confidence that the integrated nature of British Gas would no longer inhibit competition. Once you get that degree of confidence in the market and the competitive downstream grows significantly, British Gas's own interests were to make sure it was focusing on the business in which it was going to compete. Therefore, its view moved towards complete separation.

On the industrial and commercial markets, I was told two years ago that 'we are in danger of having a success on our hands here'. There have indeed been quite remarkable developments in that market. (Incidentally, we will be doing a 1997 competitive market review. We left it towards the end of the year so that we can combine it with a review of the domestic market.) Not everything is rosy; the customers are not entirely satisfied. Many of the issues they raise with us actually relate to the network code, a problem which George raised. A difficulty is that the network code is only about shippers and does not involve the suppliers as a separate group. In particular, the customers are not directly involved. We have tried indirectly to involve the customers and put out explanations to them about what modifications are all about. We have also tried to develop a principle that says that there should not

87

be blockages in the transportation arrangements in order to protect supply arrangements as there tends to be. A particularly controversial issue that has been discussed quite recently is the idea that more than one shipper should be able to ship to one supply point: at the moment the idea is that you can only have one shipper per supply point, even if it is a huge industrial customer, and getting that blockage out of the way has proved quite controversial. So I do agree with George: I think a lot of industrial and commercial customers' concerns are really about that issue.

If we go on to the domestic market, perhaps the best I can do is to bring you up to date on where we are in terms of the number of switches. Switching overall is now about 24 per cent and the second phase of competition which was opened earlier this year has just overtaken the percentage of switches in the first phase which was opened in April 1996. It was always expected that the second phase would go a bit faster, just because of the nature of the properties in the area (quite a lot of commercial people, such as hoteliers). As George said, the intimations for the next phase which starts on 1 November in Scotland and the North East is that there are probably more than 400,000 waiting to switch on day 1 which is a bit over 16 per cent of that market – quite a big difference from the first phase. In that phase, only 5 per cent switched on the first day, so there is a certain momentum that is being developed. Moreover, we have increased the size of successive phases. The first was only half a million customers, the second phase was about one and a half million, and in Scotland and the North East there are about two and a half million. The next phases are of similar magnitudes.

At the moment it looks as if everything is in place for 1 November. All the systems seem to work, and TransCo – which I do not always praise – have done awfully well and so have all the others, such as the suppliers and BGT, and systems have really worked remarkably well. Other sorts of problems have been ironed out along the way and we are going to consult by the end of this week about whether the next phase is going to come in late February. We are intending to consult on the next two *tranches* to get those two in place in February and March.

The later tranches are somewhat more uncertain not because of the systems but in terms of the sheer volume of customers that might transfer at any one time: there are peak constraints.

Therefore, if there are a lot of customers transferring from the next tranches there may be a bow-wave that blocks the possible transfers later on; we will come to that closer to the time. It may be that we could help things by opening more than one of the later tranches together at a later time. The roll out is certainly very much on target.

George mentioned the MORI survey. We are going to do that again but one of the surveys that I found particularly interesting of late was a survey from the Electricity Association which showed that the switches were as likely to be low-income, low-consumption prepayment customers as they were to be high-income, high-consumption direct-debit customers. I suspect that that is partly because of the success of doorstep selling. Doorstep selling is one of the surprise success stories of opening the domestic market. Customers seem to like it very much, perhaps because of the novelty of having gas competition. They like it to be explained to them and the supplier seems to find it a very successful way of getting customers. Doorstep selling has had a bad press because of a few cases where there are problems. Of course it is not nice to have problems on your doorstep and that is one reason why we are introducing a licence condition on marketing, to make sure people behave properly.

On the prepayment issue, that is a future potential concern because at the moment, as George says, we have price caps on all the payment methods including the standing charge and the unit and the per-therm charge. Competitors are offering quite substantial discounts to prepayment metered customers but they are not quite as large as to other groups. The real issue is whether, if costs unravel in the future, does that discount disappear? We have been doing quite a lot of work at OFGAS to try to understand different aspects of the prepayment market. One question is: Are suppliers using prepayment meters as a soft option instead of doing more creative things to manage their cash flow and their debt problems? We are also trying to get competition into prepayment meters and into the prepayment system because at the moment there is no competition in those areas at all. We are very interested in at least making sure that costs are as low as possible before we begin to work out whether or not there is a serious divergence between the benefits of competition to different groups.

On TransCo and the network code, I think of it in two different parts: one is about transporting gas and the other is about all the services that TransCo provides that directly facilitate the competitive markets (such as the transfer of customers between suppliers and indeed meter reading). One of the surprises of our 1995 competitive market review was that the main impediments to competition were the services that TransCo was providing to suppliers, and especially opening meter reads which were particularly poor at the time. So we put in place a package of service standards for all the services that were really important in the competitive market and also put liabilities on TransCo to meet those service standards. I think we did reasonably tackle the quality of service issues.

I think it is more difficult on the transportation side because service issues there tend to be safety related and so it is quite difficult to improve quality. But that is something that has to be tackled. On unbundling, we are moving ahead to unbundle as much as we can from the basic transportation monopoly, including metering, etc. In this area, and indeed others, I think there is a tendency for shippers to want to leave things as they are: the more you unbundle the supply chain the more the opportunities are, but also the more you have to work to better your competitors.

4

REGULATORY ASSET VALUE

AND THE COST OF CAPITAL

Geoffrey Whittington[1]

University of Cambridge

The Regulatory Context

THE UK UTILITY COMPANIES WERE PRIVATISED on the understanding that they would be regulated on a price-cap basis, rather than the rate of return basis prevalent in the USA. It was believed that the price cap would provide an incentive for companies to cut costs and increase profits within the period for which the price cap was set. When the price cap was re-set, at the end of a regulatory period, the information revealed by the economies achieved in the previous period could be used to benefit the consumer over subsequent periods.

Experience since privatisation has shown very clearly that price-cap regulation does not avoid the need for calculating the rate of return, with its attendant difficulties. When the price cap is reviewed, projections are made of the prospective cash flows resulting from alternative price caps. In choosing an appropriate price cap, a critical factor will be whether the resulting cash flows available to shareholders are excessive, and one method of checking this is to look at the resulting rate of return on a measure of shareholders' funds, that is, the regulatory asset base (RAB). This process has now become a routine aspect of regulation in telecoms, gas, water, electricity and airports. The disparate circumstances of different industries have led to the precise methodology used being different, for example in water, the availability of comparators has meant that studies of comparative efficiency across different companies has been an important part of the regulatory process,

---

[1] The author is grateful to Richard Barker, Michael Beesley, Richard Green, Geoff Meeks and Michael Pollitt for comments on an earlier draft, but any remaining errors are the sole responsibility of the author.

whereas in gas distribution this has not been possible because TransCo has a virtual monopoly of the pipeline network. However, there is a fundamental similarity between the bases used in different industries, and this has become more apparent as a result of appeals to the Monopolies and Mergers Commission (MMC) by regulated industries. The MMC has sought to be consistent in its decisions and this has led to a degree of convergence across industries, not least in the rate of return allowed on the RAB. Some key points of recent MMC decisions in this area are summarised in Appendix 1.

The most important recent MMC pronouncement on this topic has been its 1997 Report on British Gas, which largely followed the 1993 report but amended it in some important respects. British Gas will be the main focus of the practical illustrations in this paper, although the principles apply to other regulated industries. The object of the paper is to discuss the critical issues relating to the establishment of a regulatory asset base and, to a lesser extent, the selection of an appropriate rate of return. It is not intended to discuss whether price-cap regulation in its present form is the most appropriate system, but it should be noted that its two principal rivals, rate of return regulation and profit sharing, involve using the rate of return on regulatory assets more frequently than does the price-cap approach. Hence, the difficulties of measuring the asset base and establishing a fair rate of return will tend to be compounded under these alternative regulatory régimes.

1. The Regulatory Asset Base (RAB)

In establishing the RAB upon which a rate of return is allowed, four distinct issues have emerged in the development of the regulatory process over the past decade.[2] These are, first, the valuation of the initial regulatory base, second, the up-dating of the regulatory base to allow for price changes, third, the treatment of depreciation, and fourth, the treatment of new investment. These will be considered in turn, with comments on their treatment in the recent British Gas report.

1. Valuation of the Initial Regulatory Asset Base

By the initial RAB, we strictly mean its value at the time of the flotation of the company, although it is possible to fix it at a later date.

---

[2] See, for example, para 2.105 of the 1997 MMC Report on British Gas.

There are two competing valuation concepts which can be used: the flotation price paid by shareholders, and some measure of the valuation of assets (usually at current cost or replacement cost) less current liabilities.[3] The latter has not found favour with regulators in cases in which it gives a notably higher answer than the former, that is, the market-to-asset ratio (MAR, which is the ratio of stock market value to asset value) is less than one. The two leading examples of this are gas (where the MAR on flotation was about 0.4) and water (where the typical MAR was much lower). Despite some hopeful claims by water companies that they should be regulated on the Indicative Values set at privatisation, there has been general acceptance of the market value approach adopted by the regulators and the MMC. To adopt a replacement cost or current cost approach at this late stage would involve a very large transfer of wealth from the consumer to the shareholder, which would be inconsistent with the requirement that the regulator strike an appropriate balance between these interests by allowing a return sufficient to justify the shareholders' investment but not excessive from the perspective of the consumer.

Thus, the accepted purpose of the regulatory base is to establish the amount of funds on which the shareholder is entitled to a return, and this amount is established, at least initially, by reference to the funds attributable to the shareholder, that is, the amount originally subscribed on flotation or some variation of that. The variations which have been implemented have been designed to cope with the instability of the share price at the time of privatisation and the belief that the initial premium should be regarded as part of the shareholders' initial stake. Thus, the water regulator uses the average share price for 200 days following privatisation as the initial value. The 1993 MMC report on British Gas went much further than this and used the 1991 share price (five years after the 1986 privatisation and immediately before the MMC inquiry was initiated) on the ground that gains up to that time represented the initial discount on privatisation and subsequent efficiency improvements obtained by the company which could reasonably be

---

[3] For simplicity, the subsequent arguments and illustrations are framed in terms of an RAB which is attributable entirely to shareholders. Other sources of long-term finance, such as loan stocks and convertible securities, would, of course, add to the RAB in practice, and the rate of return should be adjusted to take account of the cost of such finance.

expected to benefit shareholders. It was, however, recognised that this was essentially an *initial* valuation which could not be repeated as part of the future regulatory process. Otherwise, there would be circularity in the process, share prices depending on expected regulatory decisions, and regulatory decisions depending on the expectations embodied in the share price.

By focusing on share price at flotation or some later time to establish the initial value of the regulatory asset base, the regulatory system recognises that it is concerned with establishing an appropriate return *of* (in the case of depreciation) and return *on* (in the case of profit) capital to the shareholder. It is therefore concerned with establishing an appropriate valuation of shareholders' funds, rather than a valuation of specific assets, or net assets, of the business. The difference between the two is captured by the MAR. It might be thought that the failure to award a full return on the current value of assets would lead to inefficient investment decisions, but this does not apply to the initial RAB, which relates to assets which were already invested when the regulatory process started. Given the nature of the investment, it is not readily liquidated or transferred to some more profitable unregulated use. In the case of *marginal* investment decisions (decision to make new investments) it is more important that, if the investment is desirable,[4] the regulator should allow a reasonable return on current cost, which will give the regulated company an appropriate incentive to make the investment. This is addressed in 4 below.

The 1997 MMC report on British Gas endorsed the approach of the earlier (1993) report in using a measure based on the 1991 stock market price to establish the initial regulatory value of British Gas.

2. Adjusting the RAB for Price Changes

Having established an initial value of the RAB, it is necessary to consider how this should be adjusted for price changes when it is

---

[4] There is, of course, a judgement about desirability which will have to be made by the regulator, in the absence of any signals which would be provided by the market in an unregulated environment. In some cases, it might be possible to develop a pricing structure based on charging long-run marginal cost which would provide appropriate signals as to the marginal demand for investment in the industry.

carried forward to future periods. The second adjustment which must be made is that for depreciation: this is considered in 3 below.

The regulatory régime based on an RPI minus x formula is essentially defined in real terms (hence the RPI component). Thus, the consumer bears any risk arising from inflation. Equally, the standard methods of allowing the cost of capital (which will briefly be considered later) are designed to produce estimates of the appropriate real return. Thus, for the sake of consistency, we need to adjust the RAB to yield a value which is of constant real value (measured in £s of the particular year) through time. The natural index to use to adjust the initial RAB to a constant real value is a general purchasing power index such as the RPI. This would ensure that the capital fund on which shareholders are given a return is of constant purchasing power through time. It is also consistent with the use of the RPI in the price formula. The use of the RPI to re-state RAB in current prices was adopted by the MMC in its 1997 British Gas report (but not in the 1993 report, so that for purposes of consistency, the later report applied the RPI only from 1997). It had earlier been used by the MMC in its 1996 report on the BAA London airports.

The alternative index, favoured by the MMC in its earlier report on British Gas and by OFGAS in its early years, is a current cost (CC) index, which attempts to capture changes in the current cost of replacing the services embodied in the specific assets underlying the RAB. This description shows the inappropriateness of a CC index if we believe that the RAB represents a capital fund representing the shareholders' investment *in* the firm (which is implied by the MAR adjustment) rather than the specific investments made with those funds *by* the firm. The effect of using the CC indices is to tie investors' returns to the replacement prices of firm-specific assets. As a consequence of this, real holding gains (those representing specific price rises in excess of the RPI) will benefit shareholders (by increasing the RAB) and real holding losses (such as are often caused by technical progress in industries such as British Gas) will disadvantage shareholders. Such a system penalises technical progress (which might be expected to cause holding losses on existing capital assets) in a company which aims to maximise shareholder value. It can also lead to extensive regulatory uncertainty and possibly to dispute over the identification of the appropriate specific index or asset price, which was why OFWAT decided at an early stage to use general rather than specific indices for the re-statement of the RAB.

In summary, by accepting a general index basis for re-stating the RAB, the MMC has adopted a method consistent with the view that the RAB represents a pool of shareholders' funds, rather than a collection of specific investments. The general index has the further advantage of simplicity and objectivity. Its use also removes the risks to shareholders which would otherwise arise from inflation (if no price adjustment were made to the RAB) or from relative price changes (if price adjustments were based on a CC index or specific prices). It might be expected that insuring shareholders against these risks would reduce the rate of return that they would require.

3. Depreciation

The most difficult aspect of the RAB has proved to be depreciation, particularly in so far as it relates to replacement investment. Here, the MMC made an unfortunate decision in 1993 and reversed it in 1997.

The issue of depreciation is quite simple, so long as we start from a clear view as to what depreciation is for. There are two views of depreciation: first, that it represents a return of capital subscribed; second, that it represents a charge for the replacement of assets consumed. The former view is consistent with the use of the RAB as a basis for assessing the investment *in* the firm, attributable to shareholders. The latter view is consistent with the use of the RAB as a measurement of the investment *by* the firm in real assets, and is the view implicit in current cost accounting (CCA). Both approaches to depreciation are relevant to particular problems. For the purpose of establishing an RAB for fixing the price cap, the return of capital approach seems to be the more relevant, because we are concerned with giving shareholders an adequate (but not excessive) return of (in the case of depreciation) and (in the case of profit) on the capital which they subscribed.

If we adopt this approach and apply it to the initial RAB, the depreciation charged will be based on regulatory value, rather than the full current cost of the underlying assets, because it is the regulatory value on which returns to shareholders should be based. Thus, the depreciation charge will be based on the numerator rather than the denominator of the MAR. Alternatively, we can regard it as being based on the denominator (full current cost of the underlying assets), multiplied by the MAR, which gives an identical result. In other words, full current cost depreciation is abated by the MAR. This is the approach adopted in the 1997 British Gas report of the MMC. This is illustrated in (1) of Appendix 2 (below, p.111).

However, assessing the time pattern of depreciation is essentially an arbitrary process. It is, therefore, fortunate that the amount of depreciation that is deducted from profit in any year for regulatory purposes does not affect the value of total returns to shareholders so long as consistent adjustments are made to the RAB, that is, all depreciation which is charged in the regulatory profit and loss account is also deducted from the RAB, so that it will reduce the capital on which and of which shareholders are allowed a return in the future. This is an important property which accountants call *articulation*: the charge to the profit and loss account should also have an equivalent effect on the relevant item accumulated in the balance sheet.

Provided that articulation with the RAB is enforced, there is no reason why full current cost depreciation cannot be charged in the profit and loss account: the effect of this will be to allow higher prices to consumers now but lower prices in the future, and shareholders will not gain by this re-profiling of the cash flows if the regulator is successful in allowing only a normal rate of return on the RAB. However, in extreme cases, as David Newbery has pointed out (Newbery, 1997), this might lead to the RAB becoming negative, because the accumulated total of depreciation allowed exceeded new investment to such an extent that the shareholders' investment was effectively refunded in full. This is illustrated in (2) of Appendix 2 (below, p. 112). In such a case, the shareholders would ultimately have to refund the over-payment (and interest thereon) to the company, for the benefit of consumers.

The 1993 MMC report on British Gas encouraged the logical error (which was recognised apologetically in Volume 2, paras 7.78 to 7.80) of breaking the articulation between the depreciation charge and the RAB. A full current cost depreciation charge was allowed as a charge against profit, but only that proportion attributable to regulatory value (full current cost abated by the MAR) was deducted from the RAB. This is illustrated in (3) of Appendix 2 (below, p. 112). This did not affect the overall judgement made about the price cap in 1993 (and the subsequent performance of British Gas shares does not suggest that this price cap was over-generous, for example, see Figure 6.2 of the 1997 report), but it did lead to some misguided expectations, or hopes, by the regulatee, which were dispelled by the 1997 report.

4. The Treatment of New Investment

New investment, that is, investment taking place after the initial RAB is established, should be added to the RAB at cost and rolled forward by whatever price index is applied to the initial RAB. Any subsequent depreciation of the investment should be charged against profit for regulatory purposes.

This treatment of new investment is consistent with the concept of the RAB as representing shareholders' investment *in* the company, and it is also the treatment adopted by the 1997 MMC report on British Gas. New investment represents an additional investment *by* shareholders in the regulated business: if it did not qualify for an adequate return as an addition to the RAB, the funds might well be invested outside the regulated business. Equally, depreciation charged against regulatory income represents a return of their investment *to* shareholders and therefore reduces the size of the fund on which they are entitled to a return. Provided that depreciation and investment are treated symmetrically, it is not necessary to make a distinction between replacement investment and new investment. All investment (including replacement) adds to the RAB and all depreciation is deducted from it, so that a regulated firm whose investment equals its depreciation charge has a constant RAB. In retrospect, it seems that the 1993 MMC report on British Gas did not express this point clearly enough. Equally, there has been an unnecessary anxiety expressed by OFGAS and others (particularly the shippers), that the depreciation charge should not exceed investment: provided that the depreciation charge is deducted from the RAB, the lack of replacement investment means that the RAB will decline and, with it, regulated profits. A supporter of British Gas might well argue that OFGAS should have no anxiety about the adequacy of investment (replacement or otherwise) if it really is offering an adequate rate of return on RAB and a stable regulatory environment within which British Gas can invest with confidence. These issues will be taken up later.

There is one other important issue with respect to new investment. This is the choice of anticipated or actual expenditure. Clearly, at the beginning of the regulatory period, it will be necessary to include anticipated investment in the budget on which the price cap is based. However, at the end of the regulatory period, the regulator has three choices: first, add *actual* capital expenditure for the past period to the RAB and claw back any excess returns due to under-spending of the budget (possibly with compensation where there is over-spend); second, add actual expenditure to the RAB without claw-back or compensation; and third, add *anticipated* expenditure to the RAB with no adjustments for deviation of the actual spend.

Which of these is appropriate depends on the circumstances of the time and the industry. Full claw-back (the first option) removes any incentive for the industry to exaggerate anticipated expenditure relative to actual, but it also removes any incentive to find real economies in capital expenditure. It is therefore inconsistent with the principle of price-cap regulation and would be resorted to only if the regulator did not trust the industry's good faith in making its projections, or if there were some drastic change in circumstances (as in the case of water companies being given compensation for having to invest to meet new environmental requirements). The second option provides some incentive, within the regulatory period, to economise on investment expenditure and is broadly the stance taken in the 1997 MMC report on British Gas. The third option has merit where there are large, long-lived investment projects which offer large potential savings if they are well designed and managed. This approach has been used by OFWAT, and it should be noted that, although it gives the companies a greater incentive to be efficient, it also imposes greater risks on them, if their anticipations are not fulfilled.

The treatment of new investment will, in part, depend upon the confidence felt by the regulator in the information which is available about investment needs. This raises the important issue of *learning*: regulators are continuously accumulating more information about the industries that they regulate, and improving their insight into the underlying financial and productive processes, whether through models or by less formal processes. This means that regulation is a dynamic rather than a static process, so that we should not attempt to freeze it at a particular stage of its development. Hopefully, the learning process is not confined to the regulator, and the regulatee also learns more about its own business by responding to the regulator's questions. Thus, regulation may perform a positive role in making efficiency improvements possible, as well as providing incentives for them to be realised.

Summary on the RAB

The discussion of the RAB has supported the general approach of the 1997 MMC report on British Gas. This involves an initial RAB based on a stock market valuation of shareholders' interests. New investment is added to the RAB and full depreciation (the same as is charged against regulatory income) is deducted. It is preferable that this depreciation be based on RAB rather than some larger CCA valuation, but the articulation between the income statement and the RAB should ensure that shareholders do not gain in the long term, whatever depreciation schedule is adopted (provided that it is understood that the RAB might become negative in extreme cases[5]). What is wrong, or at least inconsistent, is to follow the MMC's 1993 methodology of deducting full CCA depreciation from the regulatory income but deducting only a proportion of it from the RAB. In carrying forward the RAB we need to adjust for price changes, and a general index is to be preferred to a specific (CC) index for this purpose. This and the other conclusions are all derived from the fundamental assumption that the RAB, and the return on it, are supposed to reflect the investment in the firm rather than investment by the firm in the regulated activity.

2. The Regulatory Rate of Return (RRR)

The RAB is combined with a regulatory rate of return, RRR, to establish the acceptable level of regulatory profit. The RRR has therefore attracted as much attention and discussion as the RAB in regulatory cases. However, the MMC's response to the RRR question has been much clearer than its answer to the RAB question. The answer, according to the 1997 report on British Gas, is 7 per cent per annum, and this is consistent with earlier reports (see Appendix 1, below, p. 109). This is supposed to be a fair pre-tax real rate of return on long-run investment in a privatised utility. It represents a weighted average cost of capital (WACC), including

---

[5] A negative RAB would imply negative returns and would ultimately have to be discharged by further contributions from shareholders, if consumers were to be treated equitably.

both the debt and the equity elements in long-term financing.[6]

It would be easy to mock the 'magic' number 7 per cent as being arbitrary and lacking a sound theoretical or empirical underpinning, rather like 42, which was the answer to the Ultimate Question in *The Hitch-Hikers Guide to the Galaxy*. However, there are two important differences. First, the Ultimate Question was not known, whereas we do know the question that we are trying to answer in the case of the rate of return: What is the minimum rate of return which providers of finance will require in order to undertake this particular investment? Second, the MMC's rate of return does have an empirical underpinning which is at least as good as that of the alternatives.

The basis upon which the rate of return is calculated is the widely accepted weighted average cost of capital. This weights the components of the financial structure according to their contributions, in terms of market value. Debt instruments are fairly easily dealt with, because interest payments and redemption terms are known. The more difficult component is equity, because future dividends are variable and unknown. In estimating the cost of equity, it is common practice to use the Capital Asset Pricing Model, CAPM, which has respectable theoretical underpinnings in portfolio theory, although it is by no means the only model available.[7] The CAPM estimates the return on equity using three components: the risk-free rate of return, the equity premium, and a parameter β which relates the risk of the individual security to that of equities in general as expressed in the equity premium. There is little controversy about estimating the risk-free rate of return or β. It is generally accepted that the latter is rather less than unity, that is, the regulated utilities are rather less risky than equities in general, as might be expected, although some regulatees have complained that they are subject to high regulatory risk: a natural feeling at the time of a price determination or an appeal to the

---

[6] Although the earlier discussion of the RAB referred to shareholders, this term was defined rather loosely to include all providers of long-term finance (see note 1).

[7] One alternative is the Arbitrage Pricing Model proposed by Ross (1976). A variant of the CAPM which has a sound basis in micro-economic theory but does not perform so well empirically is the consumption-based asset pricing model. A useful review of the alternatives is Brennan (1992).

MMC! It is the equity premium which has been the real source of uncertainty and contention.

The equity premium is the return which shareholders *expect* to receive above the risk-free rate. It is therefore an *ex ante* measure, and this is where the difficulty arises. Much time and effort has been expended analysing *ex post* historical series dating back as far as 1919, but, as we are regularly warned, past performance of shares is not necessarily a guide to the future. There has also been much discussion of such issues as the appropriate time period, survivorship bias and the virtues of arithmetic versus geometric averaging.[8] The result is that the empirical estimates offer a wide range of outcomes, depending on the preferred assumptions. Thus, the MMC in its 1993 British Gas report tried to cut through the elaborate tissue of modelling and estimation and instead asked leading investors what rate of return they expected to earn on investment in a utility share like that of British Gas. Although the sample was small, the respondents included major shareholders in British Gas, and they were influential in the MMC's final determination in this case which, as Appendix 1 shows, has been followed fairly consistently in subsequent cases. Unfortunately, it is unlikely that the exercise could be repeated, because fund managers might now believe that a high estimate of the required rate of return could improve the actual return on their investment.

However, the validity of the MMC's estimate of the cost of capital does seem to have been confirmed, or at least not contradicted, by the response of the stock market to its recommendations. Typically, the immediate reaction of the stock market to the publication of MMC reports has not been negative. Admittedly, there are many elements in such reports (such as the measurement of the RAB) which affect prospective returns, but it would surely be expected that the recommendation by the MMC of a return substantially below the acceptable level on the utility's current assets and future investment, would lead to an immediate fall in share price (unless the market had anticipated an

---

[8] See, for example, Scott (1992) and Jenkinson (1993). A recent British contribution to the empirical literature on the equity premium is O'Hanlon and Steele (1997): it estimates a premium in the range 4 to 5 per cent. This is lower than estimates obtained by traditional methods which gave rise to the so-called 'equity premium puzzle' (surveyed by Kocherlakota, 1996).

unacceptable recommendation, in which case the fall in share price would occur earlier). Certainly, the handsome premia paid in recent electricity and water take-overs do not suggest that a prospective 7 per cent real rate of return is seen as a threat.

Thus, the range of rates of return set in the 1993 British Gas report seems to have stood the test of time. It must, however, be admitted that it should be regarded as a robust rule of thumb rather than a precise measure. This arises not only from the uncertainty arising from estimating the elements of the CAPM, but also from the treatment of taxation. It is not clear from a theoretical standpoint that it is sensible to try to define a consistent *pre-tax* rate of return, where the tax referred to is corporation tax, yet the rate-of-return calculations made by regulators are usually on a pre-corporation tax basis. Shareholders presumably require a consistent post-corporation tax return, because it is that which determines their dividends. Some water companies have indeed been tax-exhausted, as a result of investment programmes, so that their pre- and post-corporation tax returns have been identical, although they may still be allowed to make notional tax charges for accounting purposes.[9] In such circumstances, allowing a pre-tax rate of return which matches a cost of capital grossed up for notional corporation tax might seem to be unduly generous to the company.

A disputable assumption commonly made in grossing up the cost of capital for corporation tax, is that the whole equity stream attracts imputation relief. In fact, only the proportion distributed as dividends receives imputation relief, and retentions do not, so that assuming full imputation relief reduces the grossing up factor and therefore the pre-tax cost of equity capital. The 'full distribution' assumption might be justified on the ground that ultimately all equity returns are distributed and should be valued as if they currently attract imputation relief. However, it is surprising that regulated companies have not disputed this assumption more strongly in the past, because it reduces the pre-tax rate of return which the regulator allows. In the future, the expected withdrawal of imputation relief will remove this particular problem, but another

---

[9] The current UK Accounting Standard, SSAP15, allows provision only when crystallisation of the liability can be foreseen. This standard is currently under revision, and the UK may follow international practice which requires full provision for all notional tax charges. However, this does not reflect the real economic benefits of deferral of the tax payment.

effect of this will be to increase the grossing up factor and, with it, the importance of establishing a proper treatment of taxation.

Concluding Thoughts

The RAB and the RRR raise quite complex and absorbing technical issues which may distract attention from the main point, that they provide useful rules of thumb but not a precise determination of what price cap should be set. For the latter purpose, they need to be combined with other information available to the regulator.

One important aspect of this process is the *time period* over which the regulator drives the expected rate of return down to the minimum level. This determines the period over which the regulatee is allowed to benefit from any excess rate of return which occurs. In so far as such a return results from innovation and cost saving by the regulatee, it is desirable that it be continued long enough to provide an appropriate incentive for further improvements. It has been argued that eliminating excess returns at the beginning of each regulatory period provides little incentive to improved performance in the later part of the previous period. Insofar as excess returns are due to the positive efforts of the regulatee, it is important that they be phased out over a long enough period to provide adequate incentives. On the other hand, insofar as excess returns are the result of mis-judgement by the regulator, unduly pessimistic cost or demand projections by the regulatee, or merely strokes of good fortune outside the control of either, there is no reason to adopt a 'soft landing' approach in adjusting future returns to more normal levels. Recent MMC reports, notably those on South West Water and Portsmouth Water, have adopted a fairly sceptical view as to the need for excess returns to persist and have therefore preferred a relatively rapid adjustment (for example, in the water cases, the adjustment proposed by the MMC was over the following 5-year period, whereas the Regulator had previously adopted a 10-year adjustment). Recent pronouncements by the regulators, notably OFGAS and OFWAT, have expressed similar views. However, this is an area in which the circumstances of the case, interpreted by the regulator's judgement, should determine the outcome. Precise rules would inevitably be arbitrary.

A second important aspect of the process of setting the price cap is *cash flow* forecasting. This was emphasised by Michael Beesley in his 1995 lecture in this series, which dealt with setting the price cap for British Gas. This provided considerable insight into the thinking behind the 1993 MMC report on British Gas, but it has more general application to the regulatory process. Budgets are a crucial element in the process, because the prospective revenue generated by the price cap must be adequate to meet the prospective expenses. The difference between the two, the profit or loss, is a relatively small item and depends upon the accurate determination of the larger items. One of the areas of contention and possible error in determining the larger items is the accountant's estimate of accrued amounts and changes in them, the obvious examples being asset valuation and depreciation. A *cash* budget avoids this problem by cutting out the accruals: there are therefore no problems of revaluing assets or assessing depreciation. The cash flows of the business thus give an alternative insight into the underlying transactions which are of help to the regulator. A cash-flow alternative to the RRR/RAB approach asks the question: Are the prospective cash inflows of the business adequate to meet the necessary cash outflows? The outflows will include operating expenses, replacement investment, and interest and dividend payments necessary to reward existing investors in the firm and any new investment which is required.

Although cash-flow projections can provide the regulator with a very useful cross-check on more traditional accrual accounting methods of the RRR/RAB variety, they are not a substitute for these and are not complete in themselves. There are two crucial gaps in the description of cash-flow regulation given above. First, the costs of financing which are allowed must relate to the capital sum which they are servicing, that is, to something resembling the RAB. Second, cash-flow projections over a fixed regulatory period of, say, five years are not sufficient to establish whether shareholders have been given a reasonable reward in terms of dividends: the value of dividends, and therefore of other cash flows, beyond the regulatory horizon is also relevant. This is captured by the terminal value of the RAB, at the end of the regulatory period. This is the amount upon which the regulator intends to base future returns, and is therefore one useful estimate of the value of investors' capital at that time. As the experience and skill of the regulator improve, the period over which cash flows can be reliably forecast may lengthen, and the importance of the terminal value of the RAB will diminish, but it will not disappear.

Thus, we cannot entirely escape the use of the RRR and the RAB. What we should do is to recognise that they are only two elements in a larger set of information which is used in the regulatory process. Moreover, their use involves a degree of subjective judgement by the regulator and is not as precise as is hoped for by those who press for clarification of the 'regulatory contract'. This imprecision is not necessarily a bad thing. The regulatory process is, after all, intended to act as a substitute for the discipline of the market-place, and few markets signal their future behaviour very precisely in advance. Regulated firms do expect to receive an equity premium in their shareholders' returns and this can be justified only if they are subject to a degree of risk and uncertainty.

The clarification of the 'regulatory contract' may also be undesirable from another perspective – that of change. The regulatory process is not static. Regulators have accumulated considerable experience and insight during the past decade or so, and it is reasonable to expect that this process will continue. As a consequence, the precise form of regulation may change, and it would be unfortunate if progress in this direction were inhibited by an unduly legalistic and static view of the nature of the regulatory contract.

References

Accounting Standards Board (1992): SSAP15: *Accounting for deferred tax* (amended December 1992), ASB, London.

Beesley, M. E. (1996): 'RPI-X: Principles and their Application to Gas', pp.207-22 of M.E. Beesley (ed.), *Regulating Utilities: A Time for Change?*, IEA Readings No. 46, London: Institute of Economic Affairs.

Brennan, M. J. (1992): 'Capital asset pricing model', pp.287-92 of P. Newman, M. Milgate and J. Eatwell (eds.), *The New Palgrave Dictionary of Money and Finance*, Vol.1, London: Macmillan Press.

Jenkinson, T. (1993): 'The cost of equity finance: conventional wisdom reconsidered', *Stock Exchange Quarterly with Quality of Markets Review*, Autumn, pp. 23-27.

Kocherlakota, N. R. (1996): 'The Equity Premium: It's Still a Puzzle', *Journal of Economic Literature*, Vol. XXXIV, No.1, pp. 42-71.

Monopolies and Mergers Commission (1993): *British Gas plc* (4 Volumes), Cm.2314-7, London: HMSO.

Monopolies and Mergers Commission (1995): *South West Water Services Ltd*, London: HMSO.

Monopolies and Mergers Commission (1995): *Portsmouth Water plc*, London: HMSO.

Monopolies and Mergers Commission (1995): *Scottish Hydro-Electric plc*, London: HMSO.

Monopolies and Mergers Commission (1996): *BAA plc*, MMC4, Monopolies and Mergers Commission, London.

Monopolies and Mergers Commission (1997): *Northern Ireland Electricity plc,* London: The Stationery Office.

Monopolies and Mergers Commission (1997): *BG plc*, London: The Stationery Office.

Newbery, D. M (1997): 'Determining the regulatory asset base for utility price regulation', *Utilities Policy*, Vol. 6, No.1, pp. 1-8.

O'Hanlon, J. and A. Steele (1997): *Estimating the Equity Risk Premium using Accounting Fundamentals*, Working Paper No. 97/003, Department of Accounting and Finance, University of Lancaster.

Ross, S. A. (1976): 'The arbitrage theory of asset pricing', *Journal of Economic Theory*, Vol. 13, No. 3, pp. 341-60.

Scott, M. F. (1992): 'The cost of equity capital and the risk premium on equities', *Applied Financial Economics*, Vol. 2, No. 1, pp. 21-32.

Whittington. G. (1994): 'Current Cost Accounting: Its Role in Regulated Utilities', *Fiscal Studies*, Vol.15, No. 4, pp. 88-101.

Appendix 1: Some recent MMC decisions on the RAB and the RRR

Report	Initial RAB	Price change adjustment	Depreciation	RRR
British Gas (1993)	Stock market value in 1991 (MAR 0.6).	Current Cost	Current cost charged to revenue, but abated by MAR before deduction from RAB.	6.5 to 7.5 per cent, real, pre-tax.
British Gas (1997)	As in 1993, plus additional investment and price changes, less depreciation, as agreed in 1993.	RPI	Based on RAB for old assets and cost for new assets. Amount charged to revenue is deducted from RAB.	7 per cent, real, pre-tax.
South West Water (1995) and Portsmouth Water (1995)	Market value for over 200 days following flotation (SWW), 50 per cent of indicative value (Portsmouth).	RPI	Current cost charged to revenue and deducted from RAB.	6 to 8 per cent, real, pre-tax.
Scottish Hydro-Electric (1995)	CC Value in 1991, less depreciation, plus new investment.	RPI	Based on RAB, charged to revenue and deducted from RAB.	7 per cent, real, pre-tax (range 6 to 7.75 per cent).

[continued on p.110]

Appendix 1 (cont'd)

Report	Initial RAB	Price change adjustment	Depreciation	RRR
BAA, London Airports (1996)	Book value (replacement cost) in 1991, plus subsequent investment, less depreciation.	RPI	Accounting depreciation (modified HCA) charged to revenue and deducted from RAB.	6.4 to 8.3 per cent, real, pre-tax.
Northern Ireland Electricity (1997)	Initial flotation value, plus subsequent investment, less depreciation.	RPI	Current cost abated by MAR for initial assets, and full depreciation on new investment charged to revenue and deducted from RAB.	7 per cent, real, pre-tax.

Appendix 2

Illustration

Assume that Current Cost net asset value is   £500m
  Market-based initial value (RAB) is   £200m

MAR is therefore   £200m/£500m= 0.4

Depreciation rate d is 5 per cent p.a. straight line

Assume no price adjustments or new investment.

(1) **If depreciation is based on RAB**, the charge D against regulated income should be
$$£200m \times 0.05 = £10m.$$

Alternatively, we can characterise this in CC terms as

$$CC \times d \times MAR, \text{ie } £500m \times 0.05 \times 0.4.$$

The **closing RAB** should be reduced by D to reflect the **return of capital** which it represents,

$$\text{i.e. closing RAB is } £200m-£10m = £190m.$$

This is the amount upon which future allowable rates of return will be calculated. The future cash flows (from D and profit), discounted at the regulatory rate of return, have a present value equal to the initial RAB, i.e. net present value is zero and there are no excess profits. This is because the sum of depreciation is equal to RAB and the profits exactly offset the discount factors (the rate of return being the discount rate).

The **closing CC** valuation should be reduced not by D but by the amount before MAR abatement, i.e. by £500m x 0.05 = £25m., so that the closing CC valuation is £500m - £25m = £475m.

But the CC valuation has no direct relevance to regulatory profits or charges.

(2) If depreciation is based on CC without abatement for the MAR, it is essential that the resulting higher return of capital be reflected in the closing RAB, which is the basis for calculating future allowable returns on capital.

Under this régime, D = CC x d = £25m.

But the **full amount** of D is deducted from RAB, so that closing RAB is

£200m - £25m = £175m.

Thus, CC provides a basis for allowing higher depreciation against income, but this is reflected in a more rapid reduction in the RAB and consequently lower future allowable profits. The present value of the future earnings streams, discounted at the regulatory rate of return, should be the same under (2) as under (1) i.e. equal to initial RAB.

If there is no new investment, the RAB will be completely written off after 8 years (8 x £25m = £200m). After that, no further depreciation should be allowed against profit and no further rate of return will be allowed (because RAB is zero). Otherwise, provision would have to be made for a negative return based on a negative RAB and ultimately for refund of the negative RAB.

(3) If depreciation is based on CC as an income charge but on RAB as a capital adjustment, as in 1993 MMC report, the result is a generous charge against regulatory income, constituting a return of capital, which is not fully reflected in the capital base.

Under this regime, D would be £25m as in (2) but the closing RAB would be £190m as in (1). Thus, future allowable returns would be higher than in (1) because the charge D against regulatory income would be higher, and higher than in (2) because the closing regulatory base, RAB would be higher. The present value of the future cash flows implied by (3) is therefore higher than that implied by (1) and (2) (which would be exactly equal to initial RAB). (3) therefore awards excessive returns to shareholders (the present value of future cash flows, discounted at the regulatory rate of return, exceeds the initial RAB, so that net present value is positive).

Further illustrations of alternative depreciation schemes and their effects on the MAR and the RAB will be found in Whittington (1994).

CHAIRMAN'S COMMENTS

Ian Byatt

IT IS A GREAT PLEASURE FOR ME TO BE CHAIRING THIS SESSION because this is in my old stomping ground when I worked in the Treasury. I am interested that Geoffrey uses the words RRR in the paper, if not in the slides. The RRR was, of course, something we invented in 1978 in relation to the Nationalised Industries. It is also a great pleasure to have Graham Houston here tonight because he is the person who taught me how most of these things should work.

What you said is music to my ears. As I see it, you are drawing attention to a number of sound theoretical propositions: current cost accounting should be done on the basis of the maintenance of financial capital, and one should think about the investment *in* the industry and not the investment *of* the industry. From these, a large number of things fall into place, in particular the articulation of the profit and loss account and the balance sheet including the regulatory asset base. I wish that practice was as well advanced as the theory of the matter. I think you are absolutely right that once depreciation is accounted for in the right way, many of the problems concerning it fall away.

I also agree with you that the return on capital is essentially a forward-looking concept. Though unknowable (at least to human beings), we have to make various estimates of it. I was also interested in what you said about cash. I am not quite sure whether the reference was to theory or practice. As I understood it, you were saying cash does not quite deal with all the intergenerational points that can be made. If that is true, it also applies to some of the things that you said about depreciation. I think that you were suggesting that the rate of depreciation did not really matter. I do see the enormous difficulties in estimating the right rate of depreciation, but on the other hand you will have quite significant differences between consumers at different points of time unless depreciation is handled correctly.

The importance of getting a correct estimation of net returns over time is illustrated by events in the early days of the privatised water industry. Then people talked about getting a rate of return which in effect advanced the return on capital very considerably. That was pretty unpopular and I think with very good reason. I used to describe it as 'advancement' but I was admonished for putting it in that way. I remain pretty unrepentant. In our next price review we are proposing to establish what we call 'broad equivalence'. Is the expenditure on capital maintenance broadly equal to depreciation? Over what period of time should broad equivalence apply? That is as much a judgement about generations, a political or social judgement, as it is a technical judgement.

On the return on capital, I should confess that at the last price review we also asked the kind of people to whom you referred about their expectations of the returns on their financial investments. We got much the same answer as you got. This implied that what had gone on in the past about estimating the return on equity by adding a historical equity premium to a forward-looking return on debt was, in a sense, crazy. This becomes quite clear when you ask the very simple questions, does anybody expect a return on equity in the future which is equal to the current redemption yield on gilts plus what the capital asset pricing model said the equity premium had been in the past? Some very odd theoretical things were going on there. I believe we have cracked those now. There is a broad consensus that the equity premium is around 3-4 per cent or possibly lower.

You talked about incentives. A particular one was the question of remuneration for actual investment or that allowed for in setting price limits. In 1993 OFWAT published a paper which I think was largely your position 3, but last summer we published a paper which suggests moving towards your position 2. So we got less rather than more trusting! In February we will set out our firm proposals for the 1999 Price Review. I would be reluctant to move to 1. This seems to me clearly to be retrospective and undesirable. You also raised the question of 'do you have a glide path', in other words a slow phasing out of whatever excess profits there may be in the system? There were excess profits in 1994, arising out of the use of the regulatory capital base that you talked about, rather than the initial value. At least one person in this room regarded this decision as confiscation of shareholders' money. But any such 'confiscation' did not take place abruptly.

As well as the question of specific incentives, there is the question of the credibility of the régime. RPI–x is highly desirable in that it has very strong incentives to greater efficiency. On the other hand, the general public has still to be persuaded it works, in the sense that efficiency gains eventually finish up in the pockets of customers rather than in the pockets of shareholders and others. For those reasons, in addition to the points you were making, there are strong arguments for a fairly rapid and visible transfer of efficiency gains to customers. Hence my proposal of a P_0 adjustment at the next Price Review.

I entirely agree with you about the need for discretion. How can you have a regulatory contract which is set in concrete for five years ahead? God has not told us how to predict the future. Most human predictions turn out to be pretty poor over a five-year period. Setting a framework within which people can act sensibly must involve quite a lot of judgement. Then the question is how do you check and test that judgement? I think that the only answer is a reasonable amount of transparency. The test that should be applied to regulators is: Are they explaining what they are trying to do as well as they should, and are they being fully open to challenge on these matters?

5

POOL REFORM AND COMPETITION

IN ELECTRICITY

David M. Newbery

University of Cambridge

Introduction

IN OCTOBER 1997 PROFESSOR STEPHEN LITTLECHILD, the Director General of Electricity Supply, was invited by Mr John Battle, Minister for Science, Energy and Technology, to consider how a review of electricity trading arrangements might be undertaken and to draw up terms of reference. On 5 November Littlechild issued his consultation document, setting out the objectives of the review as follows:

> 'The starting point is to consider what kinds of electricity trading arrangements will best meet the needs of customers and command their confidence. As the Electricity Act points out, these needs include prices, continuity and quality of supply. The arrangements should enable demand to be met efficiently and economically. They should enable costs and risks to be reduced and shared efficiently. In general, these aims will be promoted by competition in the market, by ease of entry into and exit from the market, and by widening the range of choices available to all market participants. Appropriate trading arrangements play an essential role in facilitating such developments.'

The Electricity Pool of England and Wales is the centrepiece for the trading arrangements in electricity, and represents an ambitious attempt to create a genuine market in an industry that in the past has almost invariably operated as a regulated or publicly owned vertically integrated monopoly. Competition provides better incentives for efficiency than regulation, but is impossible or ineffective for the core natural monopolies of electricity transmission and distribution. The guiding principle in restructuring the electricity supply industry (ESI) in Britain in 1990 was therefore to introduce competition into generation and supply and to restrict regulation to transmission and distribution. Competition requires a market, but creating a spot market for wholesale or bulk electric power is difficult, and most earlier attempts to introduce competition into the ESI in Britain and the US were both modest and of distinctly limited success.

The design, development and creation of the Pool in 1990 were not only a remarkable conceptual innovation; they were also remarkably successful in meeting the main objective of creating a market while facilitating a smooth transition from the former state-owned vertically integrated Central Electricity Generating Board (CEGB) to an unbundled ESI in which generation was potentially competitive, without causing the lights to go off (as some feared), nor causing the immediate collapse of the coal industry (which was delayed until after a critical election). Yet the Pool has been singled out for some of the fiercest criticism in an industry most parts of which have been under attack at some time or another. What do these critics claim is wrong with the Pool? Can its faults be remedied by modest reforms or is the whole concept fundamentally flawed? For other countries contemplating the creation of a power market, what lessons should be drawn from the experience of the British Pool,[1] and what lessons can Britain in turn draw from the experience of other pools operating in the Nordic countries, Victoria, and elsewhere?[2]

Before turning to the list of criticisms, it is worth rehearsing some of the successes of the Pool, and the challenges it has had to face. Consider what it sets out to do – create a daily spot market that can match demand and supply at an efficient price, into which any licensed generator (above a modest size) can sell, and from which any buyer of above a certain size (100kW in 1997, but with no restriction from 1998) can buy at the same price. (Certain additional ancillary services are bundled with the raw power, which buyers pay for through uplift, but that does not alter the price-like nature of the Pool Purchase Price at which transactions take place.) Potential generators must make their best guess about the future evolution of pool prices in

---

[1] The Pool is open to generators in England, Wales and Scotland (and France via the Interconnector) but not yet to Northern Ireland.

[2] Barker, Tenenbaum and Woolf (1997) compare Britain, Scandinavia, Victoria and Alberta. Argentina also has been operating a power pool since 1995 (Perez-Ariaga and Henney, 1994). I am grateful to Allan Fels of the Australian Competition and Consumer Council for arranging meetings with participants in the Victoria electricity markets.

deciding whether to enter, and take upon themselves (or share with contracting counter parties) the risk that their forecast is wrong, with little comfort from regulators or the government. Consumers can decide whether to buy spot power, or to buy on contract, either from their local Regional Electricity Company (REC), or from some other licensed supplier, and can choose between the various contracts on offer. They can hedge their choice through the contract market and possible adjust the specific contract terms in the Electricity Forward Agreement (EFA) market, and hence overlay any physical trade with a financial contract, just as commodity traders can through futures and options.

Independent Power Producers (IPPs) operating gas-fired combined cycle gas turbines (CCGT – overwhelmingly the most economic choice for new generation in Britain in the 1990s) can decide whether to burn gas to generate electricity for sale in the pool or whether to sell gas in the gas spot market and be available to generate only if the price is sufficient to cover the cost of substitute gas-oil, or even to sell spot gas and not be available at all for despatch. All these decisions are guided by the pool price, which therefore exercises a powerful influence over both the short- and long-run decisions of producers and consumers. In short, the Pool appears to operate as a classic commodity market with all the potential advantages this has over central planning.

Why Are Power Markets Problematic?

Electricity, even more than almost every commodity traded sight unseen, is remarkably homogeneous (all electrons are identical), but, like other commodities, must be distinguished by time and place – a MWh at 5.30 p.m. on a winter weekday is very different (and has on occasion been 100 times as valuable) as a MWh at 3 a.m. the following morning.[3] Likewise, electricity in the Northeast may not be substitutable with electricity in the Southwest during periods when transmission between the two is constrained. The key difference is that electricity cannot be stored (though water in storage hydro systems can provide a good proxy form of storage), and supply must

---

[3] The Pool transacts in MWh or Megawatthours, where 1 MWh = 1000 kWh, the kWh being the standard unit paid for by domestic consumers. Thus a price of £10/MWh is equal to 1p/kWh.

be equated to demand second by second. In addition, the quality of electricity (frequency, voltage, phase angle) must all be maintained within tight limits, making refined power (meeting these quality standards) different from raw power (MWh), and requiring a host of ancillary services to transform raw into refined power. Most of the complications which make the Pool opaque and raise suspicions of market manipulation derive from the use of the computer scheduling programme GOAL which takes information from each generating set and computes a central despatch schedule that minimises cost while ensuring system integrity and quality. Many of these complications can be avoided where there is adequate storage hydro under dispersed control which allows self-despatch and which can provide rapid load following and maintain quality at low cost. Such pools, and the Scandinavian pool is an excellent example, are relatively simple and appear to offer an attractive alternative model, but they are designed to solve a quite different, and much simpler set of problems. Lessons drawn from them may not be readily applicable in Britain.

The Institutions Required to Support a Power Market

The English electricity market is not the only way to organise a market, but its structure gives an idea of the range of functions performed. The Electricity Pool, or more precisely, the Pooling and Settlement Agreement (PSA), is a contractual arrangement signed by generators and suppliers which provides the wholesale market mechanism for trading electricity. It defines the rules, and requires almost all parties wishing to trade electricity in England and Wales to do so using the Pool's mechanisms. It provides the supporting financial settlement processes to compute bills and ensure payment, but does not act as a market maker.

National Grid Company (NGC) owns and controls high voltage transmission, and as the Grid Operator, is responsible for scheduling and despatch. Elsewhere the Systems Operator is often legally required to be independent of generation and transmission. NGC also acts as the Ancillary Services Provider, the Settlement System Administrator and the Pool Funds Administrator, though again the provision of these services can be and often is separated from the provision of transmission services.

Efficient systems operation requires a mechanism to select which plant should operate when and for how long to minimise the total cost of delivering power to final consumers, where costs depend not only on short-run avoidable generation costs (mainly fuel), but on transmission losses. In addition, stations are constrained in how fast they can be brought on line from cold, while their operating costs may depend on how long they have been operating, whether they are running at low or high load, etc. The capacity of the transmission system may restrict the set of power stations that can supply consumers in a given area, while pumped storage plant may reduce daily operating costs by buying cheap off-peak power to pump water up into a reservoir for release later to generate at the peak. All these constraints and opportunities must be taken into account in the despatch schedule.

In addition, systems operation requires the supply of a variety of services for stability, security and quality. Systems security is provided both through an adequately sized transmission grid and by ensuring that supply can be matched with demand in the presence of sudden, unforeseen events such as a station failure, a transmission fault, or a sudden surge in demand. It must be possible to increase generation over time periods of seconds, minutes and tens of minutes, relying on thermal lags and automatic responses, spinning reserve (plant already running whose output can be rapidly increased), and plant which can be brought on with varying degrees of rapidity or loads that can be shed. Systems operation will also need access to reactive power to ensure that voltage and current is in phase, and to emergency services such as black-start capability (the ability to restart generation without external power). As demand may vary considerably over the day, adequate reserve capacity must be available to meet peak demand (with a sufficient safety margin to cover the risks that not all plant will be available at the moment demanded).

In addition to the short-run problem of operating the existing system efficiently, the system will need to be expanded to meet growing demand. This will require decisions on the timing, size, type and location of new generation and transmission capacity, again with the object of securing least-cost expansion and delivery to final customers. The problem is difficult as time lags may be long (4-8 years for traditional thermal or nuclear plant, though 2-3 years for modern CCGT plant), and demand forecasts and future fuel prices are uncertain, as are future technologies, environmental and safety constraints.

It may help to think of two polar mechanisms which could in

121

principle meet these requirements. Central despatch in a vertically integrated industry (until recently the dominant model) is akin to central planning, using information about costs and technical capabilities to solve a computer optimisation problem, which informs the despatcher what commands to issue to station operators. Central planning similarly investigates least-cost expansion scenarios, considering the system (generation plus transmission) as a whole.

At the other extreme we can imagine organising decisions through a decentralised market. Somehow prices for each service at each future date would be revealed to decision makers, who would be guided as if by the invisible hand to choose the overall short- and long-run system optimum. The informational requirements of this decentralised system should not be underestimated. The Pool currently quotes 52,560 prices annually for bulk power into the grid,[4] while England and Wales are divided into 16 zones for charging generators for transmission. The latter oversimplifies the potential spatial diversity compared to more decentralised systems that compute prices at each node in the system, which can vary independently as congestion and power losses vary over time. The Pool bundles together a whole variety of ancillary services, each of which ought properly to be distinguished. Each of over 200 generating sets quotes five prices and 35 technical parameters each day, while the price of gas varies daily in the spot market, and Transco distinguishes gas transport costs from six entry points to over 150 exit nodes, together with costs of storage and other services. Gasoil, fuel oil and coal are traded on active and volatile spot and futures markets.

Consider the (relatively simple) task facing a station manager in a truly decentralised system. Given a forecast of the price he would receive for power in each future time period (half-an-hour in the English model), he would decide whether it was worth bringing a station on load for some time period, and what level of output to produce, given the fixed costs of firing up and holding the station ready, as well as the variable generating costs. The time-frame for such operating decisions for a large coal-fired station may be 48 hours or longer. The prices guiding this decision would need to ensure instantaneous and continuous balance of supply and demand as

---

[4] There are three prices for each half-hour: SMP, PPP and PSP.

temperatures unexpectedly vary, storms damage power lines, stations fail, and consumers tune into unexpectedly popular television shows. The efficiency standard against which to compare this decentralised operation is, in the short run, extremely high for an integrated centrally despatched system, though rather lower when it comes to delivering least cost investments over longer time periods.

In practice, electricity pools which organise the trade of raw power and services fall somewhere between these two extremes, and the central institutional question is how to design the set of mechanisms and governance structures to achieve the best of both worlds – efficient technical operation and market responsive innovative expansion. The Pool (capital letters indicate the Electricity Pool of England and Wales) is unsurprisingly, as the first experiment in a predominantly and therefore demanding thermal system, closest to the centrally planned model while embracing market signals as far as possible. Thus the despatcher in the Pool uses the CEGB's old computer programme GOAL to determine the merit order, or the order in which plant is despatched. The most obvious difference is that the merit order is based on bids and reported parameters rather than costs and technical parameters. The Victoria power pool is (in late 1997) possibly the closest to a decentralised system for a comparably dominant thermal system. Instead of the generating sets giving a computer programme enough information to optimise over the next 48 half hours, they reveal a set of bids and associated supplies that will determine a spot price (varying every five minutes). It is up to the station manager, using forecasts provided by the despatcher, to choose a bidding strategy that will lead to his plant covering its fixed and variable costs, and operating in a sensible pattern over time. The despatcher calls on generating sets in ascending order of bids to meet demand, with the marginal generating set setting the price in that five-minute period. Prices are then averaged over half-hour periods for settlement purposes.

There is a direct correspondence between the shadow prices that emerge from the solution of the centrally planned optimisation problem and the set of efficient prices that should rule on competitive markets, though the relation may be obscured in a stochastic environment, where prices may include various insurance elements, particularly for the bundled set of services involved in supplying stable, secure and reliable power. There is also a difference between the expected price the next hour, day, week or year ahead, and the realised spot price. This is most apparent in transacting for power of a given degree of security. Most consumers are clearly willing to pay a premium to be guaranteed a certain level of reliability – for example, less than a 1 in 10 chance of a power outage anytime in the next year, or less than a 1 in 1,000 chance in the next 24 hours. After the event, either the power has failed or not, so the risks are resolved into certainties. In a competitive market the cost of delivering a given level of security varies dramatically with the level of capacity relative to demand, as we shall see when discussing capacity payments later.

This suggests that most of the time the efficient price is just the short-run avoidable cost of generation, but occasionally the full cost of providing spare capacity, or of expanding the total capacity, will determine the market clearing price that rations demand to the available supply. Schematically, the supply schedule in electricity is very much like a reverse L, with a fairly flat section followed by a vertical section, facing a rather inelastic and rapidly fluctuating demand schedule. We should expect competitive prices to be low much of the time, but occasionally very high. Commodity markets with durable supply facilities like aluminium exhibit similar behaviour – even though they are able to buffer price fluctuations by storage far better than electricity.

The same point can be put rather differently. If the efficient price is avoidable cost most of the time (as there is spare capacity), and if the long-run marginal cost of expansion is close to the average cost (no significant economies of scale above a modest size of generation), then the fixed costs must be recovered in the small number of hours in the year when predicted demand comes uncomfortably close to available supply, and the price per hour to recover these fixed costs will necessarily be high. The same is even more dramatically the case for the transmission system, where the avoidable costs (marginal losses) may be less than one-third of fixed costs.

Competitive electricity spot markets should be expected to be extremely volatile. The unpredictable element in this volatility can be hedged with financial contracts, and if the timing of the peak is very uncertain, the range of contract prices may be more moderate (the chance that any hour is the peak may be quite low for a large number of apparently similar hours). Nevertheless, large price fluctuations would arise in competitive markets, and are not reliable evidence of market manipulation. Indeed, manipulation may take the form of muting price fluctuations in exchange for higher average prices.

The institutional design must decide whether bidding into the pool is compulsory, or whether to allow trading and despatch outside the pool, how payments are to be made for the various services, and the degrees of vertical integration and bundling allowed in the supply of various services – critically, whether the transmission owner also operates despatch and organises the delivery of ancillary services, as in Britain, or whether the system operator should be independent of the grid and of the provision of ancillary services, as in Victoria. It will also need to determine whether there are constraints on who can build transmission (in Britain, National Grid Company has the sole licence), on location of new generation (which in Britain only requires local planning permission after a quasi-automatic section 36 licence is granted), and whether there should be restrictions on or penalties for premature plant retirement.

Finally, the institutional design must meet exacting efficiency standards, for the gains from unbundling and creating competitive markets are likely to be modest, and could easily be lost by inefficient market design. Newbery and Pollitt (1997) estimated that restructuring and privatising the CEGB may have cut bulk electricity costs by 5 per cent. Elsewhere, for instance in the US, where the structural changes may be less dramatic (no ownership change), the gains from introducing markets may be more modest. Gains of a few percentage points could be easily lost by choosing the wrong level of reserve margin, by locating generating plant in the wrong place, or even by placing contractual restrictions on fuel use and hence on the order of despatch (as in Spain). In most developed countries vertically integrated utilities have managed the daily despatch of existing generation efficiently, and the inefficiencies lie mainly in poor investment choices and (moderately) high operating costs. For a market-based system to improve on this it should not only reduce operating costs, but improve investment decisions and maintain the efficiency of despatch. As we shall see, these are demanding requirements.

The Organisation of the Electricity Pool

The Pool (meaning the Electricity Pool of England and Wales) operates as a day ahead market in which bids are submitted by 10 a.m. the day before, and the least cost unconstrained schedule then determines the SMP as the most expensive generating set (genset) required to operate in each half hour, assuming that there are no transmission constraints. The Pool Purchase Price or PPP is the sum of the System Marginal Price (SMP) and the capacity payment, and is announced at 5 p.m. for each half hour of the following day, starting at midnight. Capacity payments are made to each genset declared available for despatch, and are equal to the Loss of Load Probability (LOLP) multiplied by the excess of the Value of Lost Load (VOLL) over the station's bid price (if not despatched) or the SMP (if despatched). Finally, the costs of ancillary services and of dealing with the costs of transmission constraints are charged through the Transmission Services Use of System (TSUoS) to consumers on the basis of gross demand,[5] (and which cover that part of uplift that NGC now has an incentive to control), while other costs, such as errors in forecasting demand (both of which require payments to stations either as compensation for not operating or for having to operate) are added to the PPP to give the Pool Selling Price (PSP), paid for by consumers. Transmission services are made up of the cost of transmission losses (which are recovered by scaling up demand equally for all consumers by the ratio of generation to demand), the Transmission Network Use of System (TNUoS), charged on capacity, £/MW, and Distribution Use of System (DUoS) charges (for capacity and energy).

Criticisms of the Electricity Pool

The Pool has been under constant scrutiny by OFFER, the House of Commons Trade and Industry Committee (which replaced the earlier Energy Committee) and the media since its launch in 1990.[6] The Energy Committee reported as early as February 1992 having decided that 'it was not too early to assess how satisfactorily the privatised industry was working' (para. 4 – references are to paragraph numbers in House of Commons or HC 1992). The report presents many of the criticisms which continued to be levelled at the Pool, and reveals the difficulty the Committee had in deciding whether the complex arrangements and behaviour observed in the Pool were evidence that it either was or was not fulfilling its tasks. Indeed, they noted that the

---

5 This is a new charge introduced on 1 April 1997, which is only levied in Table A periods, and is published daily along with PPP and PSP in the *Financial Times*. In October 1997 it was about £1/MWh. Previously it was included in uplift.

6 See especially Offer (1992a,b,c; 1994a,b).

purpose of the Pool had nowhere been set out, but they understood its three main functions to be determining the merit order, determining the prices for services traded, and ensuring sufficient capacity to maintain the system security. 'The Director General found "an element of artificiality about Pool prices which is unsettling for customers and generators alike, and which gives misleading signals to both groups" thereby casting doubt on the Pool's ability to fulfil any of its three functions' (para. 103). They attributed the artificiality both to the dominance of the two main generators and to the fact that initially 95 per cent or more of the electricity traded was covered by contracts, put in place at vesting and all due for renewal by March 1993.

Criticisms of the Pool can be grouped into a number of headings, inevitably with some overlap between them. The criticisms concern capacity payments, market design, market manipulation, payments for other services, and criticisms of the governance structure. It will be useful to take them in order.

Capacity Payments

Capacity payments are volatile, unpredictable and have increased to what are claimed to be excessive levels in the period 1994-97. Their annual level is given in Appendix Table A1; the monthly averages are shown in Figures 1 and 3.

Newbery (1995) argued that the system of capacity payment could provide incentives for dominant capacity holders to withhold capacity, raise the Loss of Load Probability and thereby drive up the payments artificially, as a form of market manipulation, and with the risk of prejudicing the security of the system. The calculation of capacity payments rests on the Value of Lost Load which has been criticised for being arbitrary, and possibly too high (HC 1992, para. 109), while the Loss of Load Probability is based on out-of-date information, and greatly over-estimates the risk of failure, thereby increasing capacity payments beyond the level required.

Market Design

The market has been criticised for being only half a market, with supply bids but no demand-side (HC 1992, paras. 114-16). In response, some limited experiments with demand-side bidding involving about 30 large customers have taken place, but have not transformed the operation of the market. The market has been

Figure 1
Prices in the Electricity Pool at 1995/96 Constant Price
(Monthly Averages)

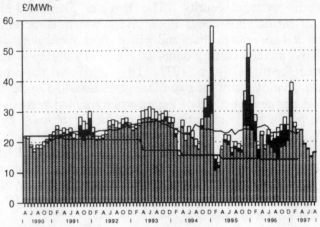

£/MWh

SMP ☐ Capacity Payment ☐ Uplift — PPP 12mth av — NP/PG fuel cost

criticised for compelling all generators to bid, and defining a single half-hourly price paid to all, rather than leaving generators to strike bilateral deals with customers and avoiding central despatch (para. 119), or, if they are centrally despatched, being paid SMP rather than what they bid. In addition, it has proven difficult to develop a liquid forward or futures markets on the back of the spot market, so that contracts remain specific, illiquid and confidential. Other commodity markets have benefitted from the increased competitive pressure that a liquid and transparent futures market brings.

Market Manipulation

The ability of generators to tailor the technical parameters as well as the individual gen set bids on the basis of information about constraints in the system, degree of tightness of demand relative to capacity, and peculiarities in the GOAL scheduling algorithm have resulted in prices that seem poorly related to costs, and have led the Director General to make a whole series of criticisms of price setting in the Pool. Part of this market manipulation can be attributed to the market power of the two main generators, who between them set the Pool price 90 per cent of the time in the first three years of operation. Figure 1 reveals the rapid widening of the margin between pool price and fuel cost from 1 April 1993 which attracted the criticism of the regulator (Offer, 1994a).

There have also been complaints that the form of contracts between RECs and IPPs and between IPPs and gas traders has resulted in bidding behaviour which does not reflect the true costs of generating from gas-fired plant. Similarly it has been claimed that the Non Fossil Fuel Obligation and the Fossil Fuel Levy bias the market in favour of Nuclear Power and against fossil generation.

Payment for Services - Uplift

The various services bundled together as uplift have more than doubled since the first year of Pool operation (as shown in Appendix Table A2 and Figure 2), and there were concerns that there were inadequate incentives to reduce these costs, and that the system of charging for various services gave poor price signals. In Figure 2 (and Table A2) *Operational outturn* is the payment to generators whose output differed from the unconstrained forecast schedule, and these generators were compensated either by their lost profit, or their bid. Thus if they were unable to run because of a transmission constraint (they were 'constrained off') they would receive SMP *less* their bid price, whereas if they had to run to satisfy demand within a transmission constrained region ('constrained on') they would be paid their bid. A large fraction of these payments was for *transmission constraints* until NGC was incentivised to control them, the balance arising from forecast errors and generator 'errors'.

Ancillary services are services required for system stability, while *unscheduled availability* is the capacity payments made to stations declared available but not called to run. Table A1 gives the yearly capacity payment per kW available, and dividing the unscheduled availability payments by these figures gives the payment-weighted amount of unscheduled capacity – which lies in the range 6,000 – 10,000 MW. Most of the variation in this component of uplift arises directly from variations in the level of capacity payment per kW. *NGC incentive payments* refer to the scheme introduced in 1994/95 under which NGC receives a fraction of cost reductions below agreed target (and pays a fraction of any excess) for Transport Uplift and Reactive Power (those parts over which it has some control). From 1997 these are collected by TS Use of System charges collected from consumers in proportion to Gross Demand (MWh). It now also receives incentive payments for Energy Uplift which are recovered through the new PSP.

Transmission losses are not included in uplift, but are part of the cost of delivering power to consumers. They were paid equally by all, regardless of location, until the Pool proposed zonal scaling factors. This was appealed against and is currently under review. Failure to charge properly for transmission losses distorts the merit order of despatch and gives incorrect locational signals for new investment. It has also been argued that NGC's Transmission Network Use of System charges give poor locational signals for new generation, though these have recently been slightly adjusted.

Governance

One of the most telling criticisms is that despite a whole series of reports by OFFER and the House of Commons Trade and Industry Committee and even by the Pool, the Pool has resisted making changes, and, because members sign the Pooling and Settlement Agreement (PSA), a commercial contract, there is no obvious mechanism to cause them to change the rules under which they operate unless enough of them agree. As most changes are likely to benefit some but disadvantage other participants, changes will be resisted. The Committee recommended that the DGES should be able to impose changes on the Pool, possibly with the Pool members having the right of appeal to the MMC (HC, 1992, para. 130). The Pool is also charged with unnecessary complexity (para. 127).

The Trade and Industry Committee returned to the Pool in their 1997 report on *Energy Regulation*, and noted that 'the DGES has no statutory authority to intervene in the operation of the Pool...The DGES may require changes to the PSA, but only in the wake of an MMC finding that the Pool operates against the public interest ... We recommend that the Government conduct a thorough review of the relationship between Offer and the Pool'. (HC 1997, para. 84) and that the Government 'consider granting powers to the DGES similar to those of the DGGS over the Network Code' (*ibid.*, para. 87).[7] On 23 October 1997, the DGES announced that he would undertake such

---

[7] The DGES is the Director General of Electricity Supply, charged with regulating the industry, while the DGGS is the Director General of Gas Supply.

Figure 2
Uplift Payments (at 1995/96 prices)

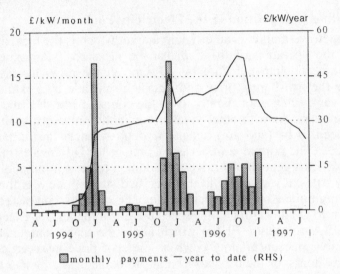

■monthly payments ─year to date (RHS)

Figure 3
Capacity Payments in the Electricity Pool

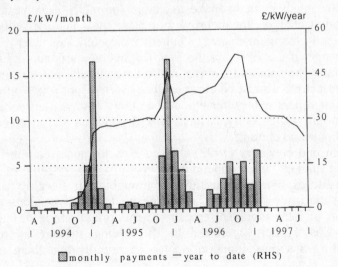

■monthly payments ─year to date (RHS)

an inquiry, and invite views on possible changes to the present Pool arrangements, including capacity payments, uplift, the timing of bids, trading outside the Pool, and even replacing the Pool by different arrangements.

Modelling Competition in the Electricity Pool

A competitive market is an efficient market which is the ideal against which the operation of the Pool can be measured. As explained, generators bid into the Pool by 10 a.m. on the previous day, and receive the half-hourly price and despatch schedule by 5 p.m. Pool prices vary, often dramatically, over the course of the day, the week and the year. As with other volatile commodity markets, such price risks need to be (and are) hedged through financial instruments or contracts. The normal contract is a Contract for Differences or CfD, under which a generator receives, in addition to the normal pool price for any sales, a sum equal to the specified strike price *less* the pool price, multiplied by the specified number of units contracted. In addition to Contracts for Differences there is a market for Electricity Forward Agreements (EFAs) which allow the main components of electricity price uncertainty (such as the spot price between certain weekday hours, or the capacity charge) to be hedged on a short-term basis.

The generators have to make three strategic choices – how to bid in their available plant each day, what level of contract cover to arrange, and how much plant to make available (normally each year when connection charges are incurred, but plant must also be withdrawn periodically for maintenance). Together these choices determine the daily range of the PPP and the long-run average around which they fluctuate. The spot and contract market are closely inter-related, and the contract price must be close to the expected spot price, otherwise buyers or sellers will prefer one to the other. Both are influenced by the amount of capacity, which will depend on the decisions of incumbents and entrants.

Green and Newbery (1992) showed how to model equilibrium in the spot market. Each generator submits a whole schedule of prices and quantities, which can usefully be thought of as a supply function (giving the price required to elicit the next unit of generation as a function of total supply offered up to this price). Indeed, National Power has explicitly referred to its bidding strategy as one of submitting a supply function. Suppose initially that there are no

132

contracts. A generator with a small fraction of capacity at each price is unlikely to set the price in any period, and thus acts as a competitive price-taker. His best strategy is to bid at short-run avoidable cost. A generator with a significant share of capacity in some active (that is, price-setting) part of the aggregate supply function sets price for some fraction of the time, and can, by raising his price over this range, increase the SMP and his revenue from all despatched plant. If the bid price of the set is too high, then another generator would undercut, set the SMP, and the plant would not be despatched. The spot market is in equilibrium when each generator is content with its own supply function, given the chosen supply function of all other competitors. Green and Newbery (1992) showed that in the absence of contracts and any threat of entry, the market power of the main generators in the Pool as it was in 1990 would enable them to raise Pool prices substantially above the efficient level.

Contracts significantly alter this picture of market power. If a generator has sold CfDs exactly equal to the amount despatched in some period, then its income is entirely determined by the strike price of the CfD. It would have no incentive to manipulate the pool price either to raise or lower the SMP, as this would not affect its revenue. Indeed, if it bid a set above its avoidable cost, it would run the risk that it would not be despatched and would lose the difference between the SMP and the avoidable cost, while if it bid below avoidable cost it might have to run the set at a loss. It would therefore do best by behaving as a competitive price-taker and bidding at short-run avoidable cost.

The extent of market power that a generator has in the spot market is related to the excess of its supply at the SMP of that period over its contracted output. Its incentive to bid a supply function above the schedule of short-run avoidable costs is thus decreasing in the volume of CfDs signed. On vesting, the three generators were provided with CfDs for virtually their entire forecast output, for periods of between one and three years, and matched with comparable (take-or-pay) contracts to purchase British coal, thus making their income and expenditure streams highly predictable for the prospectuses on which they were to be sold. It also reduced their incentive to exercise spot market power to negligible levels, though not their ability to take advantage of transmission constraints and to game capacity availability.

When the time came to renew contracts, the generators were faced with a difficult choice. If they reduced contract cover, they would have the incentive and ability to increase their bids in the Pool, and raise the average level of prices, revenue and profits. Meanwhile, IPPs, usually with equity participation by RECs, had demonstrated a technique for making the electricity market contestable. They could sign 15-year contracts with their REC for the sale of electricity, provided the REC could demonstrate to the DGES that these contracts met the economic purchasing condition of their licence (Offer, 1992c). Given then prevailing pool prices, forecast coal and gas prices, the risk of carbon taxes and other environmental restrictions likely to raise the price of coal-fired generation, and the desirability of encouraging entry and competition, the DGES was prepared to accept that the contracts met that test. The electricity contracts in turn provided security for signing 15-year contracts for the purchase of gas, issuing debt to finance the purchase of the plant, creating a highly geared financial structure with low risk, and hence relatively low cost.

Such a package made the generation market contestable, as the potential entrant could lock-in future prices and hence avoid the risk of retaliatory pricing behaviour by the incumbents. So attractive was this package that within a few months contracts had been signed for some 5,000 MW of CCGT plant, which, in addition to the incumbents' planned 5,000 MW of similar plant, would displace about 25 million tonnes of coal, compared to the 1992 generation coal burn of 60 million tonnes. The new CCGT capacity amounted to about one-fifth of existing capacity, which was in any case more than adequate to meet peak demand.

Every MW of additional capacity created by entry would displace a MW of existing capacity and hence result in the loss of the difference between average pool price and cost for the owner of that MW of capacity. Faced with this credible entry threat, incumbents had an incentive to commit themselves to bidding in such a way that the time-averaged PPP was just below the price at which contract-backed entry of IPPs was attractive. This they could do by signing contracts, which both were directly comparable to those offered by IPPs, and which would induce the incumbents to bid more competitively into the Pool, ensuring that contract and Pool prices converged. Newbery (1995, 1997) showed that the best strategy for the incumbents was to use contracts to lower the time-averaged price, while increasing the spread between peak and off-peak prices, raising the demand-weighted price and increasing price volatility in the Pool. Table A1 shows that in the first four years the demand-weighted PPP was 3 per cent higher than the time-weighted PPP, but it jumped to 11 per cent higher in the following two years. Figure 1 shows the monthly volatility increasing in the winter months. The reason why this strategy is attractive is that the incumbents have almost all the mid-merit and peaking plant, which they can use to increase their output in periods of high price. The main constraint limiting mid-merit and peak prices is the risk that IPPs may find it attractive to build plant specifically to meet these parts of the load duration curve, if the price rises sufficiently high.

The third decision the generators have to make is the amount of capacity to connect to the system (which incurs an annual connection charge) and how much to declare available each day (which influences the LOLP). The amount of capacity connected will be the best estimate of the amount that should be declared available on the day of maximum demand. The amount declared available determines the amount of capacity payments, which, together with the bids that set the SMP, gives the PPP. Capacity declarations provide the final instrument needed to set the time-average PPP, which is constrained by the entry price.

Capacity Payments

How does the system of capacity payments adopted by the Pool influence price levels, bidding behaviour and reserve margins? Stations despatched receive capacity payments equal to LOLP x (VOLL-SMP). Figure 3 shows the monthly capacity payments per kW of capacity, assuming that the capacity was available on all the days when capacity payments were made, as well as the total received over the previous 12 months, showing a peak of over £50/kW. The level of annual capacity payments needed to keep a generator on the system or to induce entry will depend on the excess of average value of the SMP over avoidable (fuel) costs, which will depend on the age and fuel use of capacity in use, and the annual connection charges, which Appendix Table A3 shows vary from £8/kW to -£10/kW. If reserve is provided by an open cycle gas turbine costing perhaps £150/kW and located in a capacity-constrained zone with negative connection charges, then the target of £35/kW set at vesting could surely be lowered to nearer £15/kW. Critics argue that both VOLL and LOLP have been exaggerated.

LOLP is intended to measure the probability of having insufficient capacity available to meet demand, and is estimated from the standard error in the demand forecast, and probabilities of 'disappearance' of each genset between the date from which availability was deduced and the time of the forecast (Green, 1997). For pre-1990 plant, these disappearance ratios were set equal to their historical pre-1990 values, even though subsequent capacity payments have provided strong incentives to improve reliability and sustained availability.[8] The reliability of post-1990 plant is based on the previous year's operating performance, and is thus updated appropriately, but it is important to realise that the disappearance ratio is just the probability of a plant not being available on any random day of the year, given that it was available in the previous week. It makes no allowance for the various reasons why plant is not now available. There is the world of difference between withdrawing a genset in the summer lull for routine maintenance, and a genset failing at a time of maximum system stress, which arguably is the statistic of relevance in computing the reliability of the system at such moments when capacity payments are actually needed.

The computer programme that computes the risk of failure takes some account of demand responses that the day-ahead forecast high prices might elicit. It also takes a modest account of possible supply-side responses to high prices, but nothing like as large as those observed in practice (for example in the winter of 1996/7 as generators were told the day before of immensely attractive prices to be paid if their gensets were able to deliver).[9]

The meaning of 'loss of load' is either a blackout, or, far more probably, a brown-out, in which voltage or frequency drops below

---

[8] The DGES wrote to the Pool on 15 September 1997 noting that 'the improved performance of AGR plant is not reflected in Pool procedures. In consequence, the Loss of Load Probability seems likely to be overstated, leading to ... higher prices to customers'.

[9] The assumed demand elasticity is -0.0085 and the supply elasticity is 0.003. Taken at face value these would imply that if the reserve margin were predicted to be as low as 10% without adjusting for demand and supply responses, SMP were £40/MWh, then without allowing for any response the PPP might be £247/MWh (using the data displayed in Figure 5), but taking account of responses would fall to £142/MWh and the reserve margin would rise to 11.5 per cent. If, however, the unadjusted margin were 15 per cent, the PPP would only fall from £54/MWh to £52/MWh and the margin increase to 15.3 per cent.

operational limits but does not fail. The inherited CEGB standards were to ensure blackouts on no more than nine winter peaks in a 100 years and brown-outs 30 winters in 100. The value of lost load or VOLL is therefore a mixture of the value of an avoided blackout, taken as £2/kWh, or a brown-out, taken as 30p/kWh. These figures were taken from a 1985 CEGB paper which in turn cited evidence from Finnish consumer willingness to pay to avoid power cuts (in a rather frostier climate). The final choice for the 1990 VOLL of £2/kWh or £2,000/MWh (to be uprated in line with the price level) might then seem high as ignoring the cheaper and more likely event of a brown-out, and was based on the assumption that brown-outs would occur on 20 hours per year, which, at £2/kWh would give an annual capacity payment of £40/kW, thought to be the required level (Henney, 1994, p. 345). National Power argued to the House of Commons that this estimate of VOLL was too high (HC 1992, para. 109).

Although each of the calculations of VOLL and LOLP might seem somewhat arbitrary, it is their combination that matters, and they were adjusted and tested out by simulating possible winter scenarios to meet the old CEGB standards, if anything erring on the high side to guarantee that the lights would not go out and take the gleam off privatisation. Some years later it seems sensible to consider whether their values are appropriate in the light of experience.

Figures 4 and 5 show that LOLP and the associated capacity payments are a very non-linear (indeed exponential) function of the margin of available capacity to maximum demand. Figure 4 gives the daily average payments in £/MWh[10] for the first five years of pool operation, showing payments on a truncated logarithmic scale (the very large number of observations less than £0.1/MWh is not shown, but is used to fit the linear regression line). Figure 5 shows the maximum half-hourly payments, again plotted logarithmically against the peak reserve margin, computed as excess of the maximum value of PPP over that of SMP, giving values roughly 10 times as large (suggesting that the capacity payments are concentrated into short periods, in accordance with the smoothing algorithm applied to determine the payments).

The LOLP almost certainly overestimates the chance of a power failure, as this can be deduced from the payments made. The

---

[10] Presumably time-weighted as they are derived from the daily average PPP and SMP.

137

Figure 4
Capacity Payments vs Reserve Margin
Daily averages, Electricity Pool, 1990-95

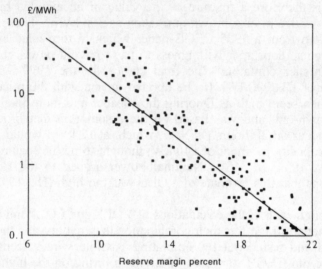

Reserve margin percent

Figure 5
Maximum Half-Hourly Capacity Payment
Electricity Pool, 1994-95

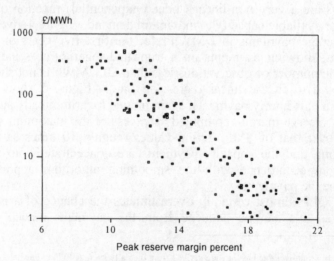

Peak reserve margin percent

probability of failure per day can be roughly estimated from the daily maximum difference between PPP and SMP using the data for 1994/95 shown in Figure 5, and divided by (VOLL - SMP) using the formula above.[11] The estimated probability of a loss of load or failure on one of the 10 peak days is greater than 99.88 per cent, while the chance of failing sometime during the whole year is greater than 1 - 4×10^{-8}, essentially certain.

If the system were operating to the old CEGB standard of 39 failures (9 blackouts or 30 brown-outs) per 100 years, the annual risk of failure should be less than 39 per cent. Since vesting, the system has not failed through inadequate capacity,[12] so it follows that the calculated LOLP greatly overestimates the risk of system failure. The reasons are obvious – LOLP is not an estimate of the risk of failure on peak days, but on randomly chosen days, assuming negligible supply response, little demand response, and based on out-dated information. The consequence is that VOLL.LOLP will be too large unless VOLL has been seriously underestimated.

In the Victoria Power Pool, generators submit bid prices and outputs which determine the SMP, and a set of negative prices, indicating the amount they are willing pay to remain on the system, rather than having to close down. Generators when formulating their bids must ensure they bid high enough to cover their fixed costs and any costs of starting from cold, for the pool price is set from the marginal bid with no capacity payments every 5-minute period. Because the market is truly a real-time spot market there is therefore no day-ahead schedule, no constraint payments to generators, and no need to predict the probability of a loss of load. The VOLL in Victoria was set at the same value ($A5,000) as in England, but generators only receive the VOLL for capacity declared available if

---

[11] VOLL was taken as £2,500, and k is defined as (Max PPP -Max SMP)/(VOLL -Max SMP). The two extremes which bound the daily risk of a loss of load or failure are to either assume that the entire risk falls in a single half hour, or at the other extreme, that the risk is equal in three adjacent half hours. In the first case, k must be multiplied by three, as the raw LOLP is smoothed by a centred moving average of three adjacent half-hour values, and the daily probability of no failure is $1-3k$, while in the second case the daily chance of no failure is $(1-k)$. If the resulting risk of not failing on day i is $1-p$, then the cumulative probability of no failure after n days is $\prod (1-p)$, $i=1..n$.

[12] The risk of a brown-out or black-out in 7 years on the CEGB security standard is 97 per cent, so the present system appears to do even better than the CEGB aimed at.

capacity is actually inadequate to meet demand, and the lights go off. This avoids the need for the System Operator to estimate the probability in advance, and leaves that calculation to the generators, who will consequently decide whether it is worth having capacity available given the probability that the lights will go off. The generators have every incentive to estimate the LOLP correctly, and could readily be given all the historical reliability information available to NGC in England.

The system had not been in operation in Victoria for very long before a series of very hot days was followed by two flood-lit sporting events – cricket and tennis, both dear to the Australian psyche. The lights went out in a most embarrassing way, partly because of heavy demands for air conditioning use, but proximately because bush fires tripped a 220kV feeder into Melbourne.[13] Irritatingly for the generators, the price in the pool failed to reach VOLL, as the reason for the failure was not inadequate generating capacity, but the blackouts caused much heart searching about system reliability and whether VOLL would ensure adequate capacity. Owners of peaking plant argued that given the actual payments received, they would need to run for over 50 hours per year to make continued connection worth while, but were lucky to run for 5 hours. The evidently unsatisfactory nature of the mechanism to ensure adequate reserves led to various reform proposals and short-run fixes. Increasing the VOLL by a factor of 10 was suggested, as was an auction to determine the amount that capacity holders would need to keep reserve or peaking plant connected.

One can do a back-of-the-envelope calculation about the cost of having an additional reserve margin of 5 per cent of total capacity at the peak, if fuel costs are half total costs, and average capacity utilisation is 66 per cent, then average electricity prices would have to rise by nearly 4 per cent. This overstates the cost, as the fixed cost per kW of peaking or otherwise obsolete plant will be considerably lower than the average, but even if fixed costs of only £15/kW are to be recovered in the 10 hours of maximum LOLP, and the risk of failure during the year (concentrated into these 10 hours) is to be less than,

---

[13] There was an earlier blackout during an Australian rules football match at Waverly Park caused by a transformer fault.

say, 25 per cent, then the implied VOLL is £50,000/MWh, or 20 times the current UK level.[14]

The problem is that whilst an insurance premium of 4 per cent to avoid a power cut sounds quite small, the number of hours that a loss of load is at all likely (with efficient capacity declarations during the year) is also likely to be small, so all the cost is loaded onto these hours, making the implied VOLL in these hours extremely high. Indirect evidence that the VOLL is probably higher than the £2,500/MWh comes from the system of charging for TNUoS, where one-third of the entire annual charge per kW is levied on each of the three triads – the three half hours of system maximum demand separated by at least 10 days. Patrick and Wolak (1997) have studied demand responses to Pool prices for large customers paying Pool prices in one REC, and for these customers, the triad charges were £10,730/MW for 1994/95. Even though the triad charges are uncertain in advance, large consumers can subscribe to a forecasting service and endeavour to reduce their demand and save very substantial sums at the expected peaks. Perfect forecasting would have allowed customers to save £7,153/MWh in each of the three triad half hours in 1994/5, but in fact forecasting accuracy is about 0.13 (on plausible peak days), making the expected value of reducing load on possible triad days about £800/MWh, higher than any capacity payments (which are known with certainty a day ahead), and one-third of the VOLL.

Patrick and Wolak (1997) estimate the own and cross-price elasticities for a number of different firms (using half-hourly consumption and price data for each firm) and find that own-price elasticities at the peak are typically less than -0.025, except for water companies who can vary the timing of their pumping demand (for which it is -0.12), and non-ferrous metals (-0.05). This suggests that the response to these high prices is not large, suggesting that customers appear to be willing to pay large sums to continue

---

[14] This calculation is very crude. Let p be the failure in each of 10 peak hours on different days, with no risk of failure at any other time. The risk of no failure is $(1-p)^{10}$, so if this is to be 0.75, $p = 0.0284$. This gives LOLP, and $10*VOLL*LOLP$ is required to be roughly £15/kW or £15,000/MW. VOLL is therefore £15,000/$(10*0.0284)$ = £53,000/MWh. A 50 per cent chance of annual power cuts would halve this figure. See the Appendix for a slightly more refined calculation.

consuming almost as much as before (which may be considerably below the willingness to pay to avoid an unexpected power cut, which is what VOLL is required to measure). It is also worth noting that most customers prefer to pay fixed prices for power, rather than exposing themselves to (hedgeable) price risks by buying at Pool prices, even though this would allow them to adjust demand and reduce their total electricity cost. This again tends to suggest that the value of not having to adjust demand (of which the extreme form is the risk of a power failure) is high, also indicating a high VOLL.

The VOLL is also relevant to managing load by reductions on the demand side. In the last two years NGC has operated an annual tender auction for the provision of standing reserve to assist in its system management function. Standing reserve is provided by open-cycle gas turbine and pumped storage plant, but also by demand reductions and non-centrally despatched small generators, though all must offer amounts in excess of 3MW. Large consumers can therefore specify their availability and willingness to reduce demand in various seasons and at various times of day, and NGC then accepts bids for which the total cost of providing load reductions is less than VOLL. In 1997/98 1,809MW of centrally despatched generation and 458MW of demand modification and small-scale generation were contracted (NGC, 1997b). Those consumers that are accepted are instructed through a PC-based mechanism, which also monitors performance and provides information to NGC's Ancillary Services settlement system on the basis of which payments are made. This mechanism is quite different from demand-side bidding (DSB), and avoids many of the apparent problems that have been encountered with DSB, including monitoring and performance. NGC is continuing to develop forms of contracting for load reduction, and presumably could be encouraged to broaden its range of services to cover those currently addressed by DSB.

The evidence from the tender auction is that for some customers for some times of the year and some periods of the day, given adequate notice, the value of reducing load is less than VOLL – but that at other times of the year or hours of the day, and for those customers who were not willing to participate, the cost of load reduction would exceed the present VOLL. (The graph in NGC (1997b) of the effective cost is fairly flat and is less than £250/MWh up to 2,250MW, and rises sharply at nearly 2,500MW, reaching £5,000/MWh at 2,750MW, mainly because of the fixed availability costs spread over a small number of hours despatched.) Clearly, unanticipated load reductions have a higher cost still and that is what is needed for avoiding outages. All this tends to suggest that if LOLP is reduced to its statistically correct level, some offsetting compensation through increases in VOLL might be warranted. It may also be that an extension of this system of load reduction more generally is more cost effective than capacity payments to generators.

If VOLL were increased and LOLP reduced, there would be a reallocation of investment away from reserve generation capacity towards reserve demand (that is, load shedding) and transmission strengthening, because transmission reliability is also valued using VOLL. It is worth noting that most customers experience power outages once a year or so because of failures in local distribution, suggesting that if local delivery is not very reliable, it may not be cost effective to increase the reliability to grid points to very high levels. Clearly, a proper investigation of trading arrangements would investigate this with the full armoury of statistical and econometric analysis.

Reforming the System of Capacity Payments

The more interesting question is what might happen in the Pool if the capacity payments were reduced, logically by a more accurate estimate of LOLP. On the assumption that entry remains contestable, the PPP is fixed by the costs of entry, in which case if the incumbents have the power to raise the SMP by the amount that the capacity element is reduced, they will do so. The amount of spare capacity will be reduced (for it must cover its fixed costs from the expected capacity payment, which has fallen), and the variability of prices might at first sight be expected to fall somewhat, as capacity payments are concentrated on a small number of hours, where the peak payments may now be lower. On the other hand, the profit maximising strategy of the incumbents is still to maximise the volatility of prices, subject to not inducing entry of peak capacity, which has been made less likely by the lower capacity payments. Incumbents may just increase base-load contractual cover to induce lower base-load prices and raise peak prices in compensation, essentially restoring the original volatility. The Pool Selling Price, PSP, should fall as the level of unscheduled availability payments, currently running at about £260 million, will fall in line with the fall in the reserve margin. If this were to fall by one-third, the PSP might

143

fall by 0.04p/kWh or by a little over 1 per cent.

The average *cost* of electricity for the incumbents will, however, fall, as capacity utilisation of the incumbents will have risen (but this will not affect any base-load IPPs), so incumbent profits should rise, as will the risk of power cuts. The end result looks like a potential public relations disaster – the generators make more profits for less reliable power at no lower price.

What would happen if there were more equally placed generators bidding into the spot market and hence making it more competitive, as in Victoria? Victoria has four generators using similar plant and fuel (opencast very cheap brown coal) and one smaller generator with peaking capacity, as well as transmission and trading links with the pool in NSW and also to the federal Snowy River hydro scheme which can sell either into Victoria or NSW, as well as a normally constrained transmission link to South Australia, making competition in non-peak periods intense. The crucial difference with England and Wales is that entry threats are not necessary to keep prices low in the pool, though at some stage as demand expands relative to existing capacity, new plant will be required, and will only be justified once the average price rises to the average cost of new plant – essentially the same condition as in a contestable market. Indeed, it should have to rise above this price, for demand is uncertain, but once investment has occurred, the capacity is available for 25-40 years, giving delay an option value. To the extent that the English market can be relied upon to keep prices tracking the entry price, the risk of premature entry is reduced, and long-run (year to year) volatility may be lower than in a more competitive market. Not surprisingly, competitive markets are uncomfortably volatile places whose risks incumbents wish to mute by horizontal and vertical integration.

A more competitive spot market reduces the ability of the bidders to raise SMP much above avoidable costs, except in tight markets, and to that extent will make adjustments to capacity payments have direct effects on average pool prices as well as on the risk of power outages. It is noteworthy that the Victorian pool revealed the possible underestimate of the cost of providing security rather rapidly, and has provoked a swifter response within the industry and by the regulator to address the question of reforming the system of capacity payments. The more difficult part will be to balance the benefit of lower pool prices against higher risks of failure. The rather generous system of capacity payments in Britain has prevented power failures, but the market power of the incumbents weakens and may eliminate the trade-off of lower prices in return for lower security.

Several conclusions follow from this analysis. First, provided entry remains contestable, and provided some new capacity would be economic, given the growth in demand and the need to replace older stations, the incumbents will be forced to keep the prices at competitive levels on average, and will be encouraged to mimic the extreme daily and seasonal volatility of a competitive market. Second, the level of the PPP, which includes the capacity payments, may not be very sensitive to the exact form of capacity payments where the incumbents retain available price-setting power. Third, the degree of system security may be quite sensitive to the exact form of these capacity payments, as will the cost of providing the security. Fourth, the main deviation of market behaviour in the Pool from competitive behaviour is likely to occur in periods when entry is not a threat, typically when there is excess capacity and no economic case for investment, or if barriers to entry appear, or if the willingness of counter-parties to sign long-term electricity contracts weakens. Finally, the relatively benign experience of the English Pool (where prices have not risen as much as was feared would follow from the unfettered exercise of market power by two price-setting generators) depends critically on the ease of entry at modest scale with CCGT plant. This in turn depends on the availability of cheap gas in the presence of ageing coal plant, and will not necessarily translate to other countries with different plant and fuel prices.

Changing the form of capacity payments to meet objections will not be easy. The advantages of a decentralised market mechanism are considerable but uncomfortable. It encourages generators to make plant available when it is most needed, but to retire plant that cannot cover its annual costs. It forces those overseeing the industry to question closely the value of lost load, and, if this is not rather high, to accept the higher implied risk of system losses of load (in addition to the existing frequency of local outages). It encourages consumers to consider the value of reducing demand at the peak, and may prompt a variety of lower cost solutions to the peak than centrally despatched plant with the attendant need for adequate transmission capacity. It moves electricity pricing closer to the efficient ideal where overhead costs are loaded onto the peak or expected peak, even where the spot market may not be very competitive – at least, provided the market remains contestable.

There are a number of possible reforms that do, however, appear timely. The LOLP should be based on a proper statistical evaluation of the relevant aspect of reliability, namely, the chance that a genset will not be available at a period of demand when capacity payments are appreciable. At present, the disappearance ratio is computed from the likelihood of a genset that was available in the previous week not being available on a given date, regardless of whether it has been taken off for scheduled maintenance, or because the plant is clearly not going to earn any capacity payments and is hence surplus to requirements. Generators that are or would be 'constrained off' are clearly not in a position to help meet peak demand, and perhaps ought not to be eligible to receive capacity payments, though they may make some smaller contribution to system security, which should be recognised by a modified value of loss of load in the constrained region. Finally, generators are currently not penalised if they are not in fact available when they have been declared available.[15] Logically, they should then be required to pay any additional costs that arise because of their failure. This would directly address the present incentive that some gas-fired generators have to decide on the day to sell their gas into the gas spot market rather than generate the electricity they claimed to be available to deliver. Whether the VOLL will need adjusting will then depend on whether adequate demand side-bids at an acceptable cost can be arranged.

Would it be possible to replace the whole system of capacity payments by some alternative? The present system has two great attractions and several drawbacks. The attraction is that it provides a decentralised and responsive signal to build more capacity and scrap obsolete plant, and it gives powerful signals to ensure that such plant is available when most needed. The drawbacks are that it fails to give the right signals for new plant to locate to maximise system stability, and the exponential nature of payments against the tightness of demand makes it hard to predict future capacity payments and hence hard for potential entrants to decide sufficiently in advance to provide

---

[15] This is not quite correct. Plant which is unavailable despite being declared available is labelled as 'unreliable', and has to demonstrate, on the evidence of actually running when despatched, that it has become 'reliable'. If such plant were 'constrained off' it would not be able to provide this evidence (but base-load CCGTs would have no difficulty in re-establishing their reliability).

needed reserve capacity. It is an interesting question in auction design to see if one could devise a mechanism in which the system operator forecasts desirable levels of capacity at peak periods in each zone (bearing in mind demand-side responses) and then accepts bids for payment for capacity availability, which would then be paid contingent on being available in all periods where LOLP was higher than some predetermined level. This might reduce the unpredictability of capacity payments, facilitate the entry of mid-merit and peak plant, while retaining a market rather than central planned element. It does, however, substitute planning for the market in determining future capacity.

Market Manipulation and Entry Conditions

In the first three years the apparent market power of the two incumbent generators caused the DGES to publish a series of reports on pricing behaviour in the Pool. Offer (1994a) criticised the growing discrepancy between rising pool prices and falling fuel costs since vesting, and specifically to the sharp increase in pool prices in April 1993, as the previous year's contracts were replaced on 1 April. The regulator observed that the duopoly fossil generators between them set the Pool price over 90 per cent of the time, with almost all the balance set by pumped storage, whose electricity had been purchased at prices set by the two majors. Figure 1 shows the pool prices and the fuel cost of the two majors, and reveals the rapid widening of the margin between them from 1 April 1993.

As a result of the inquiry, the DGES agreed with the majors that they should bid to ensure that both the time and demand-weighted Pool prices over each of the two years starting in April 1994 were kept below agreed levels,[16] and by the end of that period they should divest 6,000MW of plant (4,000MW from National Power compared to its then capacity of 26,000MW, 2,000MW from PowerGen compared to its then capacity of 20,000MW) to create more competition in the price-setting part of the market. In each of the two years they were able to bid to within 1 per cent of both price caps, despite the remarkable level of monthly pool volatility – a testament to. their ability to control the level of pool prices. In due course Eastern Group took 6,000MW of plant on 99-year leases for an

---

[16] 2.4p/kWh time weighted, 2.55p/kWh demand weighted, in October 1993 prices.

impressively high price, and agreed to pay the owners £6/MWh generated, thus encouraging bids in the price setting part of the market (and ensuring essentially no change to the pattern of bidding and generation shares of these stations and of the market as a whole).

Competition between incumbents remains somewhat muted, and the threat of entry is still the main competitive force placing an effective cap on pool prices. If entry became more difficult or costly, then pool prices would likely rise more than if there were more equally placed price-setting generators, and it follows that more regulatory vigilance is required over the conditions of entry than would be the case in a more competitive market. It was largely for this reason that the President of the Board of Trade refused permission to National Power and PowerGen in their respective merger bids for two of the larger RECs in late 1995. On 9 May 1996, Ian Lang defended his rejection of the mergers and stated clearly that the Government would use its golden shares in National Power or PowerGen to block any bid 'until competition in electricity generation has become fully established...' (*DTI Press Release*, P/96/329, 12 May).

Some market manipulations may be relatively harmless, if they affect prices payable to all, are predictable by potential entrants, and are part but only part of the method of setting the time average PPP, which in turn is constrained by entry threats. Such manipulations may affect the time pattern of prices, but not the average level, and hence can be insured against through contracts. Others are more pernicious if they confer advantages on particular generators not available to entrants. Some of the bidding behaviour for constrained plant comes into this category, and has attracted a series of reports by Offer. Encouraging NGC to contract for constrained services partly alleviates this problem. The new powers of the DGES under the proposed *Competition Bill* (HL Bill 33, 15 October 1997) may also be useful, as it shifts the nature of competition law to a prohibition-based system modelled on Articles 85 and 86 of the EC Treaty. The DGES would be able to fine companies abusing a dominant position, and dominance would be defined relative to a relevant market. Constraints greatly reduce the size of the relevant market, and make it likely that generators behind such constraints would be in a dominant position. The DGES would be required under the proposed *Competition Bill* to spell out what he considered to be abusive and benign behaviour.

There are doubtless a whole variety of ways in which generators are able to take advantage of the complexities of GOAL and of the PSA rules, most of which require the ability of the DGES to intervene to change the PSA. One such is the ability of generators to bid a modest price for 95 per cent or so of capacity, and a very high price for the remaining few per cent. When directed to generate up to a limit of 95 per cent or so of capacity, they are able under current Pool rules to over-generate up to the margin permitted, and be paid their (very high) bid price (rather than the SMP, which, if the over-generation were the fault of the company, would be the logical basis for payment).

Demand-Side Bidding

The Norwegian pool allows traders to submit a schedule of supplies and demands, typically in the form of a downward sloping net demand schedule, such that above a certain price the trader is willing to sell into the pool, and below that to buy out. The overall market clears at a price at which demand and supply are in balance, or aggregate net demand at that price is zero. The effect of allowing demand-side bidding is to make the net demand schedule appear more elastic, which would reduce the extent of market power and opportunities for market manipulation. However, it should be remembered that in Norway the traders are frequently distribution companies with their own hydro capacity, and they are effectively deciding whether to buy or sell water – a net demand means that they can supply their customers from the pool rather than their own dam, while a net supply means that they generate both for their own customers and to sell a surplus. The actual final demand may be as inelastic as in Britain.[17]

At the moment demand responses are taken into account in three ways – through the calculation of the LOLP which affects capacity payments, via NGC's tender offer to provide standing reserve for system management (described above), and through a small-scale demand-side bidding (DSB) scheme introduced in 1993, and now

---

[17] Norway has some 7 TWh/year of dual electric-oil steam raising capacity, which allows these companies to switch if the electricity price rises above the equivalent cost of oil-fired steam raising. At that point the demand does become suddenly elastic – an option not economic at British electricity prices.

involving some 30 customers. The idea behind DSB is that customers should be treated symmetrically with generators, except they bid for reductions in demand, and would receive capacity payments in proportion to the extent they offered to reduce peak demand, symmetrically with generators who offer capacity and receive payments. The system apparently is poorly monitored, though it seems that NGC's tender offer system avoids most problems of monitoring and performance, and might replace this relatively unsatisfactory arrangement, provided some market maker had the incentive to set up the service.

It is worth asking whether there is any substance in the claim that the present Pool is only half a market, as it suppresses the demand side. First, note that consumers have every incentive to reduce demand at times of peak demand, for they pay large triad payments that amount to sums comparable with peak capacity payments. Second, to the extent that large consumers can (and presumably do) sign CfDs for specified quantities, they have an incentive to reduce demand and profit by effectively selling their unsold demand (the excess of the amount specified in the CfD and what they take) back into the market. The problem seems to lie not in the incentives that consumers have to reduce demand at periods of high pool prices, but in the inability of the scheduling algorithm to model these demand responses in computing the market-clearing price. Ironically, a true spot market on the Victorian model would find the intersection of actual demand and supply, but because prices are not quoted firmly a day ahead, as in Britain, consumers are less well placed to respond.

There are several possible solutions. The simplest would seem to be to adapt GOAL to accommodate predicted demand responses, which might be improved by a knowledge of the fraction of demand facing marginal Pool prices (that is, those customers with fixed quantity CfDs), and an automatic updating procedure of re-estimating the forecasting equations of demand on the basis of out-turn demand. The PSA would have to be modified to allow this (and other) updating procedures to the scheduling algorithm – and this is not easy, as the section below on Pool governance indicates.

A more dramatic change would be to shift to a continuous spot market to determine price on the basis of actual supplies and demands, while retaining the day-ahead market for scheduling and deriving predicted prices. Generators and suppliers would have the option of choosing whether to accept the predicted or *ex-post* prices at the time of bidding, and the system operator would need some incentive to narrow the gap between *ex ante* and *ex post* prices. If LOLP were properly calculated, then presumably the same choice could be extended to capacity payments, which would have the same expected value *ex ante* as the realised average *ex post*, but, given the presence of market power and the complex determination of PPP via entry threats, contracts, and competition, this proposition should be properly tested before being accepted at face value.

An intermediate option would be to have both a day-ahead market as at present, and a balancing market operating on the day to make adjustments and ensure continuous balancing of supply to demand, thereby reducing the costs of forecast errors and possibly some other components of uplift. Whether this would be much different from the balances currently achieved from the bids of plants 'constrained on' is unclear, and it would still be necessary to reconcile the two sets of prices, perhaps again offering options to trade either at day ahead or spot market prices.

Finally, note that if pool prices are set by the costs of entry, then most of these reforms will have little effect on the average level of prices. The main effect of DSB may be to encourage consumers to be more aware of high peak prices, and actively to consider ways of reducing demand then, thereby lowering the cost (if not necessarily the price) of electricity.

Pool By-pass, WYBIWYG, and Other Pool Reforms

Several large customers have proposed direct physical trades with individual generators, and have also argued that they should be credited with placing less stress on the transmission system and having lower reserve requirements than other more fickle customers. The first point to make is that it is hard to imagine a physical trade that could not be replicated with greater security and no higher cost by a financial contract, since CfDs allow the designated generator effectively to buy power in the pool whenever the PPP is lower than the avoidable cost of generation, thereby saving costs and improving efficiency. The main arguments for allowing physical trades have to do with reforming the nature of the Pool to achieve different systemic outcomes, favourable to the proposing party, or with indirectly criticising the cost of transmission and other ancillary services. The most obvious distortions that should be corrected are that large customers in export-constrained areas (as in the north and Scotland) are paying too much, as the shadow price of power is less than the SMP. To some extent, but perhaps inadequately, this is dealt with by the regionally differentiated TNUoS charges (see Table A3 below), but it may be that these should be revisited to investigate what is the opportunity cost of supplying power to base-load consumers in export-constrained regions.

If physical trades by-pass the pool, they would be struck at negotiated prices (and the proponents hope would be charged lower uplift). A related reform that has been proposed is that generators bidding into the pool are paid their bid rather than SMP – often called WYBIWYG, or What You Bid is What You Get. It is proposed by those who wish to make the Pool less competitive, less contestable, and more opaque.[18] The larger incumbents, whose diversified portfolio of plants gives them an advantage in crafting a profitable bid structure under WYBIWYG, and market traders, who would exploit their information, would be at an advantage over the owners of single stations (IPPs) and most consumers. They could no longer rely on bidding honestly at avoidable cost and receiving the PPP set by the most expensive set, but would instead have to guess what the Pool price might be and bid accordingly. Since the Pool price varies on a half-hourly basis, either they would have to bid in a time-varying schedule of bids, or they would have to hope that most time variation were eliminated by co-ordinating bids on an acceptable level, in which case the merit order would be prejudiced and the pricing function of the Pool lost. This issue was visited by Offer (1994b) and rejected then.

Since then the arguments for a compulsory Pool with a SMP, compared with a voluntary Balancing Pool (possibly at SMP) have been rehearsed at length in the US context. The fact that such a system works quite well in the storage hydro systems of Scandinavia does not mean that it would work at all efficiently in a predominantly thermal system as in Britain. The idea that a balancing pool, which would operate on the day, might eliminate forecasting errors and reduce uplift offers a partial defence, but does not argue for either Pool bypass or a physical market, both of which run the risk of out-of-merit running for no obvious gain. Stoft (1997) has cast doubts on the

---

[18] Or by large consumers who think they will be able to strike better bargains, but who are unaware of the longer-run implications for average price levels.

motives of those arguing for it in California, and suggests that it may lead to considerable efficiency losses. Remembering that a cost rise of 4-5 per cent would eliminate all the gains from restructuring, it follows that such proposals should be treated with some scepticism.

There are other reform proposals that have been made from time to time and which bear further investigation. The most obvious is that the technical characteristics of plant should be taken as fixed, possibly subject to audit, or properly priced in the annual connection charge (reflecting their value to the system in terms of security, stability, etc). They would not then be available to manipulate and game the scheduling rules. One might also ask why it was necessary for generators to adjust their plant bids on time-scales shorter than that over which fuel prices change. Indeed, if fuel prices were particularly volatile, but marked to market in a liquid spot market (preferably one on which contracts or options could be written), then bids might better be submitted as a combination of heat rates and fuel type, to be priced on the basis of spot fuel prices. Heat rates would be adjustable as generators chose to alter the running order of gensets to optimise plant operation, though perhaps on a monthly or quarterly basis.

Whether these reforms are valuable depends on whether gaming differentially benefits some incumbents over other smaller players or entrants, and on the degree of contestability of entry. If entry costs determine average pool prices, there is little to be gained from changes (other, perhaps, than greater predictability and transparency, which might be quite pro-competitive in the contract market). If the market is not contestable, then manipulation is more likely to be anti-competitive (but might also be dealt with under the prohibition-based approach of the proposed *Competition Bill*).

Constraints, Losses, and Locational Pricing

Many of the problems of the Pool can be laid at the door of failing to accommodate locational price differences. The issue is simply stated but not so simply solved. The efficient price of electricity at any moment will vary from place to place because of losses, and, more importantly, because of transmission constraints. If a region is export constrained, the most expensive bid accepted (the local SMP) within that region will be less than the most expensive bid outside (the external SMP). Conversely, if a region cannot import because of constraints, the local SMP will be higher than the external SMP. If generators could be relied upon to bid honestly at avoidable cost, and if the local rationing price could be properly set by a VOLL*LOLP mechanism, with LOLP locally computed, then each region could set its own SMP, which would be equal to the system-wide SMP when transmission was unconstrained, but would otherwise differ.

The problem is that market power is far more of a problem in regional pools, where there are very few competing generators, than in country-wide pools. The British compromise is to set a single Pool price, to maximise the number of competing generators, at the expense of inefficient regional energy prices. In effect, generators have a guaranteed right to supply, and are paid compensation for constraints. Consumers pay a single energy price with a comparable right to be supplied.

How might this be dealt with? The problem is similar to the capacity reserve problem, but is less likely to be handled by making each regional sub-market contestable, particularly in export-constrained regions where entry is positively not wanted. What is needed is a way of rewarding capacity according to its contribution to regional security of supply, which may differ dramatically from the country level. It might be relatively simple to compute regional LOLP values, and hence regional capacity payments, though this would not eliminate the incentive to distort bids away from avoidable cost. Here it depends whether constraints bind for a large or small fraction of the time, and whether the plant is on the margin of being withdrawn. If constraints are infrequent, then they may not influence bidding behaviour much, and if the DGES publishes the Guidelines on abuse of dominant position, as he will be required to do under the proposed *Competition Bill*, then he could define a significantly different bid when constrained to unconstrained as evidence of abusing a temporarily dominant position, subject to penalty. Alternatively, the compensation for being 'constrained off' could be equal to SMP *less* the highest bid of that genset over the previous year.

If the high constraint payments are required adequately to reward and hence maintain capacity, then this should be handled automatically by the regional version of capacity payment, or by a direct contract with NGC, as at present, for system stability. Finally, although existing generators have a guaranteed right to supply, there is no obvious reason why this should be extended to new generators in constrained regions, who, perhaps for the first five years, might reasonably not be compensated for not being despatched, as they made their locational decisions in the light of existing patterns of constraints.

Similarly, if large base-load customers in export-constrained regions contribute to system stability, their TNUoS charges should be computed to reflect this, as should their regional PPP, which includes the regional capacity payment, not forgetting the regional loss adjustments, which will reduce the cost of delivering power in these regions.

Losses have increased from 1.6 per cent in 1990 to a forecast high of 2.4 per cent in 1999 (NGC, 1997a, Table 6.6), mostly because of high peak power flows from north to south, in part because generators are locating too far from load centres. NGC (1997a, Table 6.7) shows that a new power station in the North (zone 1) generating 100MW only meets 93MW of national demand averaged across the system at the predicted 2003/4 winter peak, while 100MW located in Peninsular (zone 16, Cornwall) meets 110MW of demand by alleviating power losses – or 18 per cent more than the Northern station. Since all the capital cost should ideally be collected at system peak, this differential implies that lifetime generating costs might be 12 per cent too high for an incorrectly located station (on the assumption that half the cost is capital, and operating losses add another 4 per cent).[19] The Pool proposed a system of charging generators for zonal losses but this was appealed against, as it will adversely affect Northern generators.

Until losses are properly charged, the only locational signals to guide the siting of new generation are the annual TNUoS charges. These are determined from the investment cost-related pricing (ICRP) of system expansion (as explained in the footnote to Table A3), with 25 per cent of the balance of the regulatory income of NGC being recovered from generators, and 75 per cent being charged to consumers (who in addition receive the ICRP, effectively as negative generators reducing the need for transmission), the total being collected through the triad charges. Table A3 shows the zonal tariffs for generators and consumers before and after the 1997 Transmission Price Control Review (which led to an increase in the number of generation zones and a change in several boundaries). Generators

---

[19] The average marginal loss between North and Peninsular is 12 per cent, so if the load factor is 66 per cent and half the costs are variable, the variable loss is 12 x 0.33 = 4 per cent.

who face positive charges are charged on registered capacity, while those facing negative charges are paid on the average of the three highest levels of generation separated by 10 days in the winter period. Consumers are charged on the three triad half-hours.

Between 1990 and 1996 most of the new generation located north and east of London, none in inner London, and only a small amount in outer London. Plants closed in NGC zone *South Coast* and a negligible amount located in *Peninsular* (Cornwall). Compared to last year, the range between the *North* and *Peninsular* for generation has been widened from £14.37 to £18.09/kW or by 25 per cent, while for customers the range has narrowed from £16.67 to £15.38/kW or by 8 per cent. Clearly, generation charges are attempting to signal the very high opportunities of locating new plant in the *South Coast, Peninsular* and *South Wales*, though with little success to date. Part of the problem may lie in the difficulty of adjusting charges by large amounts from year to year, given the durable nature of location decisions and the unpredictability of future charges. The obvious solution would be to give the option of long-term contracts for connection, based on current best estimates of future charges, and then adjust generation charges by possibly large amounts each year to signal changing needs more accurately. This will require a careful (but economically defensible) definition of what is meant by discrimination if charges to different generators at the same place differ – the contract reflects differing views of the future which can be revalued each year if appropriate.

The incentives for by-passing transmission (that is, by own generation) are given by the sum of the TNUoS charges, which for Northern have fallen from £10.8 to £8.86/kW or by 18 per cent, though the sum in the South West has fallen from £13.1 to £6.13 or by 50 per cent, and is now lower than in the north. It is not clear that the cost of providing security (which is primarily the service offered by TNUoS charges) is now lower there or has fallen more than in the north, and it may just be that consumers in the south have been more effective at complaining about high prices there. Again, it would be useful to know whether the price signals are muted by the felt need to make gradual adjustments which might be addressed by longer term contracts.

Finally, NGC operates to double circuit outage standards, a higher security standard than almost all other high-voltage transmission systems. Thus for any six transmission lines between two points, two

156

are active and four idle, while the more conventional single circuit standard would allow three active and three idle circuits, a 50 per cent increase in capacity. Offer (1992) found that high levels of constraint payments were made when the risk of a double circuit fault seemed low, and invited NGC to undertake a review, which they did in 1994. NGC found that relaxing the security standard might save some £35 million in constraint payments at an extra cost of £10 million in transmission losses, and that these payments would fall once NGC were given an incentive to reduce constraint costs, as subsequently happened. Offer published a short note in March 1996, inviting NGC to relax their Operating Standards (though it had no power to insist on this). This NGC chose not to do, arguing that it could achieve the same benefits at lower cost. Offer also considered whether cost-benefit techniques should be applied to transmission planning, but balked at the difficulty of evaluating environmental gains. NGC argued that very few existing transmission lines would not be needed at a lower security standard, but the real question is when new investment is required, whether the extra cost of a higher standard would be justified given the higher risk of failure. The suspicion for both publicly owned and regulated utilities, where their revenue is primarily determined by their asset base, is that there will be a temptation to over-engineer standards, and this may be a case in point. The question is whether the reliability of final delivery to customers is achieved at least cost, and whether competition in the Pool would be enhanced by lower reliability and fewer transmission constraints. At present, local distribution is less reliable than the grid, and may undermine the value of the high level of grid security. Such a review would require a careful economic and engineering analysis.

Remaining Market Concerns

The main argument of the paper is that market failures can only be assessed in the context of all the factors which bear on the determination of the price level and its structure. These in turn are affected by the spot and contract markets, the conditions and incentives for entry (of which capacity payments are an element), and the handling of spatial constraints and losses. If, as in Britain, there are few price-setting generators, then the conditions of entry must play the main role in restraining prices and encouraging generators to contract adequately. Entry alone may not be sufficient to overcome local pockets of market power, unless spatial price signals are both well designed, and can be locked into contracts by entrants choosing between zones. Anything which makes entry more difficult may reduce the competitive pressure on the incumbent large generators, and is a cause for concern.

In the past, entry has been facilitated by the long-term contracts offered by RECs to IPPs (in which they often had an ownership stake). The 1998 ending of the franchise monopoly makes these contracts less likely, and hence makes entry more risky. It would be unfortunate if the introduction of supply competition for consumers resulted in less competition in generation and higher prices to consumers. The main source of optimism is that the gas spot market and gas competition make it more attractive for gas suppliers to diversify into electricity generation as a portfolio hedge, while the low price of gas makes such entry attractive. If the gas interconnector to the Continent drives up English gas prices to continental levels and creates adequate demand to remove the gas overhang this could change. It would be worrying if as a result the incumbent large generators captured most of the market for new power stations – and they already take about half of all new capacity.

Governance

Almost all reforms require changes to the PSA, which as a contract can only be changed by agreement, or by replacement which would require primary legislation. Pool reform therefore requires major changes comparable to those introduced by the *Gas Act 1996*, which introduced the network code for gas transmission. The logical structure of a reformed Pool would be a two-tier form of governance, perhaps similar to that of Victoria and proposed for several regions of the US (Barker *et al.*, 1997). The lower tier represents the stake-holders, as in the present Pool (though perhaps with more consumer representation), and if they are able to reach agreement on changes which are not opposed by the DGES, they would be directly implemented. If not, or if they fail to propose satisfactory remedies to identified problems, then a higher tier, presumably the DGES, or whatever form of governance the utilities review proposes, would have the power to intervene, subject to the appeal procedure set out in the proposed *Competition Bill*.

There may be other satisfactory governance structures, possibly even better ones, but any structure has to combine the advantages of detailed operational knowledge without the present deadlock that those adversely affected can prevent or indefinitely postpone changes. Changing the legal basis of the Pool from a contract to a company, independent of the current Pool participants, with a legal persona subject to regulation would address the second problem, but would only meet the first requirement if it had the right staff, mandate and incentives. One of the main tasks of the Pool Inquiry will be to invite carefully articulated and supported submissions on the future Pool governance structure.

Conclusions

Judging the validity of criticisms of the Pool and electricity trading arrangements requires a proper understanding of the nature of competition in all the electricity markets – for spot power, for contracts, and for capacity. Until the number of equally placed, actively competing price-setting generators increases to four or more, the main burden of competition is placed on the conditions of entry. Where the market is contestable, reforms are unlikely to have major impacts on average price levels, and some apparently sensible reforms may have unintended consequences, such as reducing system reliability with little gain in lower prices. It follows that the main test of reforms is their effect on prices, costs, capacity, and reliability, given the actual state of competition among existing participants, and, most importantly, by potential entrants.

The set of problems which the threat of entry is least likely to remedy are those to do with transmission constraints and the need to differentiate prices by location, to signal where entry should occur, exit be discouraged, and load management best directed. If prices are to play a more active role in encouraging efficient locational decisions, they will need to be capable of more rapid and possibly larger adjustment. This will require some way of insuring agents against future price changes while still providing them with incentives for short-run efficient management of their existing capacity. Contracts for differences offer the logical solution. NGC should be asked to revisit the allocation of constraint costs, security payments, and other system management costs by zone and between generators and consumers, for although the present capital costs are allocated regionally by a defensible methodology, the balance between consumers and generators still appears arbitrary, and the underlying price signals do not appear to be translated into adequately differentiated charges.

Finally, having identified the desirable reforms, major changes to the governance structure of the Pool will be required before most of the reforms can be introduced. Without such changes the Pool Inquiry will be a purely academic exercise. If a new system of governance can be created which can respond to problems, and if the proposed *Competition Bill* confers the promised powers on the regulator, then problems can be addressed as they arise, in the light of growing experience of the variety of remedies being market tested in power pools round the world.

Appendix: Adjusting the Values of VOLL and LOLP

Suppose we wish to find what values of VOLL and LOLP would give an annual risk of a loss of load of 0.25 or less, while maintaining the same reserve margins as in 1994/95, and suppose that the required annual capacity payment needed to achieve this is £15/kW. Suppose also that the correct value of LOLP is a constant fraction α of the one used in 1994/95, and the actual risk of failure on day i is taken as $p = 3\alpha k$, where k is (Max PPP - Max SMP)/(2500 - Max SMP), as defined in footnote 12 above.[20] The resulting risk of not failing on day i is $1 - p$ and the cumulative risk of failure is $\prod(1-p)$, ($i = 1,...,365$). The value of α was adjusted to ensure that this was 0.75, giving a value of α of 0.0174 (which seems remarkably low and clearly needs to be checked). Given this new value of LOLP, and assuming that the relationship between capacity payments in non-peak hours on the day and at the peak remained the same on each day, the VOLL required to give a cumulative capacity payment of £15/kW was then computed to be £75,000/MWh, rather higher than the very short-cut method of footnote 15.

If the annual risk of failure is allowed to double to 0.5, then α becomes 0.042 (rather more than double), and VOLL falls to £31,000/MWh, rather less than half.

---

[20] The alternative $(1-\alpha k)$ gives essentially the same result.

Table A1: Annual Average Pool Prices
pence/kWh or £/kW/yr

	1990-91	1991-92	1992-93	1993-94	1994-95	1995-96	1996-97
Time-weighted p/kWh							
SMP	1.74	1.95	2.26	2.40	2.08	1.94	2.06
Capacity	0.0	0.13	0.02	0.02	0.32	0.45	0.35
PPP	1.74	2.08	2.28	2.42	2.40	2.39	2.41
Uplift	0.09	0.16	0.14	0.23	0.24	0.20	0.19
PSP	1.84	2.24	2.42	2.65	2.64	2.59	2.60
Demand-weighted p/kWh							
SMP	1.81	1.99	2.31	2.44	2.19	2.07	2.18
Capacity		0.01	0.17	0.02	0.04	0.45	0.61
							0.40
PPP	1.82	2.16	2.33	2.48	2.64	2.68	2.58
Uplift		0.10	0.18	0.15	0.22	0.27	0.24
							0.20
PSP	1.92	2.34	2.48	2.70	2.91	2.92	2.78
Demand-weighted at 1995-96 prices, p/kWh							
SMP	2.11	2.21	2.49	2.59	2.26	2.07	2.13
PPP	2.12	2.40	2.51	2.63	2.73	2.68	2.52
NP +PG Total Revenue from generation at 1995-96							
		3.90	3.87	3.52	3.56	3.42	
Capacity payments at 1995-96 prices, £/kW/yr							
	0.47	19.91	2.80	2.55	29.13	39.30	27.64

Sources: Offer (1994a), *Pool Statistical Digest*, Company Accounts.

Table A2: Uplift (1995/96 prices)
£ million

	1990-1	1991-2	1992-3	1993-4	1994-5	1995-6	1996-7
Operational outturn	183	280	270	434	364	190	213
(of which constraint costs)				(255)	(194)	(74)	(57)
(of which notional reserve)	(42)	(39)	(49)	(42)			
Ancillary services	124	135	128	170	113	141	110
Unscheduled availability	4	114	14	23	248	298	252
NGC incentive payments	n/a	n/a	n/a	n/a	26	23	9
Uplift	311	529	413	627	752	655	587

Source: Offer.

Table A3: Use of System Zonal Tariffs
£/kW

Generation Zone	Generation Tariff		Demand Zone	Demand Tariff	
Zone	*1996/97*	*1997/98*	*Zone*	*1996/97*	*1997/98*
North	7.873	7.975	Northern	2.929	0.880
Humberside	4.889		Norweb		5.328
Yorkshire	4.870		Yorkshire	7.722	4.819
Rest of Yorks		3.733	Manweb	8.631	5.584
North Wales	4.121	5.484	Swalec		14.834
South Wales		-4.936	West and Wales		15.688
West and Wales		-0.500	Inner London	17.443	
Inner London	-5.476	-9.885	London		13.457
Outer London	1.037	0.021	Outer London	13.019	
South Coast	-2.096	-4.036	Southern	14.349	12.630
Peninsular	-6.495	-10.111	Peninsular	19.602	
			South Western		16.263

Source: NGC (1997a) and fax update for 1997/98; zones aligned as far as possible. If g is the charge to generators in zone i computed from the Investment Cost Related Pricing methodology, then $-g$ is charged to consumers there, and if q is generated and d demanded, then the revenue from these charges is $\Sigma g\,(q - d)$, and the balance is charged 25 per cent to generators, 75 per cent to consumers.

References

Barker, J., B. Tenenbaum and F. Woolf (1997): 'Governance and Regulation of Power Pools and Systems Operators: An International Comparison', forthcoming World Bank Discussion Paper.

Green, R.J. (1997): 'The political economy of the Pool', in M.D. Ilic, F. Galiana and L. Fink (eds.), *Restructuring, Power Systems Engineering and Economics*, Norwell, Ma: Kluwer.

Green, R.J, and D.M. Newbery (1992): 'Competition in the British Electricity Spot Market', *Journal of Political Economy*, Vol. 100(5), October, pp. 929-53.

Henney, Alex (1994): 'A study of the privatisation of the electricity supply industry in England and Wales', London: EEE Ltd.

Henney, Alex and Miles Bidwell (1997): 'Reforming the Pool of England and Wales', a report for Mr John Battle, Minister for Energy, Science and Industry and Pool Members, London: EEE Ltd.

HC (1992): 'Consequences of Electricity Privatisation', Energy Committee, House of Commons, London: HMSO 1113-1.

HC (1997): 'Energy Regulation, Trade and Industry Committee', House of Commons, London: HMSO.

HL Bill 33: *Competition Bill*, House of Lords, 15 October 1997.

NGC (1996): Transmission LC 10 Statements of Charges for Use of System and Connection to the System 1996/97, National Grid Company plc.

NGC (1997a): *1997 Seven Year Statement*, National Grid Company plc.

NGC (1997b): *Report on the Tender for the 1997/98 Standing Reserve Service*, National Grid Company plc.

Newbery, D. M. (1992): 'Capacity-constrained Supply Function Equilibria: Competition and Entry in the Electricity Spot Market', DAE Working Paper, Cambridge.

Newbery, D. M. (1995): 'Power Markets and Market Power', *Energy Journal,* Vol. 16(3), pp. 41-66.

Newbery, D.M. (1997): 'Competition, Contracts and Entry in the Electricity Spot Market', mimeo, Department of Applied Economics, Cambridge.

Newbery, D.M. and M.G. Pollitt (1997): 'The Restructuring and Privatisation of the CEGB – Was it Worth it', *Journal of Industrial Economics*, Vol. XLV (3), pp. 269-303.

Offer (1992a): *Report on Constrained-on Plant*, Office of Electricity Regulation, Birmingham, October.

Offer (1992b): *Review of Pool Prices*, Office of Electricity Regulation, Birmingham, December.

Offer (1992c): *Review of Economic Purchasing*, Office of Electricity Regulation, Birmingham, December.

Offer (1994a): *Decision on a Monopolies and Mergers Commission Reference*, Office of Electricity Regulation, Birmingham, February.

Offer (1994b): *Trading outside the Pool*, Office of Electricity Regulation, Birmingham, 14 July.

Patrick, R.H. and F.A. Wolak (1997): 'Estimating the customer-level demand for electricity under real-time pricing', paper presented to the POWER conference, March, Berkeley: University of California Energy Institute.

Perez-Ariaga, Ignacio and Alex Henney (1994): 'The Organisation and Operation of the Electricity Supply Industry in Argentina', London: EEE Ltd.

Stoft, S. (1997): 'What should a power market want?', *Electricity Journal*, June.

CHAIRMAN'S COMMENTS

Stephen Littlechild

THIS PAPER HAS CONCENTRATED MAINLY ON HOW THE PRESENT POOL WORKS and changes that might be made in particular methods that the Pool uses, rather than looking at anything more radically different. On the former issues there is much valuable material in the paper. I am very sympathetic towards the remarks about transmission losses and regional differentiation of prices. (I note that not all the generators are as sympathetic to this line of argument as I am). The remarks on LOLP and VOLL were particularly interesting and perhaps even provocative.

It would be rather interesting to calculate whether different values of VOLL should be used. I expect Geoff Horton will have something to say about the origins of VOLL. (I recall it has something to do with Scandinavians running around in the birchwoods and worrying about the saunas going off.) You are right to point out that if one had a correct pricing mechanism and capacity element, this would not mean that all the high prices in the winter would disappear. As you point out, generators and plants that run only a small proportion of the time need to cover their costs, in that proportion of the time. Consequently the prices have to be higher, then. In other words, if you did not have a capacity element you would have to have higher bids of some kind. Whether prices would be at the present level is another matter. If I have understood correctly, your calculations show that the differentials by time of day and by time of year might now be about right and more consistent with a competitive market than they were at the beginning of the Pool's history.

The term 'volatility' is perhaps unfortunate in the context you used it. Most people associate volatility with uncertainty or unpredictability of prices. There are certainly allegations that generators may try to create unexpected movements in price as a way of deterring entry, or as a way of encouraging customers to sign up contracts for differences. But that is not the sense in which you were using it, namely of differentials between peak and off-peak periods, whether it be by time of day or time of year. You pointed out that there will be differentials in a competitive market (as there are in the present market) to reflect differences in costs and demands. It is almost certainly the case that the same differentials were too low initially, and have moved in the right direction. Whether they are at the right level now is another matter.

You argue that in a competitive market you would find price equal to short-run marginal cost almost all the time. All the other costs of operating a plant would be recovered in a few peak periods, so by implication you would have a very few very high price periods. I am not sure that I follow that particular way of arguing. In a competitive market that did not have peaks of this kind, you would not find price on average equal to short-run marginal cost; you would find prices set to cover average costs (at least over a period of time). Players in the market would find a way of doing that. Prices at any time would cover the avoidable cost at that time, but prices in total would aim to recover at least the total cost of being in the business. So I am not sure that the particular justification you gave for differences in prices is one that I would want to sign up to. This may cast some doubt on your calculations of VOLL and the other prices; but you rightly put those up for discussion.

You asked whether the Pool was only half a market, without coming to a conclusion, but said that maybe there are other ways in which that problem can be dealt with. I would have preferred you to have squared up to the issue. The generating side bids into the market, but the fact is that almost all the demand side does not bid. The price is essentially set by NGC estimating what people would be prepared to pay. I am not at all convinced that demand is replicated by the kind of arrangements we have now, even with the modifications you have in mind. We need more assessment of exactly how a market could work, in which both customers and suppliers bid: with the pool price being set at the intersection of the demand and the supply curves, what the advantages or disadvantages would be; and whether under those circumstances, one would want to stick with pricing just the day ahead or possibly on the day, or whether one would want pricing for a number of periods ahead as well.

That leads me on to the more radical sort of notions that you do not address. You raise questions of trading outside the pool, and the idea that 'what you bid is what you get', but these occupied only a couple of paragraphs in the whole of the paper. But questions of trading outside the Pool, or voluntary Pools, must surely be major aspects that we need to consider now. I am not sure whether your reference is only to what 'you bid is what you get' or whether it also refers to trading outside the pool, but you say such proposals are by those who wish to make the pool less competitive, less contestable and more opaque. I think that is a little unfair. Certainly when I last looked at it, I found difficulties and significant disadvantages in 'what you bid is what you get'. These were not that the consequence would be a pool that is less competitive, less contestable and more opaque, but hinged on the difficulties of operating such a system, and the impact on risks for generators and on uncertainty for customers.

It seems to me that we must now look not only at ways in which what you described as a planning procedure can be improved, but also at the market alternatives. You have described very well how the CEGB used to operate, how it used to plan not only which sets ran at which times but also which plants were to be built, and when and where. We have moved from that system to a partial market where the decisions about when and where to build plants are made by generators. They also make the decisions on what to bid, but the decisions on which plants run and when are effectively still made by a central planning authority. It does not seem to me that your paper has addressed the question: How would a market operate where the decisions about which plants are to run are made by the market participants themselves and not by some central co-ordinating authority? You referred briefly to how a 'decentralised market' would work. You say 'somehow prices for each service at each future date would be revealed to decision-makers, who would be guided as if by the invisible hand to choose the overall short- and long-run system optimum'. You refer to the 52,560 prices quoted on the pool each year, and to the 16 transmission zones, and to other prices, and in your lecture I think you got to a total of 21 million prices. You then ask how are these prices to be known to decision-makers and how are they going to make their decisions based on them? I sense a bit of Arrow and Debreu 'general equilibrium theory' creeping in there that needs to be excised! To set that paradigm up as the basis of a market system seems to me inappropriate. It does not seem to me that this is the way the real world works.

Basically a market system would work by generators and customers, possibly through suppliers, making contracts for supply, and generators deciding what is to run. The generator (maybe the supplier, but let us say the generator) would then arrange with the Grid to use that capacity for the period it wanted. The Grid would not say 'Well, I am very sorry but I know another generator who could operate at a lower cost than you can', it would say 'Yes we would be very pleased to take your business'. It might have to say 'We do not have any more capacity left at this time in this place but we have plenty of capacity over here and these are the prices'. People would not need to know 21 million prices; they would make decisions based on what factors they thought were relevant and it may be that only a relatively small number of prices would be relevant to their decisions.

That is the way markets work when one hires in other services. Of course there are very different things about electricity. The Grid needs to recognise that whatever capacity it is offering to one generator can have an influence on the quality of the service it can offer to another. It needs to be particularly concerned that if the generator uses a bit less or a bit more capacity, supplies a bit more electricity or a bit less than it says it was going to, that causes problems for system stability. It also causes problems for others; so clearly there has to be a system for ensuring that if bookings are not honoured, arrangements are made either to top supply, or to reduce the power put in elsewhere. The charges for this have to be put on the generator in question. Also, there will sometimes be times and places when there is not enough capacity for everybody to get on the system. Arrangements will have to be made to limit access then.

It seems to me that these are the kind of issues that need to be explored if we are to look at how a market would operate in place of the central co-ordinating Pool or Grid we have now. You make only a brief reference to the United States, but these issues are actively being discussed there at the present time, in most of the 51 states. They are coming to slightly different conclusions in each state, but the general conclusion seems to be that they are going for a voluntary pool. They are not going for a compulsory Pool as we have in Britain, nor are they abolishing pools completely. It will be interesting to see how much of the trade begins to take place or continues in a pool, and how far the pool is for marginal trades only. We cannot simply ignore the notion of a market operating with a marginal pool. That has to be one of the options for analysis.

In the United States the discussion has moved on. It is no longer focusing on pool or non-pool, it has shifted precisely to the kinds of transmission system issues I referred to earlier. Among them are: Do you have a nodal or a zonal system? I understand that there might be as many as 3,000 nodes if one went for a nodal system as in California; but that one or two zones might suffice. What are the merits of having large numbers of prices? They make far more accurate signals about efficiencies and shortages, but have the disadvantage of making it more difficult to conduct trades across the Grid. Another question is how to deal with a shortage of capacity in certain areas. What devices do you use to prevent existing incumbent players, who may have a degree of market power, snapping up all that capacity and stopping entrants? Perhaps devices such as making capacity available over time, or limiting the amount any particular player can buy?

In sum, your paper has played a valuable role in identifying a large number of the issues that are important to look at, within the present Pool, and giving us some stimulating proposals for dealing with them. But there is, as I have said, another set of issues that needs to be dealt with, involving trading outside the Pool.

ADDITIONAL COMMENTS*

Geoffrey Horton

To BEGIN WITH, I HAVE A COUPLE OF COMMENTS ON TRADING OUTSIDE THE POOL. One needs to be very careful about whether there is an oligopolistic position or a competitive one. The Pool is a pro-competitive measure in that it prevents oligopolistic firms discriminating between customers, which they would do if they did not have the Pool to constrain them. It also makes their spare capacity available to all players rather than just to themselves.

I am now safely ensconced at the OFT but I probably invented more numbers in 1989/90 when I was at the Department of Energy than most other people. David is right in saying that it is the entry price that matters. Other things tend to come out in the wash. When I was making up numbers I found that reassuring. We nearly opted for an *ex-post* pricing system. Then there would be no need to calculate the loss of load probability. Either you lost a load or you did not. But there were a number of reasons why it was rejected. I think that everybody shrank from the idea of saying to the generators that if they turned the lights out they would get a higher price.

The loss of load probability is actually a probability of demand being greater than supply. So it includes voltage reductions, which is a crucial feature. That makes putting a single price on it even odder than one might at first think, because it is a price for a brown-out with some probability of blackout attached. The probability of blackout is quite low and the probability that it will be combined with a brown-out will depend on the configuration of the system.

In quite a short time before vesting various simulations were run on the basis of plant 'disappearance ratios'. These were drawn from

---

* *Editor's Note*: Stephen Littlechild referred to Geoffrey Horton's key role in setting up the original Pool mechanism. His response will be of interest to all involved in the issues dealt with by the paper and comment.

recent observations about individual plants being available so many days previously but not available on the day. The availability calculation, then, comes from an average observed at various demand levels.

The value of lost load was calculated so as to preserve the existing security standard. Simulations suggested how many hours of lost load would occur over the whole year (whether brown-out or blackout) with different sorts of weather, and other considerations. These suggested very different levels, but supported roughly speaking 20 hours associated with the rate of loss at winter peak contained in the existing standards. A £2 value for each of these hours produced a very safe number for a capacity price. However, as you vary the price you do not change the expected margin very much because the curve of increasing risk about this point is so steep. £2 was also used by the CEGB, but as a price of a different concept, a blackout, in a different year's prices. It was derived in part, I believe, from a Finnish survey of what people said they might pay. The numbers we produced were not totally silly but we thought they were all far too high for the concepts being used.

There was an attempt to allow a demand response. There is the averaging of the LOLP calculation over surrounding half hours and there are also the S and D parameters which were attempts at supply and demand elasticities. These were plucked not entirely out of the air (but almost) as initial values so that people could observe supply and demand responses and adapt the supply and demand elasticity parameters over time. They would observe disappearance ratios and adapt those over time.

The crucial feature was that it was important to be able to say that generation security was being at least maintained in introducing what was a completely new system.

6

WHEN IS DISCRIMINATION

UNDUE?

John Vickers[1]

All Souls College, Oxford

Introduction

EXCEPT IN RELATION TO WINE TASTING, DISCRIM-
INATION SOUNDS BAD. This is unfortunate, because price
discrimination can often be good, indeed optimal. So it is much to
the credit of UK regulatory licence conditions that they prohibit
discriminatory and preferential terms only when they are *undue*.
But when is discrimination undue?

This question is important in competition law as well as in
regulatory matters, though much of the discussion below will
concern implications of regulation for the appropriate treatment of
discrimination. Article 86 of the EC Treaty, and hence Chapter II of
the Competition Bill, have discrimination – in particular 'applying
dissimilar conditions to equivalent transactions with other trading
parties, thereby placing them at a competitive disadvantage' –
among the list of exemplary abuses of dominance. But since it is
well established that conduct which has objective justification is not
abusive, there is a sense in which the competition law prohibition
applies only to discrimination that is undue.

Before tackling the question of undueness, the first task is to
define discrimination. Then I shall discuss:

- what sort of cost differences make price differences non-
  discriminatory;

---

[1] I am grateful to my discussant John Bridgeman, and to Steve Anderman, Michael Beesley,
Eileen Marshall, Tom Sharpe and Catherine Waddams for comments on an earlier version.
Particular thanks go to Mark Armstrong: much of the work reported here has been joint with
him. Of course, responsibility for all views expressed and any errors rests solely with me.

175

- why price discrimination matters for resource allocation and effective competition;

- the desirability of price discrimination when fixed costs need to be recovered;

- some economics of price discrimination under forms of price cap regulation;

- price discrimination when there is competition;

- discrimination and predatory pricing;

- non-discriminatory pricing of access to essential facilities; and

- some recent questions about pricing in domestic gas markets.

The discussion of these issues will be summarised by a check-list, which turns out to be rather consistent with the approach to undue discrimination in gas supply.

When Is Pricing Discriminatory?

I will focus on discriminatory pricing, though of course price is not the only aspect of commercial dealings.[2] In general terms, a firm's pricing is discriminatory if it sells units of its output at different prices where costs do not differ correspondingly.[3] (Arguably one should extend the definition to cover uniform pricing where costs do differ, but I will leave that issue aside.)

This definition covers the cases of (a) different terms being offered to different buyers, and (b) non-uniform pricing such as quantity discounts. Case (b) is discriminatory (except perhaps if there are fixed costs per consumer that provide cost justification for quantity discounts) in that the price of the second widget that I buy differs from the price of my first widget, and the average price paid by a two-widget consumer differs from that of a one-widget

---

[2] I will also take it that the economic analysis of undue discrimination covers that of undue preference.

[3] This definition leaves open the question of whether non-discrimination involves price level differences being equal to cost level differences, or prices being proportional to costs. George Stigler favoured the latter definition.

consumer. Cases (a) and (b) are respectively instances of third- and second-degree price discrimination in the economics jargon.

Cost Differences

An immediate consequence of the definition is that differential pricing is not discriminatory – let alone unduly so – if it is justified by cost differences. But what sort of cost differences count? Clearly, differences in direct marginal cost should count: if my consumption of a widget causes greater cost to be incurred than yours, then other things equal I ought to pay more than you, not the same.

Differences in allocated fixed costs (whatever that means) should *not* count, at least at this stage, because there is no cost causation as far as they are concerned. But fixed cost recovery will be important later on in the discussion.

Should opportunity cost differences count? For example, where a vertically integrated firm with an upstream monopoly is selling inputs to downstream competitors, is it justified in charging different prices according to the lost profit (= opportunity cost) from sales to different downstream firms and/or from different uses of the input? In most situations opportunity cost differences should not count, but in the special case where the retail prices of the integrated firm are fixed by regulation, they probably should, as discussed further below.

Why Does Price Discrimination Matter?[4]

There are two main reasons why price discrimination matters. The first is that it tends to lead to misallocation of output among consumers. If I face a higher widget price than you, and if the marginal costs of supplying us are the same, then widgets will end up being misallocated. I will buy widgets up to the point where my marginal utility from widgets equals 10 (say), while you will buy to the point where your marginal utility equals 8 (say). My gain from transferring some widgets at the margin from you to me would exceed your loss, so I could more than compensate you for such a transfer. This potential gain is not realised when there is discrimination in the sense of different buyers facing different

---

[4] Varian (1989) gives an excellent survey of the literature on price discrimination.

marginal prices. Only uniform marginal pricing avoids such misallocation of resources.

This *unequal marginal utilities effect* is central to the classic literature on price discrimination, which deals with the case of a monopolist facing no regulation, no competition, and whose customers are final consumers. The unregulated monopolist restricts output below its socially efficient level, so if freedom to engage in price discrimination causes total output to increase sufficiently, then the unequal marginal utilities effect may be outweighed by a beneficial *total output effect*. But if the total output effect is negative or zero (as in the case of linear demands and all markets served), then price discrimination certainly reduces welfare.

When price discrimination opens up new markets (for example, off-peak rail travel by students and senior citizens) the total output effect is likely to be positive. Indeed, if existing consumers get the same terms as before, price discrimination is Pareto-improving when new markets open up: no-one is worse off and the new consumers and the firm are better off.

The same principles apply, with some modification and addition, when the customers of the monopolist are independent downstream firms rather than final consumers. Unlike (envy-free) consumers, each downstream firm cares not only about the terms that it pays, but also about the terms that its downstream competitors pay, for they are a key determinant of the competitive pressure that it faces. Discriminatory pricing might lead to misallocation of resources among downstream firms. If there are 'dissimilar conditions' in that I have to pay more (at the margin) than you for supplies of widget inputs, then I will be at a competitive disadvantage in the final product market. Unless this somehow offsets other inefficient distortions, it is likely to cause productive inefficiency.[5]

Further complications arise if the monopolist is vertically integrated. It is all very well to stipulate that the monopolist must supply inputs to its own downstream division on the same terms as to independent firms, but it might not be so clear what this

---

[5] However, it does not follow that price discrimination should necessarily be banned in these circumstances. Such a ban might help the monopolist to commit not to give secret discounts to individual downstream firms. Without that commitment, its upstream market power might largely unravel – to the benefit of consumers and welfare.

requirement means in practice since the downstream division of the integrated firm might well not take internal transfer prices at face value. This question of non-discrimination as between self-supply and third-party supply is central to the debate about essential facilities, which I will come back to later.

The second broad reason to be concerned about price discrimination is that it may facilitate anti-competitive behaviour. Thus if a firm faces potential competition in one market while it has another market captive, the rate of profit loss that would result from predatory pricing in the non-captive market is higher if price discrimination is banned than if it is not. Banning price discrimination makes selective price cuts impossible. More generally, by affecting the power profitably to raise price, a firm that is dominant (over a relevant product market that is narrow) if it can price discriminate might not be dominant if it cannot (the relevant product market having broadened).

In sum, price discrimination matters for static reasons having to do with resource misallocation (including distortions of competition in downstream markets), and for possible adverse effects on competition over time. Offsetting these concerns, however, are various benefits that freedom to engage in price discrimination can bring.

Recovery of Fixed Costs

Firms with economies of scale would make losses from marginal cost pricing, so price-cost mark-ups are needed. Two-part tariffs – a form of price discrimination in the absence of cost justification according to our definition – involving a fixed fee per consumer (an 'access charge') plus a usage charge equal to marginal cost can in principle combine fixed-cost recovery with efficient resource allocation. But even if such non-uniform pricing is feasible and not vulnerable to resale among consumers, in practice it is likely inefficiently to curtail the number who consume. That is, one cannot have the efficient levels of both access and usage.

If, then, mark-ups are needed, will they optimally involve discriminatory pricing – that is, different price-cost mark-ups? Almost certainly yes. The principles discovered 70 years ago by Frank Ramsey in the context of commodity taxation broadly imply that the optimal departures from marginal cost pricing, which fixed-cost recovery necessitates, involve higher mark-ups on products for which demand is less price sensitive. More specifically, the optimal pattern of mark-ups is such as to induce an approximately equi-proportional *demand* reduction for each product, relative to marginal cost pricing (and after adjusting for income effects). Only in the special case of independent demands does this imply the 'inverse elasticity rule'.

So, to return to the example just mentioned, if participation were inelastic, then all the mark-up needed for fixed cost recovery should be on access (the fixed element of the two-part tariff). But if demand for access is elastic at least to some degree, then the optimal pattern of mark-ups will strike a balance between suboptimal access and suboptimal usage. This is an example where demands – for access and usage – are interdependent, so the 'inverse elasticity rule' does not hold.

Indeed, in the special case where usage is the same for everyone who buys access, there should be zero mark-up on usage. This accords precisely with the principle of equi-proportional demand reduction, since total usage is by assumption proportional to access in this special case. If, as is plausible in many cases, usage is higher for customers who value access more, then a mark-up on usage is optimal. Indeed it might even be optimal to have a negative mark-up – to subsidise access. Externalities associated with access and usage can be brought into the model. Maybe analysis of this kind has some bearing on the interesting question of subsidy to set-top boxes for digital TV.

Be that as it may, it seems clear that fixed-cost recovery can sometimes provide considerable scope for robust justifications of discriminatory pricing. Indeed, Ramsey principles imply that *optimal* pricing to recover fixed costs generally entails discrimination.

Discrimination, Regulation and Competition: Some Recent Research Questions

Implicitly if not explicitly, the last two sections have mostly been about pure monopoly. The underlying questions have been: (i) should a profit-maximising monopolist be allowed to engage in price discrimination, and (ii) what is the optimal structure of prices for a welfare-maximising monopolist needing to recover fixed costs? Welfare is defined in the conventional way as the sum of consumer surplus and profit. The Ramsey analysis is the same for a monopolist who places greater weight on profit than consumer surplus, for example, because profit goes into the public purse and there is a social cost of public funds.

The answers to these questions have yielded important principles, but with limitations. In particular, the case of pure monopoly excludes, both regulation and competition. But practical concern about whether discrimination is undue usually involves one or both of these elements. Interactions between regulation, competition and price discrimination have therefore been a good topic for research in the past few years. In attempting to describe some results of that research, I shall focus on the work of Jean-Jacques Laffont and Jean Tirole of the University of Toulouse, and some work with my Oxford colleague Mark Armstrong and others.[6]

Discrimination and Price Cap Regulation

Should a monopolist subject to price cap regulation be allowed to engage in price discrimination? Can price caps be designed to give a monopolist good incentives regarding the pattern of prices that they charge?

The answer to the first of these questions depends partly upon the nature of the price cap. Suppose first that price control takes the form of a single cap on an index of the firm's prices: $\Sigma w_i\, p_i \leq P$, where w_i is the weight on the price p_i of product i in the index, and P is the limit that the index must not exceed. (It will be assumed that the price cap P is the same whether or not price discrimination is allowed.[7])

It is important to distinguish between cases where the weights in the index are fixed, hence not subject to manipulation by the firm, and cases where the weights are endogenous. With average revenue regulation (see below), index weights are immediately endogenous. (With 'tariff basket' regulation, which has been used in some regulated industries in Britain, the weights are endogenous not immediately but with a lag typically of a year.)

If the weights w_i are fixed in proportion to the quantities purchased with uniform (that is, non-discriminatory) pricing, then

---

[6] See Laffont and Tirole (1993), Armstrong, Cowan and Vickers (1994, especially Chapter 3), and Vickers (1997) for accounts of this work.

[7] Arguably P might be lowered somewhat if the firm is allowed to engage in price discrimination so as to offset any profit gain from the freedom to discriminate.

price discrimination subject to the same cap would certainly be desirable compared with the situation in which all products have the uniform price P. Freedom to discriminate benefits the firm, and the form of the price cap guarantees that discrimination makes consumers as a whole no worse off, since at worst they can buy, at no additional cost, the same quantities as with uniform pricing. Therefore freedom to discriminate must increase welfare. (A corollary is that total output is higher when there is discrimination. Indeed, output must rise enough to offset the undesirable unequal marginal utilities effect.)

If the weights are fixed appropriately – in proportion to realised demands – then a single cap of the form above can induce Ramsey pricing. Thus a very simple price cap, suitably designed, can bring about efficient pricing in a decentralised manner which apparently does not require the regulator to know about demand elasticities and so on. This is the idea behind the *global price cap* proposal of Laffont and Tirole (1996), which they extend to the setting of a vertically integrated firm supplying inputs to competitors (see further below).

The idea of inducing a monopolist, who is presumably much better informed about industry conditions than a regulator can be, to implement efficient pricing by such simple regulatory methods is clearly important. However, the optimal fixing of the weights in the index would itself require a great deal of information. Thus the informational economy of the single cap might not be so great as appears at first sight.

A simple method of price control with endogenous weights in the regulated price index is average revenue regulation, which has been used in the gas, electricity and airports industries. The cap applies to total revenue divided by total output. This requires that outputs be commensurable, as are therms or kilowatt-hours or passengers in a literal (but not economic) sense. By contrast, a price index for telecommunications services, like one for fruit, would face the apples and pears problem.

Though conveniently simple, average revenue regulation appears to have rather questionable efficiency properties. Compared with uniform pricing at P, capping average revenue at P implies that consumers are worse off, because the outputs bought at the discriminatory prices could have been purchased at no extra cost with uniform pricing. The firm, however, gains from the freedom to discriminate, and total output rises. But it is entirely possible that the most profitable pattern of prices for the firm to charge will diverge markedly from Ramsey pricing. Indeed, the firm may set price above P in markets where the Ramsey price is below P, and vice versa. Under average revenue regulation the welfare consequences of price discrimination are ambiguous. However, the incentives of average revenue regulation can be so perverse that it is worse than no regulation at all.[8]

So far the discussion in this section has concerned a single aggregate price cap. Further insight into the pros and cons of giving some pricing structure discretion to a regulated monopolist may be obtained by examining the *optimal* nature of price caps when the informational disadvantage of the regulator is explicitly taken into account. Mark Armstrong and I have attempted this for some simplified settings, and the following principles emerge.[9]

When asymmetric information is about costs, it is certainly good to give the firm some discretion over pricing structure. The firm's incentives are aligned with what is socially desirable – relatively lower prices where costs are relatively lower. But when asymmetric information is about demands, matters are less clear-cut. When fixed-cost recovery is an issue, it is desirable for Ramsey reasons for price to be higher in markets where demand elasticity is lower (assuming for simplicity that demands are independent). But the firm, if it has pricing discretion, will want to charge higher prices where the demand level is higher. If demand levels and elasticities are negatively related, then the firm's incentives are again aligned with what is socially desirable, and pricing structure discretion is good. But if demand levels and elasticites are positively related, the firm will exploit any pricing structure discretion in a way that is detrimental to welfare. In that case zero discretion – a separate binding cap on each price rather than a single cap on some average price – may be optimal even though the firm has better information about industry conditions than the regulator.

Price caps need not always bind. A quite appealing possibility is to allow price discrimination by a monopolist subject to price cap regulation provided that no-one is made worse off than with uniform

---

[8] See Cowan (1997).

[9] See Armstrong and Vickers (1997a).

pricing. This is the same as requiring that the firm continue to give consumers the *option* of buying at the uniform price. The firm might particularly value the freedom to price below the uniform price cap when non-linear pricing (a form of 'second-degree price discrimination') is feasible, because demand for increments of output gets increasingly elastic at higher demand levels. While it is trivial to say that the freedom to set prices below regulated caps harms no-one (in the absence of anti-competitive concerns), there is reason to believe that the freedom would be used in some significant cases and hence bring real positive benefits.

Price Discrimination and Competition

Having considered monopolistic price discrimination, with and without regulation, let us turn briefly to the (rather neglected) topic of price discrimination in more or less competitive conditions. Can it be said, for example, that price discrimination by a firm facing competition may be presumed not to be undue? Of course that would not be caught by the prohibition of abuse of dominance, since the example assumes that there is no dominance, but regulatory licence conditions concerning undue discrimination are not always subject to there being market power, let alone dominance.[10]

It would be wrong to claim that market power is necessary for price discrimination to be sustained, and hence that the question just posed is otiose. There are various circumstances in which vigorous rivalry between firms is quite consistent with price discrimination.

For example, with multiproduct firms, product differentiation and fixed costs, there will have to be price-cost mark-ups (or quantity discounts) whether or not there is competition. It is not just fixed costs at firm level that matter in this regard. Thus an important feature of the telecommunications and pay-broadcasting industries is the considerable fixed cost *per consumer* needed to provide network access – for example, the final link to the fixed telecommunications network, the mobile handset, or the set-top box

---

[10] Thus the prohibition of undue preference and discrimination in Condition 17 of BT's licence is not conditional on dominance. By contrast, Standard Condition 13 of the Gas Supplier Licence prohibits undue preference and discrimination by a licensee in a dominant position. It also prohibits pricing terms by a licensee in a dominant position that are unduly onerous or predatory.

for digital TV. The marginal cost of usage, at least for wire-based systems, is by contrast often very low.

Work with Mark Armstrong[11] suggests that, at least if there is sufficient competition between firms, price discrimination policies that constrain the pattern of price-cost mark-ups (or discounts) charged to multiproduct consumers will generally reduce welfare. This is natural considering that constraints have the effect of increasing the cost of delivering a given amount of surplus to the consumer.

A slightly different question is whether it is good or bad to allow firms in competitive conditions to charge different mark-ups to different groups of consumers. This appears ambiguous – it depends on elasticities and such[12] – so there is no presumption that discrimination is bad, or that it is good, in these circumstances.

Even though the outcome with competitive price discrimination can be worse than the outcome if it is banned, there are good reasons to presume that price differentiation is not undue discrimination when competition is manifestly effective. First, in competitive conditions, price differentiation may well be cost-justified (and so not discrimination) but the regulator/competition authority might have limited cost information. Second, the welfare gains even from optimally targeted bans on discrimination are unlikely to be large. Third, the costs of policy discretion are likely to be considerable, not least in terms of the risks of excessively zealous intervention, and lobbying by would-be beneficiaries of intervention.

In sum, price discrimination in competitive conditions (i) can happen, (ii) should be presumed not to be undue.

Predatory Price Discrimination

Having considered price discrimination in competitive conditions,

---

[11] See Armstrong and Vickers (1997c).

[12] In Armstrong and Vickers (1997c) we show that the conditions in which it is desirable for *competitive* firms to discriminate are in some sense the opposite of those in which it is desirable to give pricing discretion to a *regulated* firm. The reason is that with competition price tends to be *lower* where markets are larger, because average cost tends to be lower in larger markets, whereas the regulated monopolist likes to charge *higher* prices in larger markets.

let us turn to the issue of price discrimination by a dominant firm that might undermine competition. The simplest framework for considering this question has a dominant firm facing a price-taking rival, or competitive 'fringe'. If the dominant firm seeks always to maximise profit, then much of the analysis above carries over to this competitive case with minor modification. Analytically the rival(s) can be amalgamated with consumers – as if consumers were partly supplying themselves – and the relevant demand curves facing the dominant firm are the *residual* demands after netting off rival supplies from total consumer demands.

However, this simple case excludes the possibility of predatory pricing because a necessary condition for predatory behaviour is short-run sacrifice of profit. Temporary profit sacrifice is a feature also of some non-predatory pricing behaviour, for example price promotions, so this necessary condition is by no means sufficient to establish that pricing is predatory.

The presence of regulation can affect both the cost and the benefit of predatory pricing to a dominant firm. As regards the cost – the rate of temporary profit sacrifice – it is important to distinguish between cases where the price cut in one market (a) allows prices to be higher in other markets, as when a cap applies just to some average price, (b) has no effect on prices permitted in other markets, as in the absence of regulation or when separate caps apply in different markets, and (c) requires prices in other markets also to be cut, as when price discrimination is banned.

Note that in case (a) regulation has the effect of reducing the cost of predatory pricing relative to the unregulated case.[13] Regulation might be expected also to limit the firm's benefit from successful predatory pricing, since regulation remains even if rivals are eliminated. However, the elimination of rivals, in addition to its direct benefit to the dominant firm, might have the further advantage of reducing the effectiveness of regulation by depriving the regulator of useful comparative performance information.

The two leading EC cases on predatory pricing – *AKZO* and *Tetra Pak II* – do not involve regulation but are pertinent nonetheless.

---

[13] This is quite consistent with a global price cap having the efficiency properties described above, since those were premised upon continuous profit maximisation, whereas here we are considering temporary profit sacrifice.

The judgements of the European Court of Justice (ECJ) in those cases establish that for a dominant firm:

(1) prices below average variable costs must always be considered abusive; and

(2) prices below average total costs but above average variable costs are only to be considered abusive if an intention to eliminate competitors can be shown.

Intention to eliminate need not be shown in case (1) because, according to the ECJ, such pricing has no conceivable economic purpose other than the elimination of a competitor. (It will be apparent that I am among those who question this.) Neither is it necessary to show that the alleged predator had a realistic chance of recouping its losses from below-cost pricing.

These criteria may be contrasted with Standard Condition 13(3) of the Gas Supplier Licence, according to which pricing terms are predatory if and only if (i) they do not cover avoidable cost, *and* (ii) they have the purpose or likely effect of unfairly excluding or limiting competition between the licensee and other gas suppliers. Note that average avoidable cost exceeds average variable cost unless all fixed costs are sunk.

Avoidable cost – cost that 'can be escaped in the pertinent period of time' – is also the benchmark advocated by Baumol (1996) in his development of the famous Areeda-Turner test of predatory pricing. However, I think that Baumol would say that (i) and (ii) above are essentially the same, since jeopardizing the existence or entry of efficient rivals is precisely the basis for his average avoidable cost test.

Baumol dismisses 'average total cost' as a quite useless concept for multiproduct firms, but he stresses that his avoidable cost test applies to combinations of products, not just to products individually. Thus 'any combination of the firm's products must be priced so as to yield an incremental revenue that exceeds the avoidable cost incurred by that combination of products' (Baumol, p. 61). Where a firm sells different units of a product at different prices, this rule can be applied by treating the sales at different prices as sales of different products. For Baumol, failure of the avoidable cost test is by no means sufficient for pricing to be predatory: there must also be a reasonable prospect of recoupment and a lack of 'legitimate business purpose' such as a sales promotion.

Comparisons between cost standards for predatory pricing, such as those above, involve two main issues: what is the right cost floor, and is pricing below cost by a dominant firm necessarily predatory? The answer to the latter question should be negative, because non-predatory purposes for below-cost pricing are conceivable, but I would place a heavy burden of proof on a dominant defendant to rebut the presumption that pricing below cost is predatory. As for the prospect of recoupment, it seems almost true to say that dominance implies such a prospect, since (re-)entry barriers, which are – or at least ought to be – necessary for a finding of dominance, are the key to recoupment. Thus if the 'prosecution' has properly discharged the burden of showing dominance, it has at least gone a long way towards showing that there is a reasonable prospect of recoupment, and so has no (or not much) *further* need to establish such a prospect.

The cost standard is the hardest part. For example, depending on the length of the 'pertinent period of time', Baumol's average avoidable cost test can mean very different things. To paraphrase Keynes, in the long run we are all avoidable, and so too are costs. So for a single-product firm, average avoidable cost approaches average total cost as the time-period extends. In the short-run, however, avoidable cost might be very much lower. For Baumol (p. 62), logic compels the conclusion that the pertinent time-period is that 'over which the price in question prevailed or could reasonably have been expected to prevail', for a rival would not quit unless price was lower than the per-unit cost that the rival could not escape in the period of low pricing. Therefore a rival who was no less efficient than the incumbent over that period would not quit.

Quite apart from the difficulty of establishing how long the pricing might have been expected to prevail (without inducing exit), Baumol's cost test focuses on productive efficiency, which is but one aspect of economic welfare, and, like the Areeda-Turner rule, it does not reflect the dynamic strategic context of predatory pricing – see Ordover and Saloner (1989). Thus, for example, it is easy to think of situations where a higher floor than avoidable cost would sustain competition that would otherwise not be sustained, to the benefit of consumers and economic welfare generally, albeit with some loss of productive efficiency. But the higher the floor is set, the greater is the risk that inefficient firms will be protected. There is no clear-cut answer to this dilemma. My inclination (it is no more than that) is that avoidable cost is a reasonable standard, though with scope to rebut presumptions, and that the pertinent time-horizon should not be too short, subject to the key proviso that the existence of a dominant position is properly established before any questions of predatory pricing arise.

Non-Discrimination in the Supply of Inputs to Competitors

Perhaps the most controversial issues in price discrimination concern situations in which a vertically integrated firm is supplying inputs – say, access to an essential facility – to rivals with whom it is competing in the downstream market. A prohibition of undue discrimination, or of abuse of dominance more generally, may well require the integrated firm not to discriminate against rivals when setting terms of access. This must mean more than a requirement that the transfer price notionally paid for access by the downstream part of the integrated firm is the same as the actual price charged to rival firms, since the internal transfer price may be no more than book-keeping. But what more does it mean?

Baumol and his collaborators[14] argue that only the efficient component pricing rule (ECPR) gives competitive neutrality, which I will take to be the same as non-discrimination in this context. The ECPR says that access prices should include the integrated firm's opportunity cost in terms of lost profit occasioned by the supply of access to competitors. This has aroused great controversy, much of which has been rather unnecessary. Leaving aside the issue of how to measure opportunity cost,[15] some key conclusions from debate about the ECPR can be summarised as follows:

- the ECPR is a necessary condition for productive efficiency (just as marginal cost pricing is a necessary condition for allocative efficiency);

---

[14] See, for example, Baumol and Sidak (1994, especially Chapter 7).

[15] Armstrong, Doyle and Vickers (1996) discuss this for the case of given retail prices. When retail prices are endogenous, the relevant measure of opportunity cost should certainly not include profit loss due to retail price reduction caused by increased rival supply. Also see Laffont and Tirole (1994).

- in situations where productive efficiency is the only objective (for example, where retail prices are exogenous and there is no fixed cost recovery problem), the ECPR is therefore optimal;

- otherwise (for instance, if retail prices are deregulated and hence influenced by access pricing[16]) the ECPR is generally not optimal.

While overall economic efficiency – as distinct from just productive efficiency – is a suitable aim for regulatory policy as a whole, it would appear unreasonable to say that failure by a dominant firm to maximise economic welfare constitutes undue discrimination. In some cases it might be good for welfare to admit rivals who are less efficient downstream than the integrated firm – for example, because they bring downward pressure on excessive retail prices – but it would seem inappropriate to condemn the integrated firm for *undue discrimination* if it failed to set prices so as to admit them. (This is certainly not to say that a *regulator* should ignore the effect on retail prices when determining access prices.) Thus a good test of whether there is undue discrimination against rivals is whether more efficient rivals are squeezed out of production. This is what the ECPR aims to do.

In fact, in the context at hand, breach of the ECPR can be seen as equivalent to predatory pricing downstream by the integrated firm, *assuming* that the integrated firm supplies access to its retail division on the same terms as to rivals (whether or not it actually does so). Efficient rivals are shut out precisely when the integrated firm's retail price fails to cover its avoidable retail cost – with the access price charged to rivals reckoned as part of that cost. That is, the ECPR is equivalent to the predatory pricing rule assuming non-discrimination as between self-supply and supply to others.

It may be objected that if the integrated firm is not dominant downstream, and if its allegedly predatory behaviour there does not strengthen its dominance upstream, then that behaviour cannot constitute an abuse of dominance. But the ECJ in *Tetra Pak II* held that conduct in a non-dominated market can be an abuse of a dominant position in another market, even if it does not strengthen that dominant position, if there are close 'associative links' between

---

[16] Armstrong and Vickers (1997b) analyse this case.

the two markets so that the situation is comparable to one in which the firm holds a dominant position on the markets in question as a whole.[17] Without being certain what this means, I dare say that downstream conduct by the integrated firm in our example could be found to be abuse of a dominant position.

Domestic Gas Pricing

Several questions concerning undue discrimination have recently arisen in the market for domestic gas supply, where liberalisation will soon be complete throughout Great Britain.[18] Thus in 1995 controversy arose over the rebalancing by BG of its domestic tariffs in favour of customers paying by direct debit and against those on prepayment meters. After investigation Ofgas found the rebalancing to be cost-justified. Here I will briefly discuss two schemes introduced in 1997 by British Gas Trading (now part of Centrica): the ValuePlus tariff offered in liberalised parts of the country, and participation in the Goldfish credit card joint venture.[19]

ValuePlus, which offers substantial discounts relative to BGT's standard and direct debit tariffs, is available to all BGT customers in the relevant areas who pay by monthly direct debit and accept a 12-month contract with 28 days notice. Assuming that the price differentiation implied by ValuePlus is not cost-justified, it must be asked whether it is unduly discriminatory (a) between customers in the liberalised areas and others, and (b) between different classes of customer within the areas where the scheme operates. In assessing these issues it is important to note that the supply price control for BGT for 1997-2000 has an individual tariff cap on each of BGT's

---

[17] If interpreted loosely, this doctrine appears to expose multimarket firms that are dominant in a subset of their markets to the hazard of anti-trust action on an unreasonably broad front. On a narrow interpretation, which I would favour, it would be necessary to show (not just assert) that the firm did hold a dominant position on the markets as a whole. There would appear to be no logical inconsistency in saying, as it were, that a firm held a dominant position in the market for apples, and in the market for fruit, but not in the market for bananas taken in isolation. Then abusive conduct involving bananas could be an abuse of dominance in the fruit market. This seems more satisfactory than saying that it is an abuse of dominance over apples taking into account the close associative links between apples and bananas.

[18] See Waddams Price (1997) for an account of regulatory and competitive developments in the UK gas industry.

[19] See Ofgas (1997a,b).

four tariff categories. So discounts for some customers cannot directly harm others, as could happen if, for example, any discounts counted towards compliance with caps on average prices.

Standard Condition 13 of the gas supplier's licences prohibits, among other things, undue preference and discrimination by a supplier in a dominant position. Ofgas (1997a, Appendix 3) explains that the condition applies uniformly nationwide in the absence of 'established competition'. However, a supplier may supply on terms which are reasonably necessary to meet established competition in an area (or for a class of customers) provided that those terms are not predatory (which involves an avoidable cost test), not unduly discriminatory, and not unduly onerous towards other customers over whom the supplier has a dominant position.

Leaving aside the ample scope for argument about what constitutes 'reasonable necessity', 'established competition', a 'class of customers' and so on, this seems a rather sensible approach. Except when competition is in its infancy, a dominant supplier is not hamstrung by a requirement of nationwide uniformity, but its freedom to discriminate is limited to guard against predatory pricing or exploitative pricing against other customer groups. The tariff caps contain the latter danger, and Ofgas (1997a, p. 25) has expressed the preliminary view that the level at which ValuePlus has been set is not predatory, though it intends to keep matters under review.

BGT has a 50 per cent share of the Goldfish credit card joint venture. Customers spending money using the card get points which may be redeemed against the cost of purchases from the redemption partners, who include BGT, BT, Boots, Asda and TV Licensing. Most points so far have been redeemed against BGT. Since Goldfish compensates BGT for the discounts, and BGT's transactions costs are not significantly increased by the scheme, it is not discriminatory in a formal sense. But BGT's co-ownership of Goldfish raised the possibility, rejected by BGT, that BGT is effectively giving discounts to Goldfish card-holders.

Ofgas (1997b) found that Goldfish was indeed compensating BGT properly for its costs, but asked BGT to extend the scheme to prepayment customers and small business users. To help avoid the risk of customers perceiving switching costs as a result of the scheme, Ofgas also had BGT agree to insert a bill message to make customers aware that Goldfish points can be redeemed against closing accounts with BGT. Ofgas rejected the suggestion that other gas suppliers should be granted access to the scheme on the same terms as BGT. These remedies are not draconian, and the general regulatory tolerance of the scheme seems entirely appropriate.

Summing Up

Two necessary, but by no means sufficient, conditions for price differentiation to be undue discrimination are that

(1) the firm in question has some market power, and

(2) the price differences do not correspond to differences in direct marginal costs.

If (1) and (2) both hold, the next question is whether

(3) the price discrimination makes some consumers worse off.

In the absence of price regulation, (3) is likely to hold unless new markets are opened up by price discrimination. But if there is regulation in the form of separate price caps, (3) may not hold, in which case the price discrimination is not undue unless

(4) the price discrimination is predatory,

in which case consumers will lose out in the longer run. Avoidable cost is a good benchmark for assessing whether pricing is predatory, though subject to the points about time-scales and rebuttable presumptions discussed above. Predatory price discrimination, if not otherwise prohibited, should be prohibited as undue discrimination.

Where a vertically integrated firm is supplying inputs to competitors, predatory pricing rules should be applied on the assumption that the downstream part of the integrated firm obtains inputs on the same terms as independent firms. Then predatory pricing rules *imply* the ECPR. The ECPR illustrates that:

(5) in some circumstances opportunity cost (that is, lost profit) differences should count towards the cost justification of price differences.

Those circumstances include fixed retail prices when there is a need to recover fixed costs.

We are left with cases where (1), (2) and (3) hold, but (4) does not. Here a rule-of-reason approach seems appropriate, in which price discrimination is condemned as undue only if it may be expected to reduce 'economic welfare' compared with uniform pricing. 'Economic welfare' could be defined in various ways, which necessarily involve value judgements, for example as aggregate consumer surplus, the sum of consumer surplus and profit, a weighted sum of the two, or a welfare criterion that accords different weights to different consumer groups.[20] In any event, important points to keep in mind are that:

(6) efficient recovery of fixed costs generally involves price discrimination,

(7) a firm subject to price cap regulation is likely to have better pricing structure incentives if price index weights are fixed than if they are endogenous, and

(8) the more that price discrimination expands demand, the more likely it is to be beneficial.

Finally, two general themes of this discussion have been that, rather in keeping with the current competition law reform, price discrimination should be judged in terms of economic effect rather than form, and that, especially when there are fixed costs to be recovered, the economic effects of price discrimination are quite often good.

---

[20] This last possibility would allow distributional considerations to be taken into account, and perhaps also fairness, which some might regard price discrimination as jeopardizing. However, it can be debated whether regulatory policy is well suited to the pursuit of distributional aims.

References

Armstrong, M., S. Cowan and J. Vickers (1994): *Regulatory Reform: Economic Analysis and British Experience,* Cambridge, MA: MIT Press.

Armstrong, M., C. Doyle and J. Vickers (1996): 'The Access Pricing Problem: A Synthesis', *Journal of Industrial Economics,* Vol. 44, pp. 131-50.

Armstrong, M. and J. Vickers (1997a): 'Multiproduct Price Regulation under Asymmetric Information', LBS Regulation Initiative Working Paper No. 8.

Armstrong, M. and J. Vickers (1997b): 'The Access Pricing Problem with Deregulation: A Note', *Journal of Industrial Economics.*

Armstrong, M. and J. Vickers (1997c): 'Competitive Price Discrimination', mimeo, Nuffield College, University of Oxford.

Baumol, W. (1996): 'Predation and the Logic of the Average Variable Cost Test', *Journal of Law and Economics,* Vol. 39, pp. 49-72.

Baumol, W. and J.G. Sidak (1994): *Toward Competition in Local Telephony,* Cambridge, MA: MIT Press.

Cowan, S. (1997): 'Tight Average Revenue Regulation can be Worse than no Regulation', *Journal of Industrial Economics,* Vol. 45, pp. 75-88.

Laffont, J.-J. and J. Tirole (1993): *A Theory of Incentives in Procurement and Regulation,* Cambridge, MA: MIT Press.

Laffont, J.-J. and J. Tirole (1994): 'Access Pricing and Competition', *European Economic Review,* Vol. 38, pp. 1,673-1,710.

Laffont, J.-J. and J. Tirole (1996): 'Creating Competition through Interconnection: Theory and Practice', *Journal of Regulatory Economics,* Vol. 10, pp. 227-56.

Ofgas (1997a): *Extension of British Gas Trading's 'ValuePlus' Tariff to the Area Covered by the Second Phase of Competition: A Consultation Document,* London: Ofgas.

Ofgas (1997b): *Goldfish: British Gas Trading's Credit Card Joint Venture: A Decision Document,* London: Ofgas.

Ordover, J. and G. Saloner (1989): 'Predation, Monopolization and Antitrust', in R. Schmalensee and R. Willig (eds.), *Handbook of Industrial Organization,* Amsterdam: North-Holland.

Varian, H. (1989): 'Price Discrimination', in R. Schmalensee and R. Willig (eds.), *Handbook of Industrial Organization,* Amsterdam: North-Holland.

Vickers, J. (1997): 'Regulation, Competition and the Structure of Prices', *Oxford Review of Economic Policy,* Vol. 13(1), pp. 15-26.

Waddams Price, C. (1997): 'Competition and Regulation in the UK Gas Industry', *Oxford Review of Economic Policy,* Vol. 13(1), pp. 47-63.

CHAIRMAN'S COMMENTS

John Bridgeman

I WOULD LIKE TO THANK PROFESSOR VICKERS for a most interesting, indeed fascinating, and stimulating talk. As Director General of Fair Trading, I am acutely aware of the need for the practical implementation of competition law to rest on a solid and well-reasoned theoretical basis. The issues merit it. Professional advisers ask for it and businesses need it. In establishing effective competition legislation vigorous, on-going and informed public debate about the underlying issues is essential, and evenings such as this form an important part of this process.

Robust discussion about the theory and practice of competition are of particular relevance at the moment in the light of the impending changes to our competition law in the United Kingdom, and it may be appropriate for me to say a few words about these.

As you will be aware, following the election in May, the Government announced its intention to reform competition law. In August, the President of the Board of Trade published her draft Competition Bill. After public consultation, this was introduced into Parliament in October.

The new law will have two main features: the Chapter I prohibition of anti-competitive agreements, and the Chapter II prohibition of abuse of a dominant position in a market. The prohibitions are based closely on Articles 85 and 86 respectively of the EC Treaty, and are to be interpreted so as to be consistent with them.

I warmly welcome the new law. For the first time in the 25 years of an Office of Fair Trading, I shall have at my disposal effective powers of investigation and sanction. I will also have new powers to allow me to impose interim measures to suspend alleged anti-competitive behaviour and preserve the status quo while an investigation is in progress as well as providing temporary protection for parties who may be victims of this behaviour.

Again, this will bring UK law into line with the European law. It will remove one of the major loopholes in the existing legislation:

that by the time I have concluded my investigation, a company which is the victim of an anti-competitive agreement or conduct may already have suffered irreparable damage, or even have been driven out of business altogether.

The new law will be governed by general principles. It is important that these be as transparent as possible. I will therefore have a duty to issue guidelines on their interpretation. What will this involve?

The first step will be to develop OFT's internal procedures. Considerable work has been done on this already. The law may be new, but the principles behind it are established and tested. Because the new law will be closely aligned with EU law, there is an established body of jurisprudence and experience on which we shall be able to draw.

In producing guidelines, I will draw on the European Commission's Notices (as far as they reflect current jurisprudence) as well as on internal OFT guidance material. In addition to UK versions of relevant EC Notices, other areas which guidelines may cover include those such as the meaning of conduct amounting to an abuse of a dominant position. I intend, of course, to consult widely on these guidelines and procedural rules in draft and I intend to be ready to initiate this consultation as soon as practicable.

But legislation can do no more than lay down a set of general principles, which I and my officials must interpret according to the circumstances of each individual case, taking into account all the relevant factors.

As Professor Vickers has shown, the line dividing competitive from anti-competitive behaviour can sometimes be a surprisingly narrow one. At the same time, it is vital that the authority responsible for enforcing competition law should distinguish clearly between the two. Where a firm devises a novel but competitive strategy, and its rivals lose business as a result, they may cry foul every bit as loudly and sincerely as genuine victims of abuse of a dominant position.

Conversely, abuse of a dominant position may sometimes seem – in the short term – to be very much to the benefit of customers, where for example a company reduces its prices to force a smaller competitor out of the market. Not until the predation has been successful, and the monopolist raises its prices, may the damage to competition be seen for what it is.

It is the function of the competition authority to distinguish between anti-competitive and pro-competitive behaviour. Only by careful economic analysis of the situation in the light of economics are we able to discriminate – to borrow a word – between the anti-competitive, the pro-competitive, and the neutral.

In his concluding remarks, Professor Vickers said that we need to judge price discrimination in terms of economic effect rather than form. Indeed, this is generally applicable across the wider spectrum of competition.

Of course, discrimination does not only take the form of price discrimination – for example, in fine fragrances it is reasonable for a supplier to demand that dealers have appropriate displays and well-presented and knowledgeable sales staff. In this market, the European Commission has allowed quantitative restrictions of outlets under Article 85(3), where it has accepted that this can enhance the distribution of goods. But in either case, discrimination is undue when the selection criterion is not objective or is inconsistent.

It is the approach taken by the new legislation. One of the advantages of the approach taken in the new law (and indeed in the Competition Act and the monopoly provisions of the Fair Trading Act) is its flexibility: this analysis can be undertaken unhampered by any inbuilt assumptions as to the harmfulness of price or other discrimination.

The current régime for restrictive agreements well illustrates the defects of a form-based approach. The Restrictive Trade Practices Act, which is undoubtedly the weakest element of the present system, obliges parties to furnish many agreements which do not affect competition. This represents a burden, both to business and the OFT. It requires many thousands of innocuous agreements to be formally registered with my Office. All have to be carefully scrutinised by my officials.

This is expensive and wasteful to business, and it wastes public funds. Whenever a significant restriction is detected, it must be referred to the Restrictive Practices Court which, after a cumbersome and lengthy legal process which may – quite literally – take years, decides whether or not the restriction is against the public interest. Moreover, it is even possible, through careful drafting, for some anti-competitive agreements to escape being caught by the Act at all.

The new legislation should make it easier to take effective action against seriously anti-competitive agreements, while making life easier for businesses who wish to operate agreements which are either neutral, in competition terms, or which have benefits which outweigh their anti-competitive effects.

7

THE MONOPOLIES AND MERGERS
COMMISSION AND RPI-x

Martin Howe

formerly Office of Fair Trading

IN THE LAST FEW YEARS THE ROLE OF THE MONOPOLIES AND MERGERS COMMISSION (MMC) in the various regulatory régimes set up on the privatisation of the utilities, airports and railways has come into prominence with a number of references of disputed licence modifications and determinations concerned with charging conditions. These references – and the mandatory references that must be made by the Civil Aviation Authority (CAA) before conditions are imposed on airport charges at 'designated' airports – have embroiled the MMC in the technicalities of price capping, or RPI-x in the usual shorthand.

In relation to disputed licence modifications and determinations, the MMC's role has been described as that of an 'umpire' or 'court of appeal'. Neither analogy is appropriate. Only in the case of disputed determinations in water is the MMC's verdict final, as the decision of an umpire is supposed to be, and the ruling of an appeal court can be expected to be. And even in the case of determinations in water, the analogy breaks down if 'court of appeal' is interpreted literally since the MMC is an investigatory body, charged to collect its own evidence and reach its own conclusions, not to decide, as would a court, in favour of one party or the other. Nevertheless, the tags give a flavour of the role of the MMC in the regulatory system. It is the body that can be called upon to review certain proposals of regulators (or, in airports, that has to be referred to before a decision on charging conditions can be made). The main purpose of this paper is to consider the review process rather than the technicalities of RPI-x.

This process will not be affected by the Competition Bill now proceeding through Parliament. Although the MMC will be dissolved and replaced by a new body, the Competition

201

Commission, among the functions of this body will be those, unchanged, of the MMC under the regulatory régimes. But the Competition Commission will also have an appeal function. There is to be a prohibition of conduct amounting to an abuse of a dominant position (and of agreements the purpose or effect of which is anti-competitive) and it is expected that scale monopoly references to the MMC will be largely replaced by the new provision. The MMC has recommended control of the prices of a dominant firm in a number of reports on monopoly references over the years. Indeed, it was after an MMC report in 1982 on a monopoly reference (of contraceptive sheaths) that price capping was first applied in the United Kingdom as an alternative to rate-of-return regulation.[1] Such an outcome is less likely, I shall suggest, under a prohibition system.

The prohibitions in a new competition law will be enforced by the Director General of Fair Trading and, as far as the regulated utilities are concerned, by the sectoral Directors General. Appeals against their decisions will be heard by the appeal tribunals of the Competition Commission. Here we shall have an appellate body even if the tribunals are not courts in the full sense of the word. A point to consider is how this appeal function of the Commission will relate to its work on what I might call regulatory references. But that can be left to the end of my remarks. Before I can discuss the present role of the MMC in relation to the regulated sectors, I need to give an outline of the legal framework.

The Legislative Provisions on the Review Process

All airports with an annual turnover of more than £1million need permission to levy charges. More stringent regulation applies to those that are 'designated' by the Secretary of State (currently Manchester Airport plc and the London airports of BAA plc). The Airports Act 1986 requires the Civil Aviation Authority (CAA) to impose conditions as to the transparency of a designated airport's accounts and as to the maximum amount that may be levied in airport charges during a specified five-year period. The CAA must

---

[1] Monopolies and Mergers Commission, *Contraceptive Sheaths*, Cmnd. 8689, 1982. The MMC's recommendation was that the average realised prices of the London Rubber Company Ltd should increase by no more than the increase in a specially constructed cost index minus 1.5 per cent.

make a reference to the MMC before it imposes or modifies conditions relating to designated airports. In the course of each quinquennial review of airport charges a reference to the MMC is therefore mandatory.

A reference also requires the MMC to investigate whether the airport operator has pursued any course of conduct relating to airport charges or other operational activities which has operated, or may be expected to operate, against the public interest.

The CAA is not bound by the MMC's recommendations on the maximum level of airport charges but it must 'have regard' to them and, in the notice of the conditions it proposes to impose, it must give its reasons if it has not implemented the MMC's recommendations. If the MMC find that an airport operator has engaged in a course of conduct that has adversely affected the public interest, the CAA is bound to impose conditions it considers appropriate for remedying the adverse effects and it shall 'have regard' to any conditions proposed by the MMC.

As far as airport charges are concerned, the MMC is therefore more like an advisory body to the CAA than a body to review decisions of the regulator.

There have been five reports on Airports Act references so far, three on Manchester Airport (reported on in 1987, 1992 and 1997) and two on the London airports of BAA (reported on in 1991 and 1996).[2]

In water, under the Water Industry Act 1991 the Director General of Water Services (DGWS) can determine the price limits (and infrastructure charges) of an appointed company without needing formally to amend its appointment (licence). The limits are set by an RPI + K formula laid down in the licence (K – the 'adjustment factor' – can be positive or negative but so far has been positive, reflecting the investment requirements of the industry). A licensee which does not agree to a determination of the DGWS can require him to refer the matter to the MMC for the MMC to determine the limits. The decision of the MMC will be final and will be

---

[2] Monopolies and Mergers Commission, *Manchester Airport plc: a report on the economic regulation of Manchester Airport plc*, MMC1 (December 1987), MMC3 (July 1992) and MMC5 (August 1997); and *BAA plc : a report on the economic regulation of the London airport companies (Heathrow Airport Ltd, Gatwick Airport Ltd., and Stansted Airport Ltd)*, MMC2 (September 1991) and MMC4 (July 1996).

substituted for that of the DGWS. There have been two references to the MMC so far, of Portsmouth Water plc and South West Water Services Ltd, both reported on in 1995.[3]

In telecommunications, gas and electricity price limits, which since privatisation have been set by RPI-x type formulae, can only be changed by a change in formal licence conditions. The statutory provisions are virtually identical and are to be found in the Telecommunications Act 1984, the Gas Act 1986 as amended by the Gas Act 1995, and the Electricity Act 1989. In Northern Ireland, the regulatory instrument for electricity is the Electricity (Northern Ireland) Order 1992.

Licences can be modified at any time by agreement between the relevant Director General and the licensee. Where agreement cannot be reached, the Director may make a licence modification reference to the MMC. While formally it is for the Director General to take the initiative, the effect is that the licensee has a means to appeal to the MMC against a change in the licence proposed by the Director General.[4]

On a licence modification reference the MMC must consider whether any of the matters specified in the reference operate, or may be expected to operate, against the public interest and, if so, whether the adverse effects could be remedied by a modification of the licence. If the MMC identifies adverse effects the Director General must make such modifications of the licence as 'appear to him requisite' to deal with those adverse effects, 'having regard' to the modifications suggested by the MMC. Finally, the Director General must give notice of the modifications he proposes to make and allow a minimum period of time before he finalises his decision.

So far there have been six reports of the MMC on licence modification references. Two in telecommunications were not concerned with charges.[5] There have been two references of British

---

[3] Monopolies and Mergers Commission, *Portsmouth Water plc: a report on the determination of adjustment factors and infrastructure charges for Portsmouth Water plc*, June 1995, and *South West Water Services Ltd : a report on the determination of adjustment factors and infrastructure charges for South West Water Services Ltd*, June 1995.

[4] Modification references (of appointments) can be made in similar fashion in water by the DGWS but, as mentioned, these do not apply to changes in price limits.

[5] Monopolies and Mergers Commission, *Chatline and Message Services: a report on the*

Gas plc (reported on in 1993 and 1997),[6] and two in electricity, Scottish Hydro Electric plc (reported on in 1995) and Northern Ireland Electricity plc (reported on in 1997).[7]

There are therefore three models of a review process in the legislation:

- mandatory reference to the MMC before any condition relating to charges of a regulated company is imposed or modified;

- reference to the MMC only when a condition cannot be accepted by the regulated company and the MMC's conclusions bind the regulator;

- reference to the MMC only when a condition cannot be accepted by the regulated company and the regulator is not bound to accept the condition proposed by the MMC.

It would be impracticable to adopt the mandatory reference model generally. Not only would the MMC be overwhelmed if there had to be a reference before any condition relating to charges of any regulated company was imposed or modified, but the independence of the sectoral Directors General would come to be undermined. And their independence is a key feature of the UK system of utility regulation. In fact, the Department of Transport proposed in March 1995 that the regulatory system for airports be brought into line with that of the utilities, with reference to the MMC only when there was a dispute over charging conditions between the CAA and an airport

---

provision of Chatline and Message Services by means of the British Telecommunications switched telephone network, February 1989, and *Telephone number portability: a report on a reference under Section 13 of the Telecommunications Act 1984*, December 1995.

6 Monopolies and Mergers Commission, *British Gas plc: Volume 1 of reports under the Gas Act 1986 on the conveyance and storage of gas and the fixing of tariffs for the supply of gas by British Gas plc*, Cm.2315, August 1993, Vols. 2 and 3, Cm .2316, 2317, September 1993; and *BG plc: a report under the Gas Act on the restriction of prices for gas transportation and storage services*, June 1997.

7 Monopolies and Mergers Commission, *Scottish Hydro Electric plc: a report on a reference under section 12 of the Electricity Act 1989*, June 1995, and *Northern Ireland Electricity plc: a report under Article 15 of the Electricity (Northern Ireland) Order 1992*, April 1997.

operator.[8] The department's main reason was the cost and slowness of the present system. It remains to be seen if it will be changed in any future legislation on airport regulation. What seems certain is that there will be no further examples of the mandatory reference model.

With the other models it is for the regulated company to decide whether to trigger a reference. The right to do so is one of the checks and balances in a system in which the sectoral Directors General have a considerable degree of discretion in how they are to exercise their powers and carry out their duties, including the power to control prices and the conduct of price reviews.

Reference to the MMC

It is worth recalling that the RPI-x technique was envisaged as regulation with a 'light touch' when it was recommended by Stephen Littlechild in 1983 as the means by which British Telecommunications' profitability should be controlled.[9] Prices of local telephone services which would remain a monopoly, he thought, should be capped but otherwise markets were sufficiently contestable, or potentially so, to make the regulation of prices unnecessary or at least a temporary requirement only. The technique would avoid the detailed costing exercises and intervention that had characterised rate-of-return regulation in the United States. The RPI-x type of control was adopted not only for British Telecommunications (BT) but also in later privatisations for airports and other regulated utilities whose activities included significant natural monopoly elements or at least entrenched market dominating positions. But, except for airports, in each case it was for the regulator to decide on an appropriate level of x (or of K as it would be for water companies) with the licensee, and it would be for the company to decide whether it could do better by, in effect, taking its case to the MMC.

I understand it was expected that it would be not uncommon for companies to opt for a reference. An obvious reason why that expectation was confounded in the early years is that the initial

---

8   Department of Transport, *Review of the Framework for Economic Regulation of Airports*, March 1995.

9   S. Littlechild, 'Regulation of British Telecommunications' Profitability', Department of Industry, 1983.

price controls proved, almost without exception, to be generous to the shareholders of the privatised companies. It was possible for some tightening of the RPI-x formulae to be achieved by agreement.

Another factor may be that the price reviews conducted by the sectoral Directors General have become major and lengthy exercises. In the course of a review, the regulator will set out his or her proposals in detail, and the methodology behind them, for public consultation. There will be rounds of exchanges and meetings with the licensee before a Director General reaches a final view on the licence conditions (or the price determination) that he or she thinks is appropriate in the circumstances. This can no longer be described as regulation with a light touch and it would be understandable if, after a review which can last for two years or more, a company may not want to contemplate the cost and uncertainty of a further round of the regulatory process.

Whatever the reasons, in some sectors a succession of licence amendments has been agreed without recourse to the MMC, notably to the price limits in BT's telecommunications licence and to the price limits on the supply businesses of the 14 public electricity suppliers. However, the possibility of a reference must always be in the background and, despite the elaborate price reviews that are now undertaken by the regulators, there no doubt continues to be an element of bargaining. Thus the Director General of Gas Supplies has described the run up to a licence modification as 'a game of cat and mouse with the company' and explained that she finds it easier to reach a decision with the knowledge that, if it is not satisfied, the company can 'appeal' to the MMC.[10] In the review of the price restrictions in the licence of British Gas for the transportation and storage services of TransCo, the DGGS adopted a position which she did not think was 'objectively appropriate' in an effort to make a reference unnecessary. But the company could not agree to her proposal and preferred to take its case to the MMC.[11] However, it is still a rarity for the MMC actually to be brought into play.

A consideration will be the costs of a reference. These may well be substantial, especially when the calls on senior management time

---

[10] Committee on Public Accounts, *The Office of Gas Supply: the Regulation of Gas Tariffs (The Gas Cost Index)*, First Report Session 1996-97, HC37, October 1997, Minutes of Evidence, p. 6.

[11] MMC report on British Gas (1997), *op. cit.*, para. 10.9.

during an inquiry lasting several months are taken into account. Various kinds of expert will need to be hired and the licensee also has to contribute to the regulator's costs. Scottish Hydro Electric has estimated the costs of its licence modification reference as £2million.[12] If this is a reasonable estimate of the cost of a typical reference, then I suppose at the margin it may deter a company from rejecting a regulator's proposal. But where there is major disagreement, the costs of a reference are unlikely to be decisive, particularly given the size and financial strength of most licensees.

A company will also know that the MMC's report will be published, and is likely to include a considerable amount of information on its business, not least on its plans and financial projections. But it will be able to seek the excision of commercially confidential information – and the many blanks in the published reports suggest that the success rate is high.

The crucial consideration for the company is the likely outcome if it goes to the MMC, first the outcome of the MMC's investigation and then (in the case of a licence modification reference) the response of the regulator to the MMC's report. The company may surmise that the MMC's inquiry is unlikely to reopen points on which there had been agreement with the regulator. In this sense, a company may feel that it can influence the MMC's agenda and that the MMC's conclusions are unlikely to be worse (from its point of view) than the proposals of the regulator. It may also hope that the MMC's conclusions will be taken up by the regulator in subsequent reviews, thereby reducing regulatory uncertainty. Thus Northern Ireland Electricity hoped that the MMC's report on the reference made in 1996 would give 'clear regulatory guidelines' for the Director General of Electricity Supply for Northern Ireland to follow in future reviews and the company listed no fewer than 11 points on which it wished to see a ruling by the MMC.[13] The MMC is not in the business of devising blueprints for regulators' price reviews, but it is clear that the expectation has been that MMC reports on references concerned with price control will lead to a greater degree of consistency in the actions of the regulators.

---

[12] Trade and Industry Committee, *Energy Regulation*, First Report Session 1996-97, HC 50-I, March 1997, p.170.

[13] MMC report on Northern Ireland Electricity (1997), *op. cit,*. paras. 10.41-10.42.

The reports will certainly serve to indicate how the MMC will go about its task. The procedures followed by the MMC in any reference made under the various regulatory régimes are basically the same as in a Fair Trading Act reference. But the investigation will be focused from the outset on the matters set out in the terms of reference – the disputed licence conditions or whatever – whereas in a Fair Trading Act reference it is for the MMC to identify the issues upon which it believes a public interest judgement is required. And whilst in a Fair Trading Act reference, the MMC is to have regard 'to all matters which appear to [it] relevant' in reaching such a judgement (section 84 of the Act), with references made under the regulatory régimes, the MMC must have regard to the duties of the regulator in reaching a public interest judgement. These vary from regulator to regulator but, broadly put, they include striking an appropriate balance between the needs of the company to finance its activities and future investment and the interest of consumers in the lowest possible prices. That the MMC's judgement has to be linked to the duties of the regulators is a key feature of the review process.

It means that the MMC's approach is not likely to be fundamentally different from that of the regulator. Indeed, the essential elements in the approach to how X should be determined seem now to be generally agreed, although the scope of any MMC inquiry will vary from reference to reference. There will need to be determined:

- the rate of return that a business needs in order to raise capital (cost of capital);

- the value of the capital base of the regulated business (RAB) to which the cost of capital should be applied;

- the way in which depreciation of fixed assets should be calculated;

- the capital expenditure requirements over the price control period;

- the operating expenditure requirements over the period.

Projection of these financial data will enable the MMC to calculate the revenue needed to finance the ongoing activities of the business and future investment, including the appropriate return to shareholders, compared with that generated by the current RPI-x formula, and to show the effect of modifications of that formula, whether on the net present value of revenues or accounting rate of return and other financial ratios.

While there may be a good measure of agreement about the approach and some of the uncertainties in the exercise may have been reduced in the light of the MMC's conclusions in a number of reports – for example, the MMC's estimate of the cost of capital (pre-tax, in real terms) of the utilities has generally been around 7 per cent – there remains room for debate, particularly perhaps on the valuation of RAB and the forecasts of capital and operating expenditure. The MMC is also likely to have to take a view on detailed points on the structure of the price cap formula such as cost pass through provisions, adjustments for volume variations, the use of historical or forecast RPI, and so forth.

The outcome of a reference will therefore be difficult, if not impossible, to predict, certainly at the stage when a company has to decide whether or not to accept a regulator's proposal. The question that may occur to the company at that stage is whether judgements of the MMC are not likely to favour the regulator rather than the company. After all, it may be said, the MMC and the sectoral regulators (and the CAA) are all part of the family of regulators. It would not be surprising if they were to see eye to eye on any issue.

When a reference is made the formal position is that all bets are off, so to speak, and the MMC will no doubt strive to show no favours to any party to the proceedings. Both the company and the regulator will want the MMC to do a thorough job (while continuing their 'cat and mouse game' where that is possible) and will be able and willing to provide the MMC with any information it may request or with other assistance to that end. In contrast, monopolists involved in Fair Trading Act investigations have little interest in helping the MMC to get to the bottom of issues: the incentive is to conceal rather than to reveal. But the regulator's proposals do represent the starting point to the reference and in so far as they are the result of a price review involving extensive consultations with customers and others with an interest (and may have been accepted by other companies in the industry), they can be expected to carry much weight with the MMC.

There is no easy way of analysing the MMC's reports to establish whether or not they tend to be supportive of the regulators. However, I have endeavoured to summarise the outcomes for five references. As well as the airports references, these exclude the references of gas reported on in 1993 the scope of which was far beyond the more usual licence modification reference (though the reports are significant in the development of the MMC's approach to the determination of x).

By way of preliminary, Table 1 sets out the dates of the various stages of the review process for these cases. If nothing else, it shows how protracted the process can be.

In Table 2 the RPI-x formulae sought by the regulator and rejected by the company, and the formulae derived from the modifications proposed by the MMC, are compared.

In most cases the two have not been far apart. And the DGWS expressed himself well satisfied with the MMC's conclusions in the reports on Portsmouth Water and South West Water Services (though he had no choice but to implement them), as did the Director General of Electricity Supply (DGES) with the MMC's proposals in its report on Scottish Hydro (though in South West Water Services, the MMC had allowed additional operating and capital expenditure, primarily to ensure that the cost of meeting new water standards would be met, and had also imposed a more rapid convergence of the company's high rate of return to the cost of capital than had the DGWS, and though the savings to consumers with the MMC's proposals on Scottish Hydro were slightly smaller than with the proposals of the DGES that the company had rejected).

Of course, small differences in x (or K) in a price control formula can make big differences to the accounting rate of return or allowed revenues. And in the British Gas and Northern Ireland Electricity cases, the differences were more significant, particularly with the revised proposal which the DGGS put before the MMC during its inquiry after British Gas had rejected the proposal that she had hoped would avoid a reference. These differences are more clearly seen in Table 3. But the comparisons show that the MMC's conclusions were closer to the position taken by the regulator in the two cases than to that sought by the companies.

[*continued on p. 215*]

TABLE 1
The References: Some Dates

	Price Review Starts	*Date of Reference*	*MMC Report Published*	*Outcome*
Scottish Hydro	Oct. 1993 ('began consultations')	15 Nov. 94	15 June 95	Modifications 'in line with MMC proposals' published in Sept. 97
Portsmouth Water	July 1991 ('announced')	29 Sept. 94	28 July 95	Determination by MMC
Southwest Water	July 1991 ('announced')	29 Sept. 94	28 July 95	Determination by MMC
Northern Ireland Electricity	during 1995 ('initiated')	18 Sept. 96	25 April 97	Modification proposed 6 Aug. 97 Judicial Review sought 15 Aug. 97 Judicial Review granted 29 Sept. 97
British Gas	Spring 1995 ('began work on the review')	14 Oct. 96	18 June 97	Modification proposed 14 Oct. 97

TABLE 2:
RPI-x Comparison of DG Proposals and MMC Conclusions

Scottish Hydro Report (May 1995)
Distribution

	1995/96-1999/2000:	
DG	RPI – 1	
	1995/96:	1996/97:
MMC	RPI – 1	RPI – 2

Supply

	1995/96-1999/2000
DG	RPI – 2
MMC	RPI – 2

Portsmouth Water Report (June 1995)

	1995/96-2005	
DG	RPI – 1.5	
	1995/96-1999/2000	2000-2005
MMC	RPI – 1.5	RPI – 0.5

Soth West Water Report (June 1995)

	1995/96	1996/97-1999/2000	2000-2005
DG	RPI + 1.5	RPI + 1	RPI
MMC	RPI + 1	RPI + 1*	RPI

*The K Factor to be 0.5% in 1996/97 to avoid the need for retrospective changes in the current year.

Northern Ireland Electricity Report (April 1997)

		1997/98	1998/99-2001/02
Transmission and Distribution	DG	Po 30	RPI – 2
	MC	Po 25	RPI – 2
Supply	DG	Po 43.9	RPI – 1.5
	MMC	Po 42	RPI – 2

British Gas Report (June 1997)

	1997/98	1998/99-2001/02
DG	Po 20*	RPI – 2.5
MMC	Po 21	RPI – 2.5

* In a revised proposal during the inquiry, raised to Po 29%

TABLE 3: Projections Compared

Northern Ireland Electricity Report (April 1997) Period 1997/98 - 2001/02	*MMC*	*DGES (NI)*	*NIE*
Transmission and Distribution			
Allowed revenues £million 1996/97 prices PV @ 7%	575	535	650
Asset valuation April 1997 £million 1996/97 prices	475	463	523
Cost of capital %	7	7	7.5 subsequently raised to 9
Capital expenditure gross £million 1996/97 prices	350	319	389

British Gas Report (1997) Period 1997/98 - 2001/02	*MMC*	*OFGAS Initial Position*	*OFGAS Revised Position*	*BG*
Allowed revenues £million 1996 prices PV @ 7%	11,979	11,876	10,341	13,506
Asset valuation April 1997 £million 1996 prices MMC basis CCA basis	11.6	12.4	10.9	11.8 17.0
Cost of capital %	7	7	7	8
Capital expenditure £million 1996 prices	4,054	4,025	2,389	4,476

The number of reports is too small to draw any firm conclusions. For the most part, decisions on price controls are taken by the regulator with the agreement of the company. Where a company has disputed a proposed modification or determination, and triggered a reference to the MMC, the MMC has been generally supportive of the regulator. Not uncritically so, of course, and not on every issue, but the complexity of the exercise facing the MMC, and the amount of work that the regulator will already have put in, make it unlikely that the MMC will steer a completely contrary course. It will be particularly unlikely that the MMC will do so if the reference is concerned with one or two companies only out of several that are subject to control, as in water. And where the MMC's conclusions do not echo the views of the regulator, a company still has to face up to the possibility, in a licence modification reference, that the MMC's proposals will not be implemented by the regulator.

The Follow-Up Stage

To recap on the legal position, where the MMC concludes that there are adverse effects of the present control that can be remedied by a licence modification, the Director General shall make such modifications as appear requisite for the purpose and, before doing so, shall have regard to the modifications proposed by the MMC in its report. There then has to be a consultation on the Director General's proposals. To the licensee, the discretion that the regulator has in responding to an MMC report will seem one-sided, for the regulator is most unlikely to take a view more sympathetic to the company than that of the MMC.

I imagine that one reason for this feature of the system is the possibility that the MMC might come up with modifications which the Director General might see practical difficulties in implementing. After all, this has been the experience with some recommendations of the MMC in reports on Fair Trading Act references. And it needs to be borne in mind that licence modification references are not confined to licence conditions relating to prices. The reference of telephone number portability was such a case. In its report the MMC set out how it thought the principal elements in the costs of establishing number portability should be recovered but left it to the Director General of Telecommunications (DGT) to incorporate them in a revised licence condition.[14] As the regulator has the on-going responsibility for enforcing licence conditions, there is logic in the regulators being bound by the MMC's public interest findings (as applies with other types of reference) but not necessarily by the particular modifications proposed by the MMC to remedy adverse effects. The presumption would seem to follow that the regulator should not seek to reopen in a fundamental way the issues that had been put before the MMC in the reference. This appears to be the position taken by the DGT. He has stated that he 'would not wish to depart from the substance of any licence modifications proposed by the MMC in its reports'.[15]

In two recent cases the relevant Director General has had well-publicised difficulties in accepting the MMC's proposed licence modifications. In its report concerned with price restrictions in British Gas's licence on the transportation and storage services provided by TransCo, the licence modification proposed by the MMC included an amendment to deal with the effect on TransCo's revenue of fluctuations in the volume of gas transported. After publication of the report in May 1997 and the commencement of discussions with British Gas, the DGGS announced in July that she was minded not to accept the MMC proposal because more recent forecasts of volumes than those used by the MMC showed that the modification would give TransCo a larger revenue than that considered necessary by the MMC and hence would lead to smaller reductions in gas prices than the MMC had suggested. British Gas argued that 'good regulatory practice requires that the MMC report is implemented in full',[16] while the DGGS countered that she could not do that without neglecting her duty to protect consumers. Eventually an alternative modification was devised, and accepted by British Gas, which aims to protect consumers should higher volumes than assumed by the MMC materialise (as forecast by OFGAS) while preserving some elements of the MMC's original

---

[14] Monopolies and Mergers Commission, *Telephone Number Portability: a report on a reference under section 13 of the Telecommunications Act 1984*, 1995, para. 1.16.

[15] Director General of Telecommunications, 'Submission to the Review of Utility Regulation', September 1997, para. 5.13.

[16] TransCo Press Release, July 1997.

proposal.[17]

The second case concerns the price controls in the licences of Northern Ireland Electricity and the modifications proposed by the MMC for its Transmission and Distribution business. The Director General of Electricity Supply for Northern Ireland (DGNI) had a number of reservations about the MMC's proposals but the main one proved to be the valuation put on Northern Ireland Electricity's asset base. The DGNI set an initial market value (IMV) based on the share price at the end of the first day's trading which he considered a sounder guide to the value of the shareholder's investment than either the book value of the assets or the valuation represented by the flotation price. The MMC accepted the approach but concluded that the IMV should be uplifted (by 7.5 per cent) noting, *inter alia*, that this would be consistent with the approach of other regulators.[18] In April 1997, on publication of the report, the DGNI said he was minded not to accept the MMC's recommendation and the modification he proposed in August was predicated on an IMV with no uplift. He said that he was satisfied that the company could finance its activities at the lower level of revenue (£538.5 million in net present value terms for the five-year control period compared with the MMC's £575 million) and that to allow more would be inconsistent with his duty to protect consumers. The upshot would be an initial price reduction (Po) of 29 per cent compared with 25 per cent with the MMC's modifications.[19]

The company sought, and was granted, leave to apply for a judicial review of the DGNI's decision. It said:

'The MMC is the recognised "court of appeal" for resolving differences between companies and their regulators. The DGNI's

---

[17] See OFGAS, *BG Transportation and Storage: The Director General's Price Control Proposals, April 1997 – March 2002, Notice of Proposed Licence Modifications*, 14 November 1997.

[18] MMC report on Northern Ireland Electricity (1997), *op cit.*, paras. 2.64-2.97.

[19] Director General of Electricity Supply for Northern Ireland, Press Releases, 28 April 1997, 6 August 1997.

challenge to the integrity of the MMC process is inherently very damaging to the prospects of an orderly system of regulation.'[20]

It is clear from the legislation that a Director General is not bound by the MMC's conclusions on a licence modification but the extent of his discretion in a particular case will depend upon how precisely the MMC has specified the adverse effects of the present control and the way those effects would be remedied or prevented by its proposal. The judgement in the judicial review of the DGNI's decision will clarify the position, including, no doubt, the interpretation to be given to the phrase 'have regard to' in respect of the modifications put forward by the MMC.

But the DGNI has reopened an issue (the valuation of assets) which the MMC might have been expected to resolve. It heard all the arguments of the parties and devoted a considerable part of the report to assessing them. It does seem to me an issue of more 'substance' than that raised by the DGGS's response in the Transco licence modification case. Finally, there is the point that if the same asset valuation issue had come up in a reference of a price determination of a water company (as well it might), then the issue would have been settled by the MMC. It is difficult to see any logical reason for such an anomalous situation.

RPI-x and the New Competition Law

As mentioned earlier, the Competition Bill before Parliament will make fundamental changes to the general competition law of the United Kingdom and to the institutional machinery by which the law is enforced. The changes do not affect the process I have been discussing so far by which disputed licence modifications and price determinations of the DGWS are referred to the MMC, except that the functions of the MMC will pass to the Competition Commission. The same holds for mandatory references under the Airports Act. But the way the sectoral Directors General carry out their regulatory duties may be affected by the changes to the competition law.

The important change in this context is the introduction into UK law of a prohibition of conduct that amounts to an abuse of a

---

[20] Northern Ireland Electricity, Press Release, 15 August 1997.

dominant position. The language of the prohibition closely follows Article 86 of the Treaty of Rome.[21]

The Fair Trading Act provisions relating to monopoly references are to remain on the statute book (again the functions of the MMC relating thereto will pass to the Competition Commission), not least because powers arising from a monopoly reference include that of requiring divestment, a remedy that would otherwise not be available. But it is intended that scale monopoly references will largely be replaced by enforcement of the new prohibition.[22] The sectoral Directors General may make monopoly references under the present legislation but they have not used the power, presumably because they have believed control through the licence mechanism to be more effective. The making of monopoly references has in practice been a matter for the Director General of Fair Trading (DGFT).[23]

Some monopoly references have led to the introduction of price controls. Since the contraceptives sheaths report in 1982, the MMC has recommended capping of the salt prices of British Salt Ltd. in 1986 and of the advertising rates of the Yellow Pages division of British Telecommunications plc in 1996.[24] It also recommended price capping of certain gluten-free and low-protein products in a report in 1995 on a completed merger.[25]

In none of these reports, in contrast to those on regulatory references, is there much discussion of how x was, or might be, determined. In each case, the price cap was relatively mild, with x's between 1 per cent and 2 per cent (in salt, the x was raised in 1992 from 1 per cent to 2 per cent following a review by the Office of

---

[21] To become Article 82 as a result of changes made by the Amsterdam Treaty.

[22] A scale monopoly exists where one person or firm accounts for 25 per cent or more of the supply in the United Kingdom or a part of the United Kingdom (or acquires such a proportion).

[23] A notable exception was the reference of gas made by the Secretary of State in 1992 and intended to enable the MMC to inquire into the gas market as a whole when the Gas Act references made by the DGGS were limited to the tariff market.

[24] Monopolies and Mergers Commission, *White Salt*, Cmnd. 9778, 1986; *Classified Directory Advertising Services*, Cm. 3171, 1996.

[25] Monopolies and Mergers Commission, *Nutricia Holdings Ltd and Valio International UK Ltd*, Cm. 3064, 1995.

Fair Trading). Having found the monopolist's profits to be excessive and against the public interest, largely on the basis of a comparison with rates of return elsewhere in the economy, the intention seems to have been merely to put some downward pressure on prices while preserving an incentive to improve efficiency. In the case of Yellow Pages' charges for advertising in its classified telephone directories, the MMC deliberately recommended a mild control in an effort not to threaten the survival of a competitor, Thomson, and some small producers of local directories or the prospect of any further entry into the market. There is an obvious difficulty in combining control of the prices of a dominant firm and the encouragement of competition. As the classified telephone directories market has some of the characteristics of a natural monopoly, a stronger price control might have been justified in this case.

Under the new law, it will primarily be for the DGFT to decide whether a company's prices or pricing policy amount to the abuse of a dominant position. The Bill, like Article 86, includes 'unfair prices' in the (short) list of examples of possible abuses. If he should find an infringement, a financial penalty can be imposed by the DGFT and I imagine that this will be more likely than a direction that a firm's prices be controlled whether by an RPI-x formula or otherwise. If there is an appeal against the DGFT's decision, which is likely certainly in the early days of the new law, it will be for an appeals tribunal of the Competition Commission to decide whether a price is unlawful, and the penalty or direction made by the DGFT to bring the infringement to an end appropriate.

As far as the utilities are concerned, the Competition Bill provides the sectoral Directors General with concurrent powers with the DGFT to enforce the prohibitions (although this is proving one of the more controversial features of the Bill mainly on the grounds that it could lead to inconsistencies in the interpretation and application of the law). A stronger competition law will strengthen the hand of the regulators. As and when competition develops in a regulated sector, it will be more feasible to limit the extent of the control exercised through the licensing mechanism and rely on the competition law to combat anti-competitive conduct and to protect consumers – regulation with a lighter touch as originally envisaged.

Even where control by licensing continues, a stronger competition law will be valuable not least because the possibility of financial penalties for anti-competitive or abusive conduct should be more of a deterrent than are the present arrangements. The Directors Generals' knowledge of their sector and their experience in licence enforcement should put them in a good position to decide whether conduct amounts to the abuse of a dominant position. As with enforcement by the DGFT, this could include 'unfair' pricing by a utility and, as with the DGFT, any decision taken under the prohibition would be appealable to the Competition Commission.

While, in principle, a regulator may see a new, stronger competition law as an alternative to price control through licensing, I expect that there will be relatively few cases. The prohibition will be more effective in dealing with predatory and exclusionary conduct than with so-called exploitative conduct. This is because of the difficulty of establishing a standard against which a price that seems 'high' or appears 'excessive' can be said to be unlawful.

The Bill requires that, as far as possible, questions arising under the new law should be dealt with 'in a manner which is consistent with the treatment of corresponding questions arising in Community law in relation to competition within the Community' (clause 58(I)). In the leading Community case (and there are not many), the European Court declared that a detailed analysis of costs would be required before any judgement could be reached, and added that the question to be asked is 'whether the difference between the costs actually incurred and the price actually charged is excessive, and if the answer to this question is in the affirmative to consider whether a price has been charged which is either unfair in itself or when compared to other competing products'.[26] Not very helpful; the MMC has, of course, been analysing costs and reaching its own judgement on whether prices are 'excessive' in monopoly references over many years. After he had reviewed reports on monopoly references published between 1977 and 1991, one writer concluded that

> 'as a broad generalisation ... prices were unlikely to have been found excessive unless rates of return were at least 50 per cent above the national average ... and that rates of more than twice the average could

---

[26] Case 27/76. *United Brands v Commission* [1978] ECR207, [1978] 1 CMLR429, para. 252.

escape condemnation in the absence of aggravating circumstances'.[27]

The MMC would reject any implication of a rule of thumb. A judgement has to be reached in the circumstances of the case. But the point to be made is that the UK authorities, whether the DGFT or a sectoral Director General, will no doubt be expected to apply less impressionistic criteria before a price is found to be an abuse of a dominant position and unlawful. The rulings of the appeal tribunals of the Competition Commission can be expected to be influential in bringing this about. But in adjudicating on any pricing case under the new competition legislation, the tribunals will operate quite separately from the groups of members of the Competition Commission who will be charged to conduct the regulatory references. It will be a pity if they are not able to tap the experience and expertise that has been built up from those references.

Conclusion

A number of observations about the system and how it has operated can be offered by way of conclusions to this paper. First, the MMC has consistently argued that the incentive properties of the RPI-x technique make it preferable to rate-of-return regulation or profit-sharing schemes. Thus in the 1997 report on gas, the MMC say:

'In our view the RPI-x approach provides a strong incentive to improve efficiency. We have seen no convincing evidence that any alternative system would better protect the public interest in the present circumstances of this industry. Profit sharing would represent a move towards a system of annual regulation based on rate of return which could reduce incentives to improve efficiency and give rise to practical difficulties in measuring profitability with scope for dispute and the need for constant intervention by the regulator.'[28]

This is very much in line with the views of the regulators.

Second, the MMC reports, including its reports on mandatory references on the regulation of airports, have undoubtedly contributed significantly to an emerging consensus on the principles

---

[27] N. Gardner, *A Guide to United Kingdom and European Union Competition Policy*, London: Macmillan, 2nd edition, 1996, p.147.

[28] MMC report on British Gas (1997), *op. cit.*, para. 2.18.

of how the RPI-x technique of price control should be applied, though clearly the regulators themselves have played a substantial part in this process.

Third, a company may feel that, if it comes to a reference, the MMC is likely to be supportive of the views of the regulator. In a general sense that seems to be so though, within the constraints of time and resources, the MMC does as much as it can to probe and cross-check the position taken by the regulator as well as the views of the company.

It is anomalous that the MMC makes determinations in references concerned with price controls on water companies but that with licence modification references concerned with price controls (and mandatory airport references) the regulator is not obliged to implement the MMC's proposals. Where the MMC's conclusions are binding, the regulator is likely to take particular note of the MMC's reasoning in his or her conduct of future reviews; in other words, the MMC's reports will be more telling as precedents than where the regulator has discretion. Moreover, further consideration of the issues by the regulator, and statutory consultation on his or her further proposals, extends the review process. But there is logic in the regulator having this discretion. He or she has the duty of balancing the needs of the company to finance its business and the interests of consumers and he or she has the responsibility for enforcing licence conditions. But the regulator should not seek to reopen an issue of substance that was instrumental in the case going to the MMC unless there has been a material change in circumstances relevant to the MMC's reasoning, as perhaps in the TransCo case, or the review process would be undermined. How extensive is the regulator's discretion will shortly be clarified in the judicial review of the DGNI's response to the MMC's report on Northern Ireland Electricity.

Fifth, the review process can be a protracted one, the MMC's stage taking between six and nine months (the maximum allowed by law). There have been calls for a 'fast-track' MMC procedure. It is difficult to see how an alternative procedure could be devised, given that a reference requires the MMC to look at the price control as a whole even if the dispute centred on one element, say, projected capital expenditure, and that all parties with an interest must have an opportunity to express their views (even if this duplicates consultation during a regulator's price review).

TABLE 4:
Group Members

Reference	Chairman	Members
Scottish Hydro	Odgers	Blight, Finney, Morris, Bromwich*, Kennedy*
Portsmouth Water	Odgers	Hodgson, Jenkins, Whittington, Owen*, Hughes*
South West Water	Odgers	Hodgson, Jenkins, Whittington, Owen, Hughes*
Northern Ireland Electricity	Morris	Beatson, Clothier, Jenkins, Munson, Kennedy
BAA	Morris	Beatson, Lyons, Prosser, Tracey, Whittington
British Gas	Odgers	Metcalfe, Stacey, Owen
Manchester Airport	Morris	Corbett, Halstead, Mortimer

* Members of specialist panels appointed to assist the MMC in references on disputed licence conditions or determinations in telecommunications, electricity and water. There are no such panels for gas (or railway) licence modification references or for Airport Act references.

The inquisitorial procedures of the MMC, backed by intensive staff work, may be time-consuming and demanding but I am sure they are best suited to reaching judgements on complex issues such as are involved in assessing an RPI-x price control.

In the case of telecoms, water and electricity references, the group of MMC members responsible for the case has to include members of specialist panels set up at privatisation to supplement the existing membership It is not clear why no such panel was created for gas licence modification references or later for railways. I imagine that there have not been enough references for the value of these panels to be tested. However, as useful as the technical expertise that these panel members might bring – but which could presumably be acquired in other ways – must be knowledge of regulatory issues. The RPI-x reports are a considerable contrast to others produced by the MMC in their detail and in the extent to which they involve both intellectual and practical issues. There are members with the appropriate knowledge and a further specialist panel might not be particularly useful. But the learning curve must be a steep one. Some overlapping membership in the groups tackling these references would seem desirable. No doubt this is difficult to bring about with part-time members with other commitments and a need to avoid any conflict of interest. Table 4 shows that there has been a limited amount of overlapping membership in the seven most recent regulatory references.

It will be interesting, however, to see how the appeals tribunals of the Competition Commission develop when the new competition law comes into force. The tribunals will not be investigatory bodies. They will be akin to a specialist competition court. They will hear issues as presented by the parties, documented in the evidence and exposed by cross-examination. However, while the appeals tribunals are destined to become important bodies in the UK system of competition law, I do not see them being able to take on the role of the MMC (which in the future will pass to the Competition Commission in its reporting function) in regulatory references. I do not think they can be regarded as a fourth model of the review process. Nor, in fact, do I foresee many cases of 'excessive' pricing as an alleged abuse of a dominant position under the new competition legislation, though such cases have been not uncommon under the monopoly provisions of the Fair Trading Act.

Speaking at a conference in December 1991, the then Chairman of the MMC, Sir Sidney Lipworth, mentioned that there had been only one licence modification reference (of chatlines). He predicted that the 'instances of fall-out between regulator and regulated may grow'. He went on to suggest that this 'may be beneficial to the overall regime which under different regulators may be subject to inconsistent treatment. Each industry and the regulator may, after a time, welcome a central view of its particular problems'.[29] Fall-out has certainly increased though companies still appear wary of taking their case to the MMC. It must be for those involved to say whether they welcome the MMC's rather greater involvement. But to this outsider it does seem that the 'central view', as Sir Sidney put it, has

---

[29] Sir Sidney Lipworth, 'The Developing Role of the Monopolies and Mergers Commission', Mimeo., 17 December 1991.

been invaluable not just in assisting in the development of a more consistent approach to regulatory issues, both as between sectors and over time, but also in providing a necessary check on the way the regulators use their discretionary powers.

CHAIRMAN'S COMMENTS

Colin Robinson

MARTIN HOWE'S PAPER IDENTIFIES AND EXPLAINS the key roles of both the Monopolies and Mergers Commission (MMC) and price capping in Britain's regulatory régime – even if there have been fewer references to the MMC over price caps than was apparently envisaged when the system was established. One reason for the relatively few references may be that the original price controls appear (with the aid of hindsight) on the 'generous' side. But, in addition, Martin identifies a number of reasons why companies may feel uncertain whether a visit to the Commission will be worth the opportunity cost of all the management time they will devote to the inquiry.

Martin points out some of the apparent inconsistencies of the present system. There are three models of the review process:

- a mandatory reference before any change is made (the Civil Aviation Authority and airports). Though the reference is mandatory, the MMC's conclusions are not binding on the regulator;

- a reference when there is a dispute, with the MMC's conclusions binding on the regulator (water);

- a reference when there is a dispute, with the MMC's conclusions not binding on the regulator (other utilities).

It is not clear to me that these 'inconsistencies' matter. They do not appeal to one's sense of the neat and tidy but it may be beneficial to have some such differences whilst we are feeling our way towards the best system of regulation. It is false to imagine that there is some 'correct' way of regulating all privatised industries which could have been discovered at the beginning.

In any case, as Martin argues, mandatory references may be a thing of the past. They linger for airports but the Department of

Transport has recommended they be replaced by references only in the case of disputes. If references became mandatory, the MMC would be overwhelmed and the authority of the regulators would be undermined. As it happens, in most cases the regulators and the regulated companies have agreed without MMC intervention.

A more obvious anomaly is between the ability of the MMC to resolve disputes in water (for example, over asset valuations) but, as we have seen in 1997, not in gas and electricity where the regulators do not have to accept the MMC's views. However, water is different. There is virtually no competition, unlike gas and electricity. Since water is a regulated industry, evidently with little prospect of turning into a competitive market, the regulator has more power than in the other utilities where competition is taking over from regulation. Perhaps the anomaly is more apparent than real: the MMC can be viewed as a counterweight to the monopoly power of the industry regulator!

Martin makes the interesting point that the MMC and the regulator are likely to have similarities of views. The Commission, as part of the regulatory process, seems bound to be impressed by all the work carried out by the industry regulator, including consultations with consumers, before a reference is made. Moreover, the MMC is enjoined to have regard to the duties of the regulator. Martin's tables, though limited to a few references, do indeed show that MMC conclusions tend not to be very different from those of the regulator. Out of interactions between the MMC and industry regulators has emerged a 'list' for price control references, which includes estimates of the value of the capital base, capital costs, operating costs, depreciation and the rate of return.

One of Martin's suggestions is that, as competition develops, we may see (as originally intended) the emergence of 'regulation with a light touch' – less emphasis on price controls and more on general competition law. I think everyone who was originally involved with privatisation and regulation in Britain must be concerned that there is a greater weight of regulation than had been intended. I am inclined to think that is more a consequence of misguided privatisation schemes than of regulatory failure. But that is water under the bridge. Looking forward, assuming regulators have concurrent powers with the Director General of Fair Trading (DGFT), their hands should be strengthened: their knowledge gives them better knowledge than anyone else into whether or not a dominant position is being abused. It does indeed seem appropriate that, as competition substitutes for regulation, laws which regulate competition should take over from detailed regulation.

A final issue raised by Martin is a good subject for speculation by an expert audience. How will the appeals tribunals of the MMC's successor, the Competition Commission, work in cases in which the DGFT or the industry regulator has decided a dominant position is being abused? We shall not know until they begin to operate but views are no doubt already forming on this important matter.

8

WHAT NEXT IN UK
RAILWAYS?
John Welsby
British Railways Board

Introduction

OVER THIRTY YEARS AGO I worked in the electricity industry for the well-known economist Ralph Turvey. He thought it desirable for me to undertake post-graduate work at the LSE which I duly did. He only had one stipulation: in his opinion sound micro-economists were few and far between – even at the LSE – so if I was to be released to attend the School the condition was that I could choose any optional subject I wanted as long as my tutor was Michael Beesley. I have often wondered what the impact on my career might have been had Michael been interested in agriculture rather than transport.

It was with particular pleasure therefore that I received the invitation to participate in the IEA and LBS series of Lectures on Regulation organised by Michael. Unlike most of the speakers in the 1997 series I have no particular expertise, either practical or academic, in regulatory matters; indeed I hail from a generation of economists for whom the term regulator was as dirty a word as cartel. In transportation it was the era of Geddes and the sweeping away of much regulation affecting road freight operations, at least as far as quantity licensing was concerned. In other spheres the principal issues revolved around efficient resource allocation, and the pricing, output and investment decisions that ensued. Cost-benefit analysis was beginning to emerge as a practical tool and contemporary developments in economic theory were considered useful; the theory of second-best, optimisation under indivisibility constraints and the Chicago School views on forms of competition, spring to mind. None of this could be entrusted to people called 'regulators'.

Times have changed. Regulators now rule the roost in their particular areas of what was once termed public sector economics. But I cannot help wondering if the application of economic understanding to these issues has progressed at anything like the rate at which the structures themselves have changed. An article on regulating transport in the UK by Dieter Helm[1] brought this question to mind. What struck me about the article was that it was discussing the sorts of issue I referred to above in exactly the same way we would have discussed it years ago and arriving at the same solutions. The difference was the assumption that a regulatory régime would be responsible for the implementation of the integrated charging solution proposed, whereas I believe that a hypothetical 40-year-old article would have been less prescriptive about implementation.

The difference is entirely logical. The structure of the utilities today is very different from what it was in those days. Private ownership is now the norm, as is the involvement of capital markets, and their requirements differ markedly from the previous requirements of government and the Treasury. For obvious reasons markets do not like regulation by politicians; far better to have an independent regulator adjudicating on prices and other aspects of service quality.

But the question that stuck in my mind after reading the article was why, if economists have been recommending similar solutions to transport policy problems for the past 40 years, has so little notice been taken of them? For, in practical terms, I do not believe that, in the late 1990s, the transport system exhibits much more economic rationality than it did 30 to 40 years ago. Congestion on the roads has become consistently worse as economists would forecast in the absence of a pricing mechanism; integration between public transport modes has not improved and in some instances has worsened as a result of de-regulation and privatisation of bus services; and the application of value-for-money criteria to railway operations and investment decisions has shown little, if any, progress.

In this paper I intend to discuss some of the aspects of this problem in the context of railways. I start by considering what I

---

[1]   Dieter Helm, 'Regulating Transport in the UK', *Proceedings*, The Chartered Institute of Transport, Vol. 6, No. 3, September 1997.

term 'The Railway Dilemma' and previous attempts at resolution. We then consider privatisation as a solution to the railway dilemma and conclude that, whatever its other merits, it still leaves us with many of the fundamental problems faced by the previous régime. Various aspects of economic control of the industry are examined, before suggestions are made for 'what next' for the industry.

The Railway Dilemma

Michael Beesley referred in last year's lecture[2] to the 40-year battle to control subsidy in the railway; I would re-formulate this slightly as a 40-year battle between the political imperative of sustaining an extensive railway network and the financial imperative of containing public expenditure. This is what I term the Railway Dilemma. It is a classic economic problem demanding a stable solution to a set of price/output/subsidy equations, as outlined by Helm.

Beesley expressed concern about the perceived frailty of the privatisation model in the face of a renewed battle for public funds, but expressed his hope that, even in the face of such pressures, independent assessment of required railway output and its consequent independent translation into required subsidy would be retained. I share his views about the frailty of the existing system to a renewed battle for public funds, but would go further by predicting that such a battle is likely. In consequence, we may not be much closer to attaining a stable solution to the basic equations than we were pre-privatisation, in which case I shall argue that Beesley's hopes of retaining independence on required railway output and subsidy level are unlikely to be realised.

Previous Attempts at Resolution

It has long been recognised that the social welfare function for railway services, as reflected through government, results in a substantially larger and more intensive railway network than would be the case if sole reliance were placed on the effective demand function exhibited by the travelling public. Most attempts to solve

---

[2] Michael Beesley, 'Rail: The Role of Subsidy in Privatisation', in M.E. Beesley (ed.), *Regulating Utilities: Broadening the Debate*, IEA Readings 46, 1997.

The Dilemma have centred around bringing these two functions into closer, if not complete, correspondence.

- In the late 1950s and early 1960s it was thought that investment was the solution. The argument centred round the proposition that the replacement of old worn-out equipment would release sufficient 'x' efficiency and 'y' efficiency gains (using Beesley terminology) that subsidy would no longer be required. It failed.

- This was followed by an attempt to solve the dilemma by improving allocative efficiency. Beeching proposed that a solution could be found by cutting the network size substantially and subsequently building on the healthy remaining parts. A change of government terminated these plans before they had time to work themselves through, so we shall never know whether they would have worked. What is undoubtedly true is that the subsidy bill for the railway would have been unmanageable had Beeching Part 1 not been implemented.

- The next attempt, in the late 1960s, involved the application of rudimentary cost-benefit analysis to the railway on a service-by-service basis. It collapsed in the early 1970s due to estimating difficulties on both the cost and demand sides and the weight of its own superstructure.

- By the mid-1970s attempts at economic rationality had disappeared and the Public Service Obligation system was set up. This essentially said that BR should endeavour to maintain the *status quo* in terms of output levels whilst remaining within an overall financial constraint. The level of the constraint was tightened on a year-by-year basis and it was made clear that remaining within the financial constraint was the paramount consideration.

- The dilemma flared up again by the early 1980s with the then Board claiming serious consequences from a 'crumbling edge of quality'. The consequence was the setting up of the Serpell Inquiry into Railway Finances, which concluded that balance could be maintained by greater efforts towards improving productivity on the part of the Board allied to firmer forward guidance on the availability of funds. The government responded by setting objectives for the Board for three years ahead for the amount of subsidy that would be available. Surprisingly, this was the first time that government had set unambiguous forward-looking objectives for the Board.

• The clarity did not last long. Initially targets were set in terms of performance measured on a fairly standard profit and loss basis, but government's wider economic concerns meant that emphasis quickly changed to pure cash targets, the External Financing Limit (EFL). Whatever its merits as a public expenditure control in the macro-economic sphere, it was a poor measure of the performance of the business and set up some unfortunate trade-offs between the current performance of the business and its capital expenditure programme. By the early 1990s cash was certainly king and the transport role of the railway and the efficiency with which it was fulfilling that role had slipped from view.

Although the 1980s were successfully negotiated, the onset of economic recession at the beginning of the 1990s, allied to the recommendations of the Hidden Report into the Clapham Rail Crash, meant that railway finances once more came to the forefront of government concerns. The 1980s had also seen the privatisation programme developing considerable momentum, to the point where industries that would have been judged unsellable a decade earlier could now be considered for privatisation. Why not adopt this solution for the railways?

Privatisation and the Railway Dilemma
The attraction to the previous government of using privatisation as a means of resolving the railway dilemma was obvious. First, it was thought that private sector entrepreneurialism would bring a far more innovative approach to management than had the public sector, whose managers were insulated by the fact that government will always stand behind a state corporation in the last resort. Second, by opening up the industry to on-rail competition this level of innovation would be further enhanced. Third, the government would be relieved of the substantial levels of capital expenditure that would be necessary were the railways to remain in the public sector. Finally, the centralised power of the trade unions would be

dealt a serious blow if decentralisation accompanied privatisation. Together these factors led the government to conclude that privatisation would lead to a much better railway at much reduced cost to the Exchequer on both current and capital account. The dilemma would be resolved.

I should make clear at this juncture that I welcome the injection of private ownership into railway affairs, not because there is any substance to the oft repeated suggestion that private sector management is somehow more competent than its public sector counterpart – they are in many cases the same people – but because private shareholders bring a more focused framework within which management can operate than does a government shareholder. Under state ownership government was shareholder – appointing directors, setting objectives, and reserving unto itself important decisions; banker – the only one in town and prone to idiosyncrasy; and the principal customer who provided financial support for non-commercial activities. In addition, government has responsibilities for managing macro-economic affairs and setting the climate for the economy as a whole. The result is continuous and inconsistent interference in the management of the company. These conflicts were present for all the old nationalised industries but the temptation to intervene always seemed stronger on the railways than in other sectors. Playing trains has always been seductive for politicians.

The model of privatisation for the railway spelled out in the 1992 White Paper envisaged rectification of many of these problems. It saw a relatively high level of managerial freedom being given to train operators to adjust their operations to accommodate market requirements. Control by the regulator was needed to curb a public sector Railtrack's monopoly power, but for the rest of the railway controls were to be kept to a minimum. The rolling stock companies (ROSCOs) were not perceived as requiring regulation as competitive markets were expected to develop rapidly; freight operations could safely be left to market forces, given the dis-aggregated structure envisaged, and even passenger operations were not thought to be in a position to exercise much monopoly power, with the sole exception of London commuter services. In consequence, passenger fares did not need to be controlled, except London commuter fares, and franchisees were seen as having wide discretion over output levels. A minimum service level was to be specified for franchisees, but this was seen as a 'floor' substantially below previous BR levels. Operating in this loosely regulated manner was thought adequate as market incentives would be sufficient to bring about improvements in allocative efficiency as well as 'x' and 'y' efficiencies.

The passage of the requisite Bill through Parliament, together with early attempts to implement the proposals, brought significant change. This was a period in which the benefits of the government's proposals were less than self evident, even to a number of Conservative MPs. A large number of amendments was accepted during the Committee stage of the Bill and even following Royal Assent further substantial changes were made to the proposals in the light of political or market pressure, perceived or real. The minimum service requirements were changed to passenger service requirements, which reduced franchisees' ability to reduce output levels; the adoption of controlled 'fares baskets' and the postponement of 'open access competition' for the passenger railway, and the sale of most of the freight railway to a single company are well-known examples. None of these changes arose from *ex ante* decisions to alter the basic model, rather they were adopted as expedients to circumvent particular problems that had arisen in the process of execution. The effects of these changes on the smooth operation of the privatised railway were given scant consideration and in some cases it is doubtful if the implications were even understood – for example, the franchised passenger railway finished up with fewer managerial degrees of freedom than were previously enjoyed by BR under state ownership.

The failure to execute the privatisation proposals in line with a well understood plan meant that substantial uncertainty attached to the robustness of the solutions finally executed. Consider passenger operations.

- As a result of pressure on the privatisation timetable the Franchising Director undertook no systematic benchmarking of the levels of improvement that a franchisee could reasonably be expected to deliver; indeed, to the best of my knowledge no benchmarking at all took place beyond the stage of Initial Bids. This was the case whether one looked at the issue from the point of view of what was offered by the franchisee or what was required from the Franchise Director to enable the franchisee to deliver; for instance, is the necessary capacity available?

• Initially the market was suspicious of the franchising process. With the passage of time this changed to the point where some bidders considered it essential to have one or more franchises in their portfolio for strategic reasons, almost irrespective of the terms.

The result was that the franchising programme yielded wild variations in the aggressiveness of successful bids. Table 1 shows an index, by company, of the reductions in support payments resulting from the franchising programme expressed as a proportion of passenger revenue plus own expenses. This is an unusual measure as income and costs are normally subtracted, but given that the majority of the cost base for a franchisee is fixed in the form of contracted payments to Railtrack and the ROSCOs, the absolute values of the remaining cash flows give a useful measure of the controllable sums against which reductions in subsidy must be achieved.

The Table shows the huge variability in contract conditions that emerged from the franchising process, with some companies offering over 25 times the subsidy improvement offered by Company A. It is possible to argue that this merely reflects the underlying economic strengths of the different franchises, but experience of performance under BR ownership would not substantiate such a view; indeed my own expectations would be that Company A has more potential for improvement than most.

Such variability raises obvious questions. If Companies I to L made deliverable offers why were offers A to C accepted? The answer is clearly that they were the best offers on the table, but the figures highlight the short-sightedness of refusing to allow BR to bid, if only as the benchmark against which to determine the desirability of allowing a particular franchise to proceed at that point in time. Alternatively, one can raise questions about the probability that the more onerous franchises will be successfully delivered. This is the line that has been adopted by some commentators. Where reality lies between these two extremes only time will tell. My own forecast is that it will lie between the

Table 1: Reduction in Subsidy as a Proportion of Passenger Revenue + Own Expenses (at 1996/7 Prices)

Franchise Operator	2003/4 Index
Company A	7
Company B	47
Company C	77
Company D	85
Company E	92
Company F	106
Company G	118
Company H	143
Company I	143
Company J	150
Company K	160
Company L	189
Index: total subsidy/total passenger revenue + own expenses = 100	

extremes; some companies will make a lot of money, others are unlikely to deliver what has been promised.

If we assume that all the franchise offers are capable of delivery we run into a different problem. To the best of my knowledge no-one has added up all the aspirations of the franchisees to determine if they are deliverable on the supply side.

Figure 1 shows a rough estimate of the rail passenger volume implied in delivering the franchises; carryings must rise by a third over their 1994/5 levels by 2002/3 to attain levels not seen since the end of the Second World War. To this must be added the aspirations of the freight business. English, Welsh and Scottish Railways (EW&S) has set itself the task of tripling rail freight carryings over the next 10 years, attainment of which would yield volumes not seen since the 1950s. The question raised is obvious. Can these aspirations be accommodated with the infrastructure network as currently configured and, in the case of passenger operations,

Figure 1: Rail Passenger Volume: Billion Passenger Kilometres

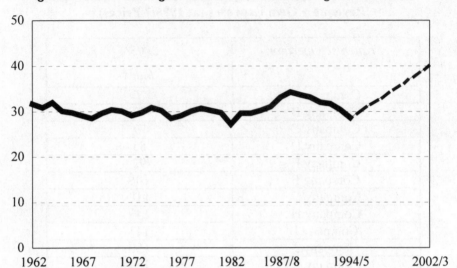

with the rolling stock currently, or likely to be, available within the relevant time-frame. If the aspirations cannot be accommodated, what are the implications for the Exchequer in bringing about the necessary equilibrium? Although there is no difficulty in posing such questions it appears impossible to give definitive answers.

This illustrates one of the serious shortcomings of the current structure; the reason that no answers are available is that no-one is responsible for providing such answers let alone ensuring that consistent solutions are delivered. Each player has a responsibility for a part of the whole, but overall strategic responsibility is missing. The lack of strategic focus is not confined to questions of consistency in the franchising process, it is a quite general problem. For example, plans are afoot to upgrade the West Coast Main Line. But who is responsible for ensuring that the result of such upgrading is in the best interests of the system as a whole, and whose criteria are they using? We hear much about tilting trains for the Inter-City elements, but what about the medium-term requirements of the other eight passenger train companies that utilise the line, or future freight requirements?

The principal point worthy of note is that if any significant changes occur to the *status quo* they will inevitably have implications for public expenditure or public policy, or both. Should any franchises suffer financial failure the options will be to re-let on the same output specification, presumably at greater cost to the exchequer, or to reduce the output specification to the point at which the franchise can be re-let for the same cost. I find it inconceivable that such decisions can be taken by other than government or its direct agent, following consultation with government. Similarly, any future developments to the system will entail trade-offs between public expenditure and output levels that can only realistically be taken by government. In this respect the privatised railway is fundamentally different from the other privatised utilities where price/output/investment decisions can be taken without having recourse to public funds.

Most economists will argue that from the point of resource use this difference is more apparent than real, and from a strict economic point of view they are correct. What matters is whether a particular decision to utilise resources is taken or not. The fact that in one case funds come from taxation whereas in another they come from consumers has little bearing on the matter; there may be some welfare implications deriving from differences in the ultimate incidence of the two funding mechanisms, but they are of second order. What such arguments fail to recognise is the constitutional difference between responsibilities for the two different funding mechanisms. Parliament has been prepared to devolve responsibility for decisions involving the level of charges to final consumers to a third party (a regulator). Parliament has *not* been prepared to devolve such responsibility in cases involving exchequer expenditures, nor in my judgement is it likely to do so. Ministers are responsible to Parliament for policy judgements involving public expenditure and accounting officers are responsible for efficient discharge of such funds. It is for this reason that Professor Beesley's hopes that the system can develop to the point of independent determination of railway output and subsidy appear to me to be unrealistic.

- This leads me to conclude that the previous government's hope that privatisation would provide a lasting solution to the Railway Dilemma will not, indeed cannot be, successful. The difficult trade-off decisions involving government expenditure and policy aspirations are present in the current system to exactly the same degree that they were present in the old. This is not to decry privatisation,

Table 2: Economic Control

	ORR	*OPRAF*
RAILTRACK	YES	NO
ROSCOS	NO	NO
TOCS	YES	YES
FREIGHT	NO	NO
OPEN ACCESS	YES	NO

Notes:
ORR is Office of the Rail Regulator.
OPRAF is Office of Passenger Rail Franchising.

as the new players may be more effective than their predecessors in improving 'x and y' efficiencies and the value of this must not be under-estimated. But to the extent that the Railway Dilemma involves questions of allocative efficiency, the privatisation process has actually made matters worse by introducing additional constraints on management, with the inevitable consequence that government and politics feature even more strongly at the centre of decisions on allocative efficiency. It is in this context that I see it as no accident that the value-for-money criteria that the Franchise Director was charged with producing have, so far, not gone into operation in any comprehensive way.

Aspects of Economic Control of the Industry
From the perspective of an interested observer there appear to be other economic aspects of the current arrangements that do not assist in resolving the Dilemma. They stem from the partial nature of the existing control framework for the industry and, within this, from the fact that responsibilities are ambiguously defined. Table 2 shows the economic controls exercised by the various parties in the current structure.

I consider each of these in turn:

Railtrack
Two years ago John Kay raised a number of fundamental questions about the future of UK regulation in an address to this group.[3] The

---

[3] John Kay, 'The Future of UK Utility Regulation', in M.E. Beesley (ed.), *Regulating Utilities:*

issue he termed 'the problem of legitimacy' has particular relevance for railways because of the involvement of both customers and taxpayers, and his strictures on the appropriate form of legal duties of corporations could well have been written with Railtrack in mind. But even if we eschew such radical thoughts there are still a number of questions about the effectiveness of the current regulatory régime.

The most obvious issue centres round the stock market valuation of the corporation and why there has been such a dramatic rise in share price over such a short period of time. Part of the explanation undoubtedly centres around the flotation price which did not fully reflect the underlying endowments, together with the fact that charges were fixed up to the point of the quinquennial review. But other factors will also have had an effect; approval of a relatively generous treatment of property profits, the financial benefits that have arisen to Railtrack from the operation of the performance régime and the efficiency gains available from their supply chain.

In the start-up arrangements for the industry provision was made for the regulator to review the level and structure of access charges and that review took place in 1994-5 ahead of privatisation. The regulator reduced the level of charges by 8 per cent and introduced a standard RPI-x formula for the remainder of the review period. The level of charges reflected his view of the level of funds required for investment and renewal over the period.

As with other regulated utilities the stage has been set for continued dialogue with Railtrack as to whether the levels of investment and renewal allowed for in the charging régime are being achieved. Concern on this score has led the regulator to seek, and achieve, a revision to Railtrack's licence which it is hoped will go some way towards rectifying matters. Nevertheless, the key issue, which has still to be resolved, is 'what does the access charge buy?' Roughly £2 billion of charges is levied but does it buy an investment and renewal programme – a set of inputs – or does it buy a modern equivalent asset railway – a set of outputs. If it is the latter, will we know it when we see it? Resolution of this issue is going to be crucial to the development of the railway.

Of equal interest is the fact that the access charging régime has economic characteristics quite unlike other regulated utility charges, with the possible exception of domestic water rates. For passenger operators access charges are almost entirely a fixed cost; some 91 per cent of the access charge is totally invariant to the level of use by the operator, and two-thirds of the remaining variable element pertains to electricity charges for traction current, where Railtrack acts as procurement agent for the industry. The consequence is that Railtrack is insulated from the final demand market for passenger services. The recently announced arrangements for the West Coast Main Line do involve Railtrack sharing revenue risk but this is a specific and voluntary arrangement covering enhancement of the system; equivalent revenue risk-sharing arrangements do not feature on the rest of the system.

From the perspective of the train operator access charges exhibit most of the characteristics of a tax; indeed, were I to feel provocative, I could be more explicit and relate the characteristics to a Poll Tax. This must lead us to expect that the regulator's decisions on the level of charge will feed through in a fairly direct manner to the level of bids received for franchises and hence to public expenditure. In effect, therefore, the regulator's decisions on access charges have direct, and potentially major, implications for the level of public expenditure needed to sustain the passenger railway. He stands in for the market-place in determining how much should be spent on the infrastructure and in ensuring that these sums are spent efficiently. This direct relationship between his decisions and requirements for public subsidy raises questions about the objectives and criteria that are brought to bear on such decisions.

These issues will be of major importance in the forthcoming quinquennial review of Railtrack's charges. The underlying profitability of the company, the strength of its balance sheet and its rating by shareholders suggest that, yet again, whatever the other benefits of privatisation, getting full value for the taxpayer is not one of them. The Regulator will have an interesting and highly significant choice to make about the regulatory asset base. I would argue that questions of charging structure rank almost as highly as questions of charging level. The current system of virtually fixed levies sends no economic signals and the question of exposing the infrastructure provider to the final market-place deserves further scrutiny.

ROSCOs

ROSCOs are not subject to regulation or any other form of economic control, other than general competition law. As indicated earlier, the previous government believed that a competitive market in the provision of rolling-stock would emerge and hence no other form of control was necessary. To date there is little evidence that substantial competition is emerging in the market for the existing rolling-stock fleet, nor are there grounds for thinking that it will in the foreseeable future. Competition can arise only when the potential supply of equipment is greater than the demand, and a number of factors are pertinent in considering the likelihood of such a condition occurring:

• The stock of equipment is large in relation to any realistic view of the net annual flow by which the size of the stock can be changed.

• Some 300 new vehicles per annum need to be purchased merely to stop the average age of the fleet rising. So far, new orders placed are barely sufficient to keep this equation in balance.

• Although the ROSCOs are being paid at a rate which would enable them to invest in new equipment, two of the three ROSCOs have not invested in any new vehicles at all. Nor does any mechanism exist to force them to invest.

• Many of the OPRAF contracts with franchisees envisage significant increases in services and carryings. Attainment of these increases will require the size of the fleet to increase.

• There are some indications that the ROSCOs are actively managing the size of the fleet available for leasing to ensure that excess equipment does not become available.

These factors lead me to conclude that there is likely to be excess demand for equipment, at least in the medium term, and certainly at the point at which most of the rolling-stock leases have to be renegotiated.

Remedial measures fall into two broad categories. It would be possible, subject to primary legislation, to bring charges for rolling-stock leases within the net of those agreements requiring the regulator's approval. This would probably only be necessary for the rolling-stock endowments received from BR at conception, that is, there are no grounds for regulating the prices of new equipment leased either from ROSCOs or manufacturers. Alternatively, reliance could be placed on creating a more competitive market by substantially increasing the flow of new vehicles into the fleet by means of the powers granted to OPRAF to underwrite vehicle acquisition under the 1993 Act. This would, of course, require Treasury approval. Manipulation of available fleet size by the ROSCOs could be addressed by an MMC referral.

It is for government to determine whether any action is needed to increase the public accountability of ROSCOs; what does seem clear is that unless some action is taken, along the lines outlined above, it will be very difficult for the Exchequer to satisfy itself that value for money is being obtained from these expenditures. The value for money issues are very similar to those outlined for Railtrack; by the time the first round of leases have expired the ROSCOs will have been repaid in full, together with interest, for the assets they purchased. Therefore capital charges should fall substantially on renewal.

The Franchises

The industry structure adopted by the previous government relieved franchisees of the requirement of funding capital-intensive operations. Assets are leased on medium-term contracts from the ROSCOs and Railtrack, with lease charges largely invariant to changes in final output over the period of the lease. This means that asset owners are insulated from risks that arise from the vagaries of the final market. Virtually all such risks reside with the franchisees.

I have suggested that Railtrack and the ROSCOs may be under-regulated. In contrast, given their risk-bearing character, questions arise as to whether the franchises are over-regulated. Table 3 outlines areas in which the regulator and OPRAF control aspects of the operation of the passenger franchises.

As can be seen from Table 3 the franchises are not only subject to detailed control, but the roles of the regulator and Franchising Director overlap, with the potential for confusion and even conflict. For example, one specifies in some detail the nature and extent of passenger services to be run, whilst the other gives detailed approval

Table 3: Regulation by ORR and OPRAF

	ORR	OPRAF
Fares Regulation		✓
National Railway Timetable	✓	
Disabled Access	✓	
Telephone Inquiry Bureau	✓	(✓)
Impartial Retailing	✓	(✓)
Routeing Guide	✓	(✓)
Through Ticketing	(✓)	✓
Multi-Modal Ticketing		✓
Discount Cards	(✓)	✓
Interavailability		✓
Information at Stations	✓	✓
Timetable Connections		✓
Passenger's Charter		✓
Complaints Handling	✓	(✓)

Note:
The absence of brackets indicates my understanding of who holds the primary responsibility; brackets indicate secondary responsibility. It would not surprise me if the principals involved were to disagree with this classification, but that merely makes my point. To this list must be added the interests of government and other official and unofficial bodies. The Rail Users Consultative Committees are an example of the former, Save our Railways the latter. The result is that the managerial degrees of freedom available to franchisees are very limited. The situation was summarised neatly by the principal of one company that had been successful in winning a franchise. Negotiations had been handled by a subordinate who attempted to explain the implications of the successful bid and the roles of the government, the regulator, and OPRAF. The principal's response was 'I fully understand the roles of government, the regulator, and OPRAF but could you explain one more time where I fit in.' The issue that must be faced is whether such arrangements are stable, particularly in the face of exogenous shocks to the system.

to the running of such services; one sets out the policy framework for ticket price caps, whilst the other rules on predatory pricing, and so on.

Although the regulator must have regard to the finances of the Franchise Director there is plainly the potential for conflict between this and his duty to promote certain policies towards the railway. I shall return to this in considering Open Access operations in the passenger business. The separation of responsibilities derives from the original privatisation model that envisaged a lightly regulated, internally competitive rail passenger industry, whereas we have finished up with a heavily regulated, non-competitive one. Unless there is to be a speedy return to the original concept, which seems extremely unlikely, there would appear to be an unanswerable case for clearing up the muddled set of arrangements that govern the franchises.

Freight

The freight business is subject to no economic regulation in the final markets other than that provided by general competition law. It does, of course, need its access contracts and associated arrangements approved by the regulator but in the field of final demand it is free of constraint. There would seem to be little case for altering these arrangements. The businesses are tackling an extremely competitive market with vigour, higher levels of investment are going into rail freight than for many decades, and the potential for open-access operators to enter the field remains. This is not to argue against policy measures designed to make competitive modes face more of the external costs they impose on society, rather to suggest that no further change to the internal structure within which rail freight operates is necessary.

Open Access (Passenger)

Open access was a central plank of the privatised railway as perceived by the previous government. Despite an initial flurry of interest, largely on the part of prospective charter operators, no substantive operations resulted and a modified (restricted) competition régime was introduced at an early stage. The result of this was virtually to free franchisees from the threat of new competition on any significant passenger flow until 1999, when limited competition might be re-introduced at the discretion of the regulator. The threat of full competition was put into abeyance until 2002. The regulator has just gone out to consultation on the implications of introducing limited competition from 1999.

The decision in 1994 to limit the possibility of open-access operations was taken to facilitate the franchising process. Although the Treasury argued that one of the benefits of the new arrangements would be to increase the transparency of the cost of supporting the railway to the taxpayer, the reality was that the franchising process embraced major degrees of cross-subsidisation in the provision of services and this remained hidden. Indeed, substantial political pressure arose to ensure that the degree of transparency was not too great; hence the abandonment of any proposals for 'micro-franchises'. It was recognised that allowing open-access operations would reduce the scope for cross-subsidisation with potentially serious implications for public finances. Rather than face these issues directly a 'fudge' of postponing the onset of competition for several years was adopted. But postponement only buys time and the same issues confront us once more. By 2002 we shall be close to the re-franchising round and the question that must be faced before then is whether the same dilemmas that were apparent in 1994 will re-emerge

Failure to recognise that decisions affecting the provision of passenger rail services cannot sensibly be taken without considering the associated public funding issues lies at the heart of the problem. No solution that fails to concern itself with the balance between public funding, service levels and quality, and the competitive framework can possibly be optimal. The temptation is to ignore the true complexity of this equation and concentrate on simpler, but partial, issues. The Foreword to the regulator's recent consultation document appears to fall into this trap. It talks of the overriding consideration being 'which system (i.e. competitive versus non-competitive) is going to produce better railway services for passengers generally?' This is not an appropriate formulation of the question. It should read: *within the limits of public finance available to support the passenger rail system* which system is going to produce better railway services for passengers generally? The difference between these two formulations reflects the difference between unconstrained and constrained optimisation. The former has no relevance in the constrained world in which we live.

The body of the consultation document acknowledges that complex interdependencies may exist but seeks to steer the reader towards the possibility of solutions approximating to Pareto optimality: 'My role is therefore to ensure that where competition develops it is in such a way that passengers and taxpayers can expect to gain overall'. Whilst not denying the possibility that such a solution might exist the generality of solutions are more likely to involve passengers benefiting at taxpayers' expense or vice versa. The document is silent on how such matters might be handled, nor does it ask for views on how such matters might be addressed. Perhaps this is not surprising as it is not clear whether such issues should not be more properly addressed to the Franchising Director rather than the regulator.

I conclude that open access is another area of passenger operations where lack of clarity between the roles of the Franchising Director and the regulator exists. It is also an issue of strategic importance. Hopefully, the forthcoming White Paper on Transport Policy will give greater clarity to government policy in on-rail competition and the respective roles of the Franchising Director and regulator.

What Next for the Railways?

There are elements of the privatisation of the railway that are unequivocally welcome. The adoption of an enforceable contract basis for subsidy is an enormous step forward. The charging régimes give a fairer representation of the true costs of operating the railway, which was masked by varying degrees of capital consumption under the old régime. Together these changes allow for much greater certainty in forward plans. This should result in major efficiency gains in comparison with the earlier 'stop–go' arrangements. I only hope that when franchises come to be re-let this benefit of certainty can be sustained.

Similarly, the externalisation of engineering and other service activities deserves unqualified support. In-house provision was always hampered by the fact such activities were limited by the powers of BR itself and hence were confined to activities associated with the provision of railway services. This often reduced the cost-effectiveness of in-house operations in comparison with external companies which did not suffer from such limitations.

I would also argue that freight operations should be left alone to ascertain whether the new owners can achieve the stringent targets they have set themselves.

A number of other areas give less cause for satisfaction. Perhaps the principal of these is that the industry is in receipt of very little strategic guidance as to where it should be heading. This may not have been of much concern to the previous government, but it is very difficult to see how rail can play a full role in an Integrated Transport Policy unless there is a sense of strategic direction which the industry can share. It has been argued, implicitly, that strategic direction is something the previous government would have had to start to concern itself with if only because of the public finance implications of franchise renewal. Will the next round of franchises simply embrace an attempt to roll forward the *status quo* or seek to introduce variation to some degree? What about investment in non-infrastructure assets and the financial implications of such decisions?

The answers will be highly dependent upon whether the current control system has been able to improve the value for money obtained from public funds prior to commencement of the re-letting programme.

Central to the introduction of greater economic rationality into such decisions is the development of criteria for the allocation of government financial support. The Franchise Director has recently published criteria but it is too soon to see the impact of their application. One senses that the problems are not technical – indeed, it has long been known that a weighted passenger miles maximising approach is both a practical tool and an acceptable approximation to benefit maximisation. One suspects that the problems centre around the fact that any rational criterion will point to significant change to the *status quo*, and that such change would bring significant political problems in its wake. But maintenance of the *status quo* also brings its own problems. My final chart (Figure 2) shows the allocation of subsidy between the old BR passenger businesses, starting in 1993/4, the last year of the pre-privatisation system, then 1996/7 and 2003/4 when the first franchises come to an end. There are two striking points that emerge. First, the absolute level of public cash going in is broadly comparable – though the definition of subsidy changed radically in the process. Second, and more

Figure 2: Subsidy by Market Segment

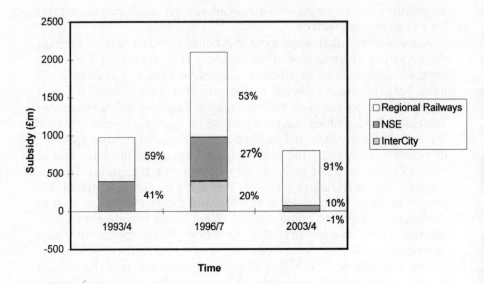

important, the distribution of subsidy between the businesses is becoming ever more skewed towards the markets in which the railway has a poor market share and little transport impact.

With a single exception, the original round of franchises all required government support and all embraced cross-subsidisation within the franchise. However, the differential anticipated performance of the franchises during the franchise period should mean that by early next decade some franchises still receive subsidy, some are breaking even, and some are returning a significant contribution to the Exchequer. At the point of re-letting, does the Franchise Director extract 'rents' from the better performing franchises and utilise these to cross-subsidise *between* franchises? This would help minimise his subsidy bill but at tremendous expense in transport policy terms. If the policy aim is to encourage the use of the railway, it is rather bizarre to tax the better-performing parts of the service in order to assist the worst-performing parts. To take the most extreme example, what is the rationale behind the government taking a premium of over £200 million a year from the West Coast Main Line franchise if the declared aim of government is to encourage an increase in the use of rail travel? Franchising has resulted in government securing the monopolist's reward regardless of the transport consequences. Unless rational criteria are allowed to play an explicit role in determining output decisions we are right back where we started with the Railway Dilemma.

Much greater effort needs to be devoted to ensuring that the monopolistic elements in the supply chain yield value for money to both passengers and the taxpayer. The magnitude of this task must not be underestimated. Together, Railtrack and the ROSCOs account for some two-thirds of the cost base of franchises, and it will be impossible for rail services to be developed fully unless monopoly profits are driven out of the supply chain. This is doubly relevant if we stay with a model that attaches virtually no risk to asset owners. John Kay outlined the difficulties that regulators face in accomplishing this task: the inevitable tendency of the utilities to overestimate costs and investment requirements and underestimate income as the time for a price review approaches, and the subsequent difficulty of establishing whether improvements in actual performance result from pessimistic estimates or from real, but unanticipated, external events. These are, of course, exactly the same problems government used to wrestle with in the context of nationalised industries. There, as a result of a lengthy learning process, control mechanisms gradually moved from a 5-year PES Review conducted in 'real' terms – which was very similar to current quinquennial reviews – to one or possibly 2-year budget reviews conducted in 'nominal' (cash) terms. It will be interesting to see whether the regulator will be able to devise an adequate control mechanism without having to resort to equivalent short-termism.

Control of Railtrack is firmly in the hands of the regulator and it is my firm belief that it is in this area that his success will ultimately be judged. ROSCOs are completely un-regulated even though many of the same issues arise. Government will wish to consider whether they are content with this state of affairs or whether action should be taken to bring them within the regulator's net before the next big round of leases is due for renewal.

Finally, I have argued that the issue of open access for passenger operators is of strategic importance. The concept of an integrated transport policy implies extra-market involvement and will most likely embrace some movement along the competition-co-operation spectrum in the direction of co-operation. It is not clear how the current conception of open access fits within this framework. As a minimum, there would seem to be a need to develop criteria to differentiate between competition that is worthwhile and that which is not. Given that such differentiation must be geared to establishing the extent to which competition actively encourages attainment of wider transport policy goals, it is difficult to see how anyone other than government, or its agent, can be responsible for the development of such criteria.

Conclusion

Privatisation has not solved, and cannot of itself solve, the Railway Dilemma. Although we are currently experiencing a relatively tranquil period, the strategic questions affecting output/investment/ pricing/subsidy will re-emerge as franchises approach renewal, if not earlier. The key to resolution of these issues centres around the systematic application of value for money criteria - defined in terms that are relevant to wider transport policy goals. Privatisation, *per se*, has nothing to contribute to this strategic debate.

Equally, there are aspects of the current model where, in my opinion, the previous government failed to get things 'right-first-time'. As regards the delivery of value for money from the supply chain, those elements of the chain that are subject to competitive markets give little cause for concern, but where significant elements of monopoly power are present the current regulatory framework could usefully be revisited and strengthened. With respect to the implications of introducing open access to the passenger business it is difficult to see how sensible decisions can be reached other than through a process of strategic assessment that is beyond the locus of existing players. Nor is anyone responsible for ensuring that the sum of the parts of a disaggregated railway equals the whole that is desired in transport policy terms. The situation is further complicated by the fact that any such summation is itself path-dependent. For example, introducing competition before re-letting franchises will not lead to the same outcome as proceeding the other way round.

It is for these reasons that I believe the current government's proposals to introduce a Strategic Authority are to be welcomed.

Such an authority should not involve itself in the running of railway services, which is best left to the private sector. What it should be responsible for is ensuring that the delivery of such services takes place within a framework that satisfies government as well as consumers of the achievement of value for money in transport policy terms.

CHAIRMAN'S COMMENTS

Chris Bolt

I AGREE WITH MANY OF THE POINTS JOHN HAS MADE. But I would like to add some comments of my own on some of the points of agreement, based in part on experience in other regulated industries, and also to identify one or two areas where, I believe, an alternative interpretation is possible.

John started by noting that the transport system does not exhibit more economic rationality now than it did 30 or 40 years ago. My own experience in another field provides another example. When Ofwat reviewed charging methods and tariff structures in the water industry in the early 1990s, the state of affairs – and the analysis – had hardly changed from the position when I had previously worked on these matters in the Department of Environment in the late 1970s. One possible reason for this is the relatively rapid turnover of the staff within government departments: between my two stints on water, I did three other civil service jobs. By contrast, many people on the other side of the table had simply been promoted – no doubt growing wiser as well as older. Quite a few are still managing the water companies today.

One of the reasons for thinking more progress in increasing 'economic rationality' may now be possible is therefore that the framework of independent regulation developed in the UK since 1984 provides much more continuity for regulatory policy than was previously possible. This has a number of results. One is reducing the asymmetry of information which was always a problem for a sponsoring department in facing up to nationalised industries. Another – and I return to this below – is that it brings a clearer separation between government policy-making and day-to-day regulatory decisions.

A second area where I would endorse John's comments is in respect of the current structure of access charges. Back in 1994, ORR had a choice: we either stuck with the existing framework of charges – with 90 per cent of Railtrack's revenue in the form of fixed annual payments – or introduced a new and untested structure. In the circumstances, the first option seemed more appropriate; and subsequent experience in other countries (for example, Germany) confirms our view that major changes in charging structure should only be introduced carefully.

Nevertheless, we made clear our view that changes were desirable, and are now discussing with Railtrack a programme to review their cost structures and to identify alternative bases for access charges which will give better incentives to use the existing network effectively, and to give Railtrack and train operators the right incentives to increase services and enhance the network where this is in the public interest. This involves not only a better understanding of Railtrack's cost structures – for example, picking up some of the points made last year by Michael Beesley[1] – but also considering whether changes in the allocation of risk through revenue-sharing arrangements will be beneficial to the development of the railway network.

In suggesting how the current framework of rail regulation might develop, John welcomed the proposal to introduce a Strategic Rail Authority (SRA), and also suggested that there was 'an unanswerable case' for tidying up the responsibilities of OPRAF and ORR in respect of passengers. As John Swift made clear in his memorandum to the Transport Select Committee, we agree on both points.

But in taking these issues forward, there are many issues to be considered, including:

- Is regulation through contract (in this case the franchise agreement) likely to be any more (or less) effective than regulation by licence? Experience in other industries has confirmed that licences can be tightened to reflect best practice and increased customer expectations, but this may not be feasible with contracts.

- Is a division of functions based on whether decisions have an impact on Exchequer expenditure too simplistic? This can be looked at from both directions: in practice, some decisions which have been devolved to the independent regulator (such as Railtrack access charges) have a direct impact on subsidy; but to

---

[1] M. E. Beesley, 'Rail: The Role of Subsidy in Privatisation', *Regulating Utilities: Broadening the Debate*, IEA Readings 46, 1997.

do otherwise would prejudice the involvement of private sector capital which is a key feature of the public sector/private sector partnership in the restructured railway. From the other direction, the fact that discussions on environmental standards and charges in the water industry do not have a direct impact on the Exchequer does not mean that the regulator should have complete freedom to take decisions on these matters, as Ian Byatt has always accepted. If a way can be found for government policy on environmental and social matters to guide the exercise of regulatory functions in the water and energy industries, can the same not be done in transport?

I feel I must react to the suggestion that Railtrack may be under-regulated. The Rail Regulator certainly took the view that the initial licence conditions did not provide adequate 'bankability' for Railtrack's investment commitments. But the new licence condition introduced in September does, we believe, give us adequate and appropriate powers in this respect. What now needs to be done is to make sure that this new framework actually delivers. A key component will be the assessment by Railtrack of future network needs, and we welcome the involvement that OPRAF will now have, under the terms of its revised Objectives, Instructions and Guidance, to provide an input to this process.

This will provide a good model for the strategic input that a future SRA can make. But there is a danger here as well. How can a central strategic view of the future use and development of the rail network be balanced with maintaining the benefits which come from private sector involvement? How can the interests of passengers and freight users best be protected and promoted?

Just because Railtrack, rolling-stock companies and train operators owe their existence to public funding, a return to a form of command structure in place of a genuine public sector/private sector partnership is not required. Direct government management of the railways in the past inevitably introduced constraints on their development. There is a real danger here of blocking fruitful, innovative risk-taking by commercial businesses.

Last year, Michael Beesley suggested that 'we should now concentrate on effective competition for passenger franchise monopolies' and that 'a vision of the future where there can be effective competition for railway slots is mistaken'. The question to both Michael Beesley and John Welsby is whether private operators should have freedom to decide whether to engage in – and withdraw from – commercial operations over and above the service levels which the Franchising Director is prepared to support, or not.

We recognise that this characteristic of private sector risk-taking is at tension with some of the other key characteristics of the public sector/private sector partnership in the restructured railway. But we believe it is compatible with it, and will bring greater benefits to passengers and freight users than simply relying on the central specification of all the services to be operated. To achieve this outcome requires· a future Strategic Rail Authority – just like the regulator – to avoid getting drawn into day-to-day management decisions. Independence of regulation, transparency of obligations and accountability are closely linked. It is obviously right that commitments by operators are properly enforced. But it is clearer now who is responsible for specifying and who is responsible for delivery, and the railway is more accountable now than it was when in public ownership. Rail users are benefiting from this change.

Does The Past Have a Future?
The Political Economy of Heritage

Many countries are proud of their 'heritage,' in terms of buildings and various artefacts from the past. In some cases, a country's heritage is of such interest that people will travel long distances to view it.

But there are resource costs in preserving the past and presenting it: the resources so employed could have been used in other activities. How are decisions made about what should be preserved and how should those decisions be made?

In Does the Past have a Future?, eight distinguished authors (from France, Italy, Switzerland, the United Kingdom and the United States) examine such questions and consider alternative means of making preservation decisions, ranging from voting rights for citizens to various forms of privatisation.

The collection of papers is edited by Sir Alan Peacock, who is internationally known for his work on these issues.

1. The Economist and Heritage Policy: A Review of the Issues
   Sir Alan Peacock
2. Public Choice, Cost Benefit Analysis and The Evaluation of Cultural Heritage
   Bruno Frey and Felix Oberholzer-Gee
3. Heritage Regulation: A Political Economy Approach
   Ilde Rizzo
4. The Evolution of Heritage Policies: The Case of France
   Françoise Benhamou
5. The National Trust: The Private Provision of Heritage Services
   David Sawers
6. Museums and Galleries: Storehouses of Value
   Sir Gerald Elliot
7. International Aspects of Heritage Policies
   Dick Netzer

The Institute of Economic Affairs
2 Lord North Street, Westminster, London SW1P 3LB
Telephone: 0171 799 3745 Facsimile: 0171 799 2137
E-mail: iea@iea.org.uk Internet: http://www.iea.org.uk   ISBN 0-255 36414-8

£15.00

The Minimum Wage:

No Way to Help the Poor

Deepak Lal

1. Controversy among economists about the effects of a minimum wage has recently been revived.
2. Recent studies apparently support the views of politicians in the United States, Britain and other European countries who would like to set or increase minimum wages.
3. These studies claim that minimum wages can increase both employment and the efficiency of the economy.
4. The claim rests on the assumption that labour markets are monopsonistic (employers have considerable market power). But no evidence is produced that monopsony is widespread.
5. 'Dynamic monopsony' (where workers have imperfect information about job opportunities) is said to be a circumstance in which setting the minimum wage can increase efficiency.
6. However, the label 'monopsony' is misapplied to situations in which employers and employees are searching for ways to adapt to uncertainty: divergences between wages and marginal products are the norm in real-world labour markets.
7. Minimum wages would have widespread effects on labour markets. They would, for example, reduce human capital formation because they would compress the wage structure and undermine incentives to acquire skill.
8. Thus support for a minimum wage is '…at odds with [the] desire to promote skill accumulation by unskilled workers – particularly the young and females'.
9. 'Revisionist' ideas which support minimum wages are an exercise in 'Nirvana economics' in which an 'imperfect' market is implicitly compared with the perfectly competitive ideal.
10. Even if labour markets were 'riddled with monopsony', technocrats could not have the information required to apply corrections: '…there is no obvious technocratic solution which would be better than that discovered by the market'.

The Institute of Economic Affairs

2 Lord North Street, Westminster, London SW1P 3LB
Telephone: 0171 799 3745 Facsimile: 0171 799 2137
E-mail: iea@iea.org.uk Internet: http://www.iea.org.uk

£4.00

ISBN 0-255 36344-3

Democratic Values and the Currency

Michael Portillo

with a Postscript by
Martin Feldstein

1. The single currency is not 'merely an economic device' but '…a project in re-shaping the way our Continent is governed'.
2. The 'federalism' now being pursued at European level is 'highly centralising and owes much to the Monnet-functionalist approach'.
3. Much of the momentum behind European integration derives from the fear of war. But Europe is more secure from inter-continental conflict than ever before because it is composed of democracies and '…it is inconceivable that democracies would go to war with one another'.
4. European integration is '…not the means to achieve the security of our Continent'. Because the form of integration reduces democratic control, rather than abolishing nationalism it risks stirring it up.
5. For democracy to work, people have to have more than just a vote. Resentment and unrest will be the result if policies are made by bodies '…thought to be too distant, or made by people who are not democratically accountable at all'.
6. Motivation for the single currency is political, not economic. It is '…a bigger step towards centralised decision-making than any that has been taken before'.
7. Monetary policy will become the responsibility of a European Union central bank. Constraints on borrowing will restrict member-countries' freedom to decide either tax rates or spending levels. Because there is no single labour market, and the flexibility of currency adjustment will have been lost, the '…full impact of recession will …fall on unemployment'.
8. Electors will feel 'resentful and cheated' when they cannot through their votes influence economic policy or change the policy-makers.
9. Trying to establish democratic accountability at European level is not the answer. 'Europe' does not constitute a nation. 'No parliament spanning from Dublin to Athens …is capable of satisfying the democratic requirements and aspirations of each of our populations'.
10. Though the EU is composed of democracies, the Union itself is undemocratic. Transferring decisions from member-states to the Union reduces democratic accountability with the danger of providing '…a breeding ground for nationalism and extremism'.

The Institute of Economic Affairs

2 Lord North Street, Westminster, London SW1P 3LB
Telephone: 0171 799 3745 Facsimile: 0171 799 2137
E-mail: iea@iea.org.uk Internet: http://www.iea.org.uk

£4.00

ISBN 0-255 36412-1

The Conservative Government's Economic Record: An End of Term Report

Nicholas Crafts

1. The first half of the eighteen years of Conservative government saw a radical departure from the economic policies of all earlier postwar governments with a new emphasis on the supply side. In the later years, the '...Thatcher experiment' was 'refined and extended'.

2. From the 1950s to the 1970s there were 'mistaken economic policies and institutional deficiencies' which had to be corrected if Britain's relative economic decline was to end.

3. In those early years, physical capital was subsidised, state ownership was widespread, 'national champions' and prestige research projects were promoted. Governments failed to reform industrial relations or taxation.

4. Vocational training was poor, labour was used inefficiently, and industrial relations arrangements increased unemployment despite government efforts to '...suppress the problem through incomes policies'.

5. The Conservatives strengthened '...incentives and market disciplines' and reduced subsidies in actions which have '...some support from modern growth economics'. They failed, however, to introduce competition in some privatised industries and (in the 1990s) to reduce the burden of taxation on growth.

6. Employment policy focussed on reducing equilibrium unemployment, abandoning incomes policies. Less commendable were efforts to 'hide unemployment'.

7. Counter-inflationary efforts were '...much less well-conceived than either labour market or supply-side policy'. The government failed to choose suitable policy targets and was reluctant to surrender political control of monetary and exchange rate policies.

8. A striking feature was a marked upturn in labour productivity growth in manufacturing which reduced the productivity gap between Britain and other countries. But there was no comparable upturn in service sector productivity growth.

9. Changes in the '...bargaining environment and associated developments in industrial relations' seem to have had a major effect on manufacturing productivity. Product market deregulation was also important.

10. The Conservative years have '...left long term growth prospects in Britain better than would have seemed possible eighteen years ago.' 'Microeconomic radicalism paid off handsomely' though macroeconomic management was less successful.

The Institute of Economic Affairs

2 Lord North Street, Westminster, London SW1P 3LB
Telephone: 0171 799 3745 Facsimile: 0171 799 2137
E-mail: iea@iea.org.uk Internet: http://www.iea.org.uk   ISBN 0-255 36413-X

£4.00

Less Than Zero
The Case for a Falling Price Level in a Growing Economy

George Selgin

1. Most economists now accept that monetary policy should not aim at 'full employment': central banks should aim instead at limiting movements in the general price level.

2. Zero inflation is often viewed as an ideal. But there is a case for allowing the price level to vary so as to reflect changes in unit production costs.

3. Under such a 'productivity norm', monetary policy would allow 'permanent improvements in productivity...to lower prices permanently' and adverse supply shocks (such as wars and failed harvests) to bring about temporary price increases. The overall result would be '...secular deflation interrupted by occasional negative supply shocks'.

4. United States consumer prices would have halved in the 30 years after the Second World War (instead of almost tripling), had a productivity norm policy been in operation.

5. In an economy with rising productivity a constant price level cannot be relied upon to avoid '..."unnatural" fluctuations in output and employment'.

6. A productivity norm should involve lower 'menu' costs of price adjustment, minimise 'monetary misperception' effects, achieve more efficient outcomes using fixed money contracts and keep the real money stock closer to its 'optimum'.

7. The theory supporting the productivity norm runs counter to conventional macro-economic wisdom. For example, it suggests that a falling price level is not synonymous with depression. The 'Great Depression' of 1873-1896 was actually a period of '...unprecedented advances in factor productivity'.

8. In practice, implementing a productivity norm would mean choosing between a labour productivity and a total factor productivity norm. Using the latter might be preferable and would involve setting the growth rate of nominal income equal to a weighted average of labour and capital input growth rates.

9. Achieving a predetermined growth rate of nominal income would be easier under a free banking régime which tends automatically to stabilise nominal income.

10. Many countries now have inflation rates not too far from zero. But zero inflation should be recognised not as the ideal but '...as the stepping-stone towards something even better'.

The Institute of Economic Affairs

2 Lord North Street, Westminster, London SW1P 3LB
Telephone: 0171 799 3745 Facsimile: 0171 799 2137
E-mail: iea@iea.org.uk Internet: http://www.iea.org.uk   ISBN 0-255 36402-4

£8.00

How Markets Work:
Disequilibrium, Entrepreneurship and Discovery

Israel M. Kirzner

1. Mainstream neo-classical economics focusses on already attained states of equilibrium. It is silent about the processes of adjustment to equilibrium.

2. Human action consists of '…grappling with an essentially unknown future', not being confronted with clearly-specified objectives, known resources and defined courses of action as mainstream theory assumes.

3. Critics of the market economy find ammunition in neo-classical theory: they '…merely need to tick off the respects in which real world capitalism departs from the requirements for perfectly competitive optimality'.

4. The theory of entrepreneurial discovery allows economists to escape from the 'analytical box' in which 'choice' simply consists of computing a solution implicit in given data.

5. An entrepreneurial act of discovery consists in '…realising the existence of market value that has hitherto been overlooked'. Scope for entrepreneurial discovery occurs in a world of disequilibrium – which is quite different from the equilibrium world of mainstream economics where market outcomes are foreordained.

6. Entrepreneurial discovery explains why one price tends to prevail in a market. Though new causes of price differences continually appear, entrepreneurs exploit the resulting profit opportunities and produce a tendency towards a single price.

7. Only with the introduction of entrepreneurship is it possible to appreciate how markets work. Without entrepreneurship, there would be no market co-ordination.

8. So-called 'imperfections' of competition are often '…crucial elements in the market process of discovery and correction of earlier entrepreneurial errors'.

9. Advertising expenditures, for example, are means of alerting consumers to 'what they do not know that they do not know'. Anti-trust laws may hamper market processes and prevent competitive entry to markets.

10. Entrepreneurial profit, far from generating injustice, is a 'created gain'. It is not '…sliced from a pre-existing pie…it is a portion which has been created in the very act of grasping it'.

The Institute of Economic Affairs

2 Lord North Street, Westminster, London SW1P 3LB
Telephone: 0171 799 3745 Facsimile: 0171 799 2137
E-mail: iea@iea.org.uk Internet: http://www.iea.org.uk   ISBN 0-255 36404-0

£8.00

Markets
in the Firm
A Market-Process
Approach to Management

Tyler Cowen and David Parker

1. Information is now the critical factor of production: firms need to be able to sense the need for change and respond before their competitors do.
2. Use of market principles within a firm can help it learn and adapt.
3. The days are numbered when rigid 'Taylorist scientific management' principles could usefully be applied. Markets now demand more variety and quality. Companies are decentralising to cope with the uncertainty and pace of change of markets.
4. 'Looser-coupled' firms, however, run the risk of anarchy. Means of maintaining the 'coherence and strategic direction of the firm' are required.
5. Economists from Ronald Coase onwards have been interested in why firms exist. Viewing the firm as a 'nexus of contracts' focuses attention on the similarities between resource allocation in markets and in firms.
6. Some companies have applied market principles '...to unlock the problems of management.' Koch Industries Inc. in Kansas has been particularly successful.
7. Its success appears to have been achieved by an integrated system of mission statements, decentralised management (profit centres and cross-functional teams), and definition of property rights within the firm so as to provide appropriate incentives.
8. 'Command-and-control' methods are as inappropriate within a firm as they have proved to be outside it. Firms need to harness the ability of markets to 'flex and change, assimilating and processing information speedily and accurately, attributes that are essential to the learning organisation.' (p 73).
9. The 'command firm' is '...subject to all the disincentives of planned economies, including the hiding of resources, aggravated shortages, the over- or under-use of inputs and the resulting inefficiencies of production.' (p78).
10. Market economies have been effective in '...encouraging learning, adaptation and innovation'. The challenge is to '...design firms that can mimic these attributes of the market economy.' (p80).

The Institute of Economic Affairs

2 Lord North Street, Westminster, London SW1P 3LB
Telephone: 0171 799 3745 Facsimile: 0171 799 2137
E-mail: iea@iea.org.uk Internet: http://www.iea.org.uk   ISBN 0-255 36405-9

£8.00

Regulating Financial Markets:

A Critique and some Proposals

George J. Benston

A000018090291

1. Financial services, financial firms and financial markets are regulated to a greater extent than most other products and services. Financial service regulation goes back centuries.
2. It provides benefits to governments (for example, from direct and indirect taxation of banks) and to regulated financial institutions (which gain where entry is restricted).
3. Consumer protection is a common reason given for financial regulation. But consumers in financial markets are probably less subject to fraud, misrepresentation, discrimination and information asymmetry than consumers of other products.
4. Concern about 'negative externalities' (costs borne by others) is another argument for regulation. However, on examination it is clear there are few genuine externalities.
5. Regulation on externality grounds is justified only for financial institutions which hold government-insured deposits; for insurance companies which provide government-mandated non-contracting third party insurance (for instance, for cars); and for companies which underwrite long-term life insurance and annuities.
6. Financial regulation incurs costs, borne by consumers and taxpayers, which probably exceed the benefits they receive. There are substantial unintended costs (such as reduced diversification of financial institutions and the absence of less costly and more innovative products because of restrictions on entry to financial markets).
7. An 'optimal regulatory system' for banks would involve substantial capital requirements, periodic reporting of assets, liabilities and capital and a 'structured early intervention' system for the authorities.
8. For government-mandated third party liability insurance, life insurance and annuities, insurance companies should be subject to capital requirements similar to those for banks.
9. If governments wish to protect consumers of financial products the best procedure is to establish an Ombudsman to which consumers who feel they have been mistreated can go.
10. The proposed regulatory system '...would be almost costless to taxpayers, the regulated companies and consumers of their products and services.' Compared with existing regimes, it has the great advantage of not restricting entry to financial markets nor the introduction of new products.

The Institute of Economic Affairs

2 Lord North Street, Westminster, London SW1P 3LB
Telephone: 0171 799 3745 Facsimile: 0171 799 2137
E-mail: iea@iea.org.uk Internet: http://www.iea.org.uk   ISBN 0-255 36415-6

£12.00